GLOBAL ENVIRONMENTAL POLITICS

DILEMMAS IN WORLD POLITICS

Series Editor
George A. Lopez, University of Notre Dame

Dilemmas in World Politics offers teachers and students of international relations a series of quality books on critical issues, trends, and regions in international politics. Each text examines a "real world" dilemma and is structured to cover the historical, theoretical, practical, and projected dimensions of its subject.

EDITORIAL BOARD

Jeffry Frieden
Harvard University

Deborah J. Gerner
University of Kansas

Vicki Golich
California State University–San Marcos

Lev Gonick
Wilfrid Laurier University

Barbara Welling Hall
Earlham College

Elizabeth C. Hanson
University of Connecticut

Barry Hughes
University of Denver

Janice Love
University of South Carolina

Vincent Mahler
Loyola of Chicago

Zeev Maoz
Tel Aviv University

Karen Mingst
University of Kentucky

Frederic Pearson
Wayne State University

V. Spike Peterson
University of Arizona

Neil Richardson
University of Wisconsin–Madison

Martin Rochester
University of Missouri–St. Louis

Georg Sørensen
Aarhus University (Denmark)

Harvey Starr
University of South Carolina

Michael Stohl
Purdue University

Douglas Stuart
Dickinson College

Donald Sylvan
Ohio State University

Sarah Tisch
Winrock International

John Vasquez
Vanderbilt University

FORTHCOMING TITLES

Bruce E. Moon
Dilemmas of International Trade

□ □ □

James A. Caporaso
Challenges and Dilemmas of European Union

□ □ □

David S. Mason
**Revolution in East-Central Europe,
Second Edition**

□ □ □

Thomas G. Weiss
**Humanitarian Action, Intervention,
and World Politics**

□ □ □

Janice Love
**Southern Africa
in World Politics**

SECOND EDITION

GLOBAL ENVIRONMENTAL POLITICS

■ ■ ■

Gareth Porter

ENVIRONMENTAL AND ENERGY STUDY INSTITUTE

Janet Welsh Brown

WORLD RESOURCES INSTITUTE

WestviewPress

A Division of HarperCollinsPublishers

Dilemmas in World Politics Series

All rights reserved. No part of this publication may be reproduced or transmitted in any form or by any means, electronic or mechanical, including photocopy, recording, or any information storage and retrieval system, without permission in writing from the publisher.

Copyright © 1991, 1996 by Westview Press, Inc., A Division of HarperCollins Publishers, Inc.

Published in 1996 in the United States of America by Westview Press, Inc., 5500 Central Avenue, Boulder, Colorado 80301-2877, and in the United Kingdom by Westview Press, 12 Hid's Copse Road, Cumnor Hill, Oxford OX2 9JJ

Library of Congress Cataloging-in-Publication Data
Porter, Gareth, 1942–
    Global environmental politics / Gareth Porter, Janet Welsh Brown.
    —2nd ed.
       p.   cm. — (Dilemmas in world politics)
    Includes bibliographical references and index.
    ISBN 0-8133-2181-6 (cloth). — ISBN 0-8133-2182-4 (pbk.)
    1. Environmental policy.   I. Brown, Janet Welsh.   II. Title.
III. Series.
GE170.P67   1996
363.7'056—dc20   95-19877
                                                                                    CIP

Printed and bound in the United States of America

The paper used in this publication meets the requirements of the American National Standard for Permanence of Paper for Printed Library Materials Z39.48-1984.

10   9   8   7   6   5   4   3   2

Contents

☐ ☐ ☐ **1 The Emergence of Global
          Environmental Politics**   **1**

☐ ☐ ☐ **2 Actors in the Environmental Arena**   **31**

☐ ☐ ☐ **3 The Development of Environmental
          Regimes: Nine Case Studies**   **67**

□ □ □

Illustrations

Tables

Figures

Photos and Cartoons

□ □ □

Acknowledgments

This book has been made possible by the inspiration, encouragement, and assistance of many colleagues. The series editor, George Lopez, had the clarity of mind to think of including a book on this topic in the series. Jennifer Knerr has patiently guided us through the entire process, in terms of both format and substance.

Global environmental politics is a vast canvas—much too broad to master without help from those who are more expert in the specific issues than we. We are grateful to the following colleagues who provided documents as well as insights on specific issues covered in the second edition: Walter Arensberg, Catherine M. Barnes, Jim Barnes, Michael Bean, Sharon Bellucci, Richard Benedick, Hyacinth Billings, Ian Bowles, Barbara Bramble, Norman L. Brown, Melinda Chandler, Kevin Chu, Sheldon Cohen, Liz Cook, Kathleen Courrier, Clif Curtis, Andrea Durbin, Denise Fisher, John Fitzgerald, Patricia Forkan, Scott Hajost, Brian Hallman, Inji Islam, Miguel Jorge, Peter Jutro, Lee A. Kimball, Charles Lawson, James MacKenzie, Joan Martin-Brown, Joseph Mendelson, Alan Miller, Deborah Moore, Franklin Moore, Felice Nguyen, Michael Oppenheimer, Michael Pope, Sandra Postel, Elizabeth Raisbeck, Walter Reid, Mike St. Claire, Nigel Sizer, Paul Speck, Michael Sutton, Marijke Torfs, Peter Veit, Jim Valette, Frederik von Bolhuis, Dana West, Carol Werner, and Brian Wood-Thomas. We are most grateful for their assistance and insights; any remaining errors or misjudgments are our own. Special thanks go to Sam Boltik, library technician at the World Resources Institute, who untiringly and cheerfully responded to many requests to track down sources for our research, and to Ramona Felts-Wonders, Virginia Jamison, and Michael Pope for researching and chasing down all the last-minute details necessary to get the revised manuscript to press. We are indebted also to our respective institutions, the Environmental and Energy Study Institute and the World Resources Institute, for their support during the rewriting of this book, for the use of their libraries and other services, and most of all for the support of our colleagues.

Gareth Porter and
Janet Welsh Brown

Acronyms

ACP	Africa, the Caribbean, and the Pacific
AID	Agency for International Development (U.S.)
AOSIS	Association of Small Island States
ASOC	Antarctic and Southern Oceans Coalition
ATCPs	Antarctic Treaty Consultative Parties
BCSD	Business Council on Sustainable Development
CANZ	Canada, Australia, and New Zealand
CAFE	Corporate Average Fuel Economy standards (U.S.)
CCAD	Central American Commission on Environment and Development
CCAMLR	Convention on the Conservation of Antarctic Marine Living Resources
CFCs	chlorofluorocarbons
CI	Conservation International
CITES	Convention on International Trade in Endangered Species
COICA	Coordinadora de Organizaciones Indigenas de la Cuenca Amazonica (Coordinating Council of Indigenous Organizations of the Amazon Basin)
COP	conference of the parties
CRAMRA	Convention on the Regulation of Antarctic Mineral Resources Activities
CSD	Commission on Sustainable Development
CTE	Committee on Trade and Environment (of the World Trade Organization)
EC	European Community
ECE	Economic Commission for Europe
ECLAC	Economic Commission for Latin America and the Caribbean
ECOSOC	Economic and Social Council (U.N.)
EDF	Environmental Defense Fund
EEB	European Environmental Bureau
EEC	European Economic Community
EESI	Environmental and Energy Study Institute
EEZs	exclusive economic zones

EPA	Environmental Protection Agency (U.S.)
ETMs	environmental trade measures
EU	European Union
FAO	Food and Agriculture Organization (U.N.)
FOE	Friends of the Earth (U.S.)
FOEI	Friends of the Earth International
FRG	Federal Republic of Germany
FSC	Forest Stewardship Council
G-7	Group of Seven
G-77	Group of Seventy-seven
GATT	General Agreement on Tariffs and Trade
GDP	gross domestic product
GEF	Global Environment Facility
GNP	gross national product
GWP	gross world product
HCFCs	hydrochlorofluorocarbons
IAEA	International Atomic Energy Agency
IBA	Industrial Biotechnology Association
ICREAs	international commodity-related environmental agreements
ICS	International Chamber of Shipping
IDB	Inter-American Development Bank
IFIs	international financial institutions
IGOs	international governmental organizations
IIED	International Institute for Environment and Development
ILO	International Labor Organization
IMF	International Monetary Fund
IMO	International Maritime Organization
INC	intergovernmental negotiating committee
INGO	international nongovernmental organizations
IOs	international organizations
IPCC	Intergovernmental Panel on Climate Change
IPM	integrated pest management
IPR	intellectual property rights
ITTA	International Tropical Timber Agreement
ITTO	International Tropical Timber Organization
IUCN	International Union for the Conservation of Nature
IWC	International Whaling Commission
JI	joint implementation
JUSCANZ	Japan, United States, Canada, Australia, and New Zealand
KENGO	Kenya Environmental Non-Governmental Organization
LMOs	living modified organisms
LRTAP	(Convention on) Long-Range Transboundary Air Pollution
MARPOL	International Convention for the Prevention of Pollution from Ships

MDBs	multilateral development banks
MMPA	Marine Mammal Protection Act (U.S.)
NAFTA	North American Free Trade Agreement
NAM	Nonaligned Movement
NASA	National Aeronautics and Space Administration (U.S.)
NATO	North Atlantic Treaty Organization
NEPA	National Environmental Policy Act of 1969 (U.S.)
NGOs	nongovernmental organizations
NIEO	New International Economic Order
NRDC	Natural Resources Defense Council
NWF	National Wildlife Federation
OAS	Organization of American States
OAU	Organization of African Unity
ODA	official development assistance
OECD	Organization for Economic Cooperation and Development
OPEC	Organization of Petroleum Exporting Countries
PACD	Plan of Action to Combat Desertification
PIC	prior informed consent
POPs	persistent organic pollutants
ppb	parts per billion
PrepComs	Preparatory Committee meetings of United Nations conferences
SIDS	Small Island Developing States
tce	tons of coal equivalent
TFAP	Tropical Forest Action Plan
UNCED	United Nations Conference on Environment and Development
UNCLOS	United Nations Convention on the Law of the Sea
UNCSD	United Nations Commission on Sustainable Development
UNCTAD	United Nations Council on Trade and Development
UNDP	United Nations Development Programme
UNEP	United Nations Environment Programme
UNFPA	United Nations Population Fund
UNGA	United Nations General Assembly
UNICEF	United Nations Children's Fund
WALHI	Wahana Lingkungan Hidup (the Indonesian Environmental Forum)
WHO	World Health Organization
WMO	World Meteorological Organization
WRI	World Resources Institute
WTO	World Trade Organization
WWF	World Wildlife Fund (U.S.)

ONE

□ □ □

The Emergence of Global
Environmental Politics

Until the 1980s, global environmental problems were regarded by major powers as minor issues that were marginal to their national interests and to international politics. But because of the rise of environmental movements in the industrialized countries and the appearance of well-publicized global environmental threats that could affect profoundly the welfare of all humankind—such as the depletion of the ozone layer, global temperature increases, and depletion of the world's fisheries—global environmental issues have assumed a new status in world politics. These issues are no longer viewed as merely scientific and technical issues but as intertwined with central issues in world politics: the international system of resource production and use, the liberalization of world trade, North-South relations, and even international conflict and internal social and political stability.

This new status of global environmental issues was reflected in the fact that the first global summit meeting in world history was the 1992 United Nations Conference on Environment and Development (UNCED), held in Rio de Janeiro, Brazil. That conference also further heightened popular and official interest in global environmental problems and their relationships with economic policies, both domestic and international. By the early 1990s, it was not an exaggeration to say that the global environment had emerged as the third major issue area in world politics, along with international security and global economics.

Growing international concern about the global environment is no historical accident. It is a belated response to the fact that the major components of the **biosphere,** including the atmosphere, the oceans, soil cover, the climate system, and the range of animal and plant species, have all been altered by the intensity of human exploitation of the earth's resources in the twentieth century. The by-products of economic growth—the burning of fossil fuels; the release of ozone-destroying chemicals; emissions of sulfur and nitrogen oxides; the production of toxic chemicals and other wastes and their introduction into the air, water, and soil; and the elimination of forest cover, among others—cause cumulative stresses on the physical environment that threaten human health and economic well-being. The costs of these activities to future generations will be much higher in both developing and highly industrialized countries than they are to the world's current population.

In the past decade, scientific understanding of global environmental issues has increased enormously. The realization that environmental threats can have serious socioeconomic and human costs and that they cannot be solved by the unilateral decisions of states has given impetus in recent years to increased international cooperation to halt or reverse environmental degradation. That realization has also unleashed a new political force—a global environmental movement that undertakes increasingly effective transnational action on various issues. But in each case some states—and certain economic interests—have opposed strong international actions to reduce or eliminate activities that threaten the global environment.

The result is an intensifying struggle over global environmental issues. As global negotiations multiply on issues affecting a wide range of interests around the globe, the stakes for all the participants in the struggle will continue to grow. This chapter introduces the issue area of environmental politics. It highlights the economic and environmental trends underlying the emergence of environmental politics as a major issue area, defines the scope of the issue area, and outlines some of its major characteristics. The chapter also traces some of the major intellectual currents and political developments that contributed to the evolution of global environmental politics.

GLOBAL MACROTRENDS

The rise of global environmental politics can be understood only within the context of the major changes in the global environment resulting from the explosive growth of economic activity and population in the latter half of the twentieth century. Global economic, demographic, and environmental macrotrends do not reveal the differences between rich and poor countries or between social strata within countries. But these macrotrends do describe the gross physical changes driving global environmental politics.

Economic Growth and Population

It is not the growth of population per se but the total world population multiplied by per capita consumption that is the important measure of total potential stress on the global environment. The per capita **gross world product** (GWP)—the total of goods and services produced and consumed per person throughout the planet—has been growing faster than world population for decades. It doubled between 1950 and 1975 and continued to rise through 1991 before dropping slightly for the first time. (See Figure 1.1.) Seventy-five percent of the world's total goods and services are consumed in the highly industrialized countries.

But population growth worldwide, by serving as a multiplier of economic activity, also has a major impact on the environment. Global population doubled between 1950 and 1987 (from 2.5 billion to 5 billion) and now stands at about 5.7 billion (see Figure 1.2). Projections of future population growth depend on assumptions about fertility trends, which will be affected strongly by actions undertaken in the coming years. If high-quality family planning information and services were readily available to all families who want them, however, world population could stabilize at as low as 8 billion around 2025 (see Figure 1.3). Whereas the most significant increases to date in consumption have occurred in the most highly industrialized, richer countries, most of the population growth (93

FIGURE 1.1 Gross world product per person, 1950–1992

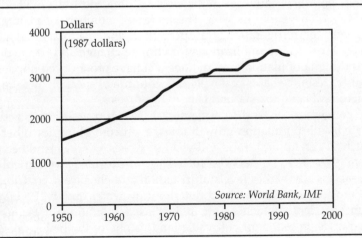

Source: Lester Brown, Hal Kane, and Ed Ayres, *Vital Signs 1993* (New York : W. W. Norton, 1993), p. 73.

FIGURE 1.2 World population growth, 1750–2150

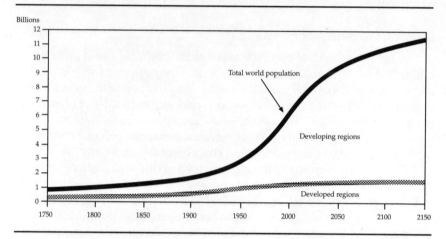

Source: Population Bulletin 42 (July 1987), Fig. 1, p. 9. Reprinted by permission of the Population Reference Bureau. Updated from United Nations Population Fund, *State of World Population 1993* (New York : UNFPA, 1993), pp. 1, 6.

percent in 1990) has been in the poorer, developing countries, with the fastest growth rates in the poorest countries.[1]

Population growth contributes to environmental degradation at the global and national levels by increasing the stress on natural resources and vital support services, such as the ozone and climate systems. The two most populous countries in the world, China and India, will add almost 34 million people in 1995. The increased numbers of people and their needs for refrigeration, transportation, and manufactured goods will have far-reaching implications for **climate change** and ozone depletion. And high population growth rates will have pronounced impacts on the natural resource bases of developing countries, especially with regard to agricultural land, forests, and fishery resources.

The conversion of land to agricultural uses appears to be positively correlated with population growth rates, even controlling for other factors such as agricultural trade and yield increases.[2] And as land becomes increasingly scarce, farmers are forced to turn to intensive agriculture, with dramatically higher levels of irrigation and chemicals, contributing to soil erosion, salinization, and deteriorating water quality. Population pressures on land, which result in increased migration of farmers to forested areas in search of cultivable land, is one of the major causes of tropical deforestation.[3] Population growth along the world's coasts is the

FIGURE 1.3   Alternative futures: Population projections to 2150

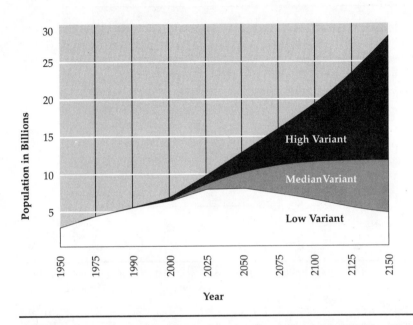

Source: United Nations Population Fund, *The State of World Population 1994* (New York: UNFPA, 1994), p. 2.

cause of much of the pollution that seriously reduces fish catch, and worldwide population growth accounts for half of the increased exploitation of coastal fishery resources in the past four decades.[4]

World population growth also affects the environment through the swelling of the population in urban areas. As a report of the United Nations Population Fund (UNFPA) recently observed, "The earth is rapidly becoming an urban planet." Half the world's population is expected to reside in cities by the year 2000, implying both heavier pollution of water and air and a higher rate of consumption of natural resources.[5] In many developing countries, for instance, one of the little-noticed costs of urbanization is added pressure on forests: Former villagers who move to the city tend to consume twice as much wood as they did before because charcoal, which is preferred by urban dwellers, has only half the primary energy of fuelwood used in rural areas.[6]

FIGURE 1. 4 Global per capita energy use, 1970–1991

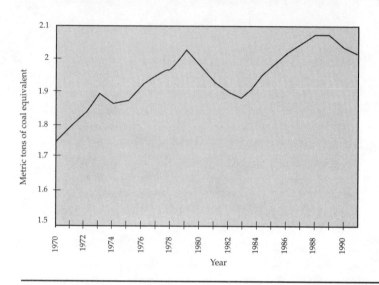

Source: Data from Lester R. Brown, Hal Kane, and David Malin Roodman, *Vital Signs 1992* (NewYork: W. W. Norton & Co., 1992), p. 77; United Nations Statistical Division, *U.N. Energy Tape* (NewYork: The United Nations, 1993).

Energy, Climate, and the Atmosphere

The enormous increase in economic activity has been reflected in the 4.5-fold increase in world energy consumption, from just over 2 billion metric tons of coal equivalent (tce) in 1950 to more than 9 billion metric tons in 1985. During the same period, per capita energy use nearly doubled, but between 1970 and 1991, it increased only about 18 percent, from about 1.75 tce to just over 2 tce per capita (see Figure 1.4). So past projections that total energy use could exceed 20 billion tce by the year 2025 now appear too pessimistic.[7] Although in the past, energy consumption was overwhelmingly dominated by the highly industrialized countries, in the next generation most of the increase will be in the developing countries.

The expansion of energy use has brought parallel increases in the emissions into the atmosphere of various chemical compounds created by the burning of fossil fuels. Annual releases of carbon into the atmosphere from fossil fuel combustion grew from about 1.5 billion metric tons in 1950 to nearly 6 billion metric tons in 1990 (see Figure 1.5). Without a concerted global effort to reduce energy consumption, annual worldwide carbon emissions could double by 2020.[8] Worldwide carbon dioxide levels in the atmosphere from fossil fuel combustion and vegetation loss have increased from 275 parts per million before the industrial revolution to about 346 parts per million in 1986.[9]

FIGURE 1.5 Global carbon dioxide emissions from fossil fuels, 1860–1990

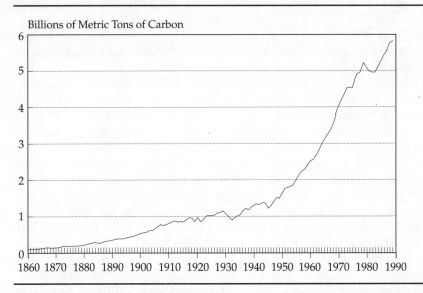

Source: T. A. Boden, R. J. Sepanski, F. W. Stoss, eds., *Trends '91: A Compendium of Data on Global Change* (Oak Ridge, Tennessee: Carbon Dioxide Information Analysis Center, Oak Ridge National Laboratory, December 1991).

Carbon dioxide as well as other chemical compounds absorb the earth's infrared radiation and trap heat close to its surface in what is called the **greenhouse effect.** The increased concentrations of these gases in the atmosphere, according to most climatologists, gradually raise average global temperatures, creating climate warming. Industrialization is believed by most scientists to have drastically sped up this natural process, putting back into the atmosphere in decades the carbon that nature had taken millions of years to store in fossil fuels.

Climate models project that, if current trends in greenhouse-gas emissions continue through 2030, the earth could experience an average rise in temperature ranging from 2.7° to 8.1°F (1.5° to 4.5°C). Even higher warming is considered possible because of feedback processes.[10] That would be comparable to the total warming since the 41°F (5°C) peak of the last ice age 18,000 years ago, which was enough to shift the Atlantic Ocean inland onto the North American continent about 100 miles (161 kilometers), to create the Great Lakes, and to alter the composition of forests.[11]

The impacts of global temperature change, according to most specialists, would include a decline of nontropical forests; major increases in air pollution, tropical diseases, and species extinction; the northward movement of agricultural production; and a rise in sea level by as much as 5 feet (1.5 meters) by midcentury (about eight times faster than the rise during the previous century). The sea-level rise would threaten coastal areas, where half the global population resides. It would also increase the frequency of severe flooding; cause the loss of drinking water and agricultural water supplies, wetlands, and wildlife habitats; and damage coastal infrastructures.[12]

Worldwide emissions of sulfur dioxide, which began in measurable amounts around 1860, reached 40 million metric tons annually by 1910 and 70 million metric tons annually by 1950. They are now estimated to be about 180 million metric tons annually and are expected to reach 200 million metric tons annually by the year 2000.[13] Sulfur dioxide and nitrogen oxide, emitted by industrial smokestacks and automobiles, turn into diluted sulfuric and nitric acid, or **acid rain**, when they come into contact with moisture and also fall as acidic gas and particles. These various forms of acid rain are carried hundreds of miles across borders and destroy buildings and vegetation, kill fish in lakes, pollute groundwater, and cause serious respiratory problems in children and asthmatics. Acid rain has been implicated in *Waldsterben* (forest death), the leaching of essential nutrients from trees, which has seriously damaged more than 28,000 square miles (70,000 square kilometers) of forests in fifteen European countries.

Other chemical compounds being released into the atmosphere, chlorofluorocarbons (CFCs), have been identified as the primary cause of depletion of the stratospheric ozone layer, which protects the earth from the sun's harmful ultraviolet rays, called UV-B. CFCs break up in the stratosphere 9 to 13 miles (14 to 21 kilometers) above the earth's surface and release chlorine, which becomes a catalyst in the breakdown of ozone and the reduction of the ozone layer. Production of CFCs for air conditioning, refrigeration, solvents, and styrofoam, among other industrial applications, increased from 86,000 tons in 1955 to 1.26 million tons in 1988 and then began to decline to 820,000 tons in 1990 because of international agreement to protect the ozone layer. (See Figure 1.6.) Until the mid-1980s, virtually all CFC-11 and CFC-12 was produced and sold in the Northern Hemisphere. Today, the developing countries are responsible for around 16 percent of production.[14]

Since the beginning of the 1970s, at least 2 percent of the ozone layer is believed to have been destroyed per decade at all latitudes outside the tropics, with the greatest losses at high altitudes and in winter. Scientists have projected that ozone depletion over North America and Europe will reach 6 percent in the summer and 10 percent in the winter by the year 2000.[15] Significant losses of ozone begin to occur when the level of chlorine in the atmosphere reaches 2 parts per billion (ppb). Even if interna-

FIGURE 1.6 Annual world production of CFCs, 1950–1992

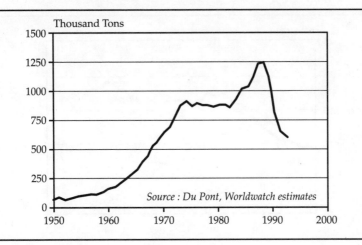

Source: Lester Brown, Hal Kane, and Ed Ayres, *Vital Signs 1993* (New York: W. W. Norton, 1993), p. 67.

tional commitments to phase out CFCs and other ozone-depleting chemicals are fully carried out, atmospheric chlorine levels will peak at 3.9 ppb after the year 2000 before declining to about 3 ppb.[16]

Although too little is known about the potential impacts of increased exposure to UV-B radiation on food crops, marine life, and the human immune system, the early research on these impacts suggests such exposure significantly reduces the productivity of most crop varieties, causes some loss of photosynthesis by phytoplankton (the single-cell base of the marine food chain), and causes animals to suffer reduced immunity to infectious diseases.[17]

Endangered Resources: Oceans, Fisheries, Soils, Freshwater, and Forests

The world's oceans and their abundant marine resources have been under increased stress as a result of overfishing and pollution. The world fish catch increased fivefold between 1950 and 1989, from 22 million tons to 100 million tons, before it started to decline, primarily because stocks were being depleted by too many boats taking too many fish.[18] On a per capita basis, world fish catch increased dramatically from about 8 kilograms (17.6 pounds) in 1948 to a peak of more than 19 kilograms (41.9 pounds) in 1989, but it then began to decline and by 1992, it was down 7 percent from that peak year. (See Figure 1.7.)

FIGURE 1.7 World fish catch per person, 1950–1993

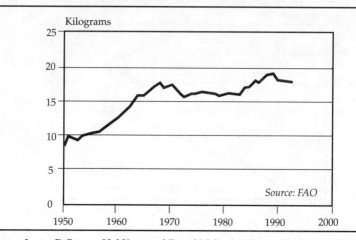

Source: Lester R. Brown, Hal Kane and David Malin Roodman, *Vital Signs 1994* (New York: W. W. Norton, 1994) , p. 33.

No overall statistics on marine pollution have been collected, but land-based sources are believed to account for nearly 80 percent of the total pollution of the oceans. The major land-based pollutants are synthetic organic compounds; excess sedimentation from mining, deforestation, or agriculture; biological contaminants in sewage; and excessive nutrients from fertilizers and sewage. Production of synthetic organic compounds increased more than tenfold from 1950 to 1985, and one of the leading examples of such a compound is formulated pesticides, whose worldwide consumption increased from 300,000 to 3 million tons from 1950 to 1985. Fertilizer consumption, meanwhile, increased more than tenfold from 14 million metric tons in 1970 to an estimated 146 million metric tons in 1989.[19]

Another significant source of marine pollution, however, is oil that has been discharged directly into the sea in the process of shipment to markets. Official data on oil discharges into the seas from shipping are lacking, but it has been estimated that by the 1980s, such discharges had reached roughly 1.5 million metric tons annually, only 10 percent of which could be attributed to tanker accidents.

The rise of nuclear power as a source of energy has led to the disposal of low-level radioactive wastes in the oceans. The cumulative volume of such nuclear wastes rose from less than 20,000 metric tons in 1967, with a negligible radioactivity, to almost 100,000 metric tons with a million curies of radioactivity, in 1984. Moreover, in 1993 Russian authorities revealed that the Soviet Union, in violation of international agreements,

FIGURE 1.8 Estimated annual world water use, total and by sector, 1900–2000

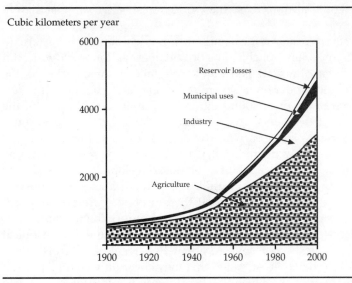

Cubic kilometers per year

Source: Sandra Postel, "Facing Water Scarcity," in Lester R. Brown et al., *State of the World, 1993* (New York: W. W. Norton, 1993), p. 23.

had dumped twice as much radioactive waste as had all the other twelve nuclear nations combined between 1946 and 1982.[20]

The impacts on plant and animal life of most wastes introduced into the seas are imperfectly understood, but oil pollution is known to interfere with the normal development of fish eggs and to harm phytoplankton communities. Toxic chemicals released into the oceans have been shown to reduce the reproductive capacity of some sea mammals and the shell thickness of the eggs of some seabirds. Chemical compounds also concentrate in marine organisms that enter into the food chain and affect human health. Oysters, for example, can increase concentrations of the pesticide DDT by as much as 70,000 times in only one month.[21]

The world's freshwater resources are in theory a renewable resource, but supplies are being used up at a faster rate than they are being replenished. The world now uses almost four times more fresh water than it did in the 1950s, primarily because of increases in agricultural and industrial uses. (See Figure 1.8.) As a result, per capita availability of water supplies worldwide is now one-third lower than it was in 1950. In twenty-six countries, water supplies available are already less than 725 gallons per person, which imposes severe constraints on economic development, food production, and natural resource conservation. If current trends continue, by the year 2010 more than a third of Africa's population is expected to live in water-scarce countries.[22] Temperature increases from climate change could also decrease the world's freshwater supplies significantly.

One of the earth's most critical and most fragile resources is its agricultural land. There are few reliable data on soil degradation worldwide, but it is estimated that almost 11 percent of the total cultivated surface of the globe has suffered moderate to severe soil degradation because of deforestation, overgrazing, or unsound agricultural practices. No part of the developing world has been spared, and many highly industrialized countries also experience soil loss. Worldwide, 3 percent of that land is believed to be so severely degraded that the land can be restored only by means that are beyond the capabilities of most developing countries. Over the next two decades, soil erosion and loss of soil nutrients could substantially reduce global food production if these processes are not slowed.[23]

The pressures of subsistence agriculture and conversion to commercial agriculture have combined with logging to threaten the world's tropical forests. Tropical forests once covered about 16 percent of the world's terrestrial surface. Today it is estimated that they cover only about 7 percent of the terrestrial surface. The annual worldwide tropical forest loss rate accelerated to 0.9 percent in the 1980s from an estimated 0.6 percent in the latter 1970s—a 50-percent faster rate of loss than was thought at the time. According to a 1991 Food and Agriculture Organization (FAO) estimate, tropical rainforests are now disappearing at the rate of 6.8 million acres (17 million hectares) each year.[24] This rate represents the annual loss of a forested area as large as Washington State.

The loss of the earth's **biodiversity** (variety of living things), encompassing both the mass extinction of species and the loss of genetic diversity within species, is taking place at a historically unprecedented rate. Scientists began warning in the 1980s that one-fourth or even one-half of the earth's species could be lost over a few decades, largely because of the destruction of tropical forests, which hold an estimated 50 to 90 percent of all species. That would constitute the sixth great "spasm of extinction" in the earth's history; natural evolution took millions of years to recover from the five previous such episodes.[25]

The genetic diversity of the world's agricultural crops has also eroded rapidly during the twentieth century. A few high-yielding hybrids have replaced the traditional varieties, and wild relatives have been lost in conversion of land to other purposes. An estimated 75 percent of the genetic diversity of crops has been lost since the beginning of the twentieth century.[26] Many of these varieties contain genes that are needed to create more productive and pest-resistant crops. Biodiversity loss reduces the ability of human societies to respond to diseases and to keep the world's food supply secure from pests and changes in climate.

AN INTRODUCTION TO GLOBAL
ENVIRONMENTAL POLITICS

The scope of the issue area of global environmental politics is defined by two dimensions of any international environmental problem: the environmental consequences of the economic activity in question and the states and nonstate actors involved in the issue. If the consequences are global, or if the actors in the issue transcend a single region, we consider it a global environmental issue.[27]

Issues that involve threats to the **global commons** (the natural resources and vital life-support services that belong to all humankind rather than to any one country) are clearly within the scope of global environmental politics. But other issues involving natural resources that are clearly under the sovereign control of nation-states are also within its scope if a group of states transcending one region seeks to promote some broad international action to address the issue. Thus the destruction of the world's tropical forests and the loss of biological diversity are also part of global environmental politics.

Threats to the survival of whale species and to the African elephant and threats to the wilderness of the Antarctic are also global environmental issues because developed as well as developing countries have negotiated on them. The issue of the international hazardous waste trade involves both developed and developing countries, with environmental consequences for both, depending on how the issue is addressed by the international community. Long-range **transboundary air pollution** (the emission of pollutants, especially nitric and sulfuric acids, across national boundaries) has been the subject of multilateral negotiations involving Europe and North America, and China and Japan.

Multilateral agreements aimed at reducing environmental threats are not the only subject of global environmental politics. The policies and actions of various international institutions affecting the environment also have become an integral part of the issue area. The development-assistance agencies of large donor countries, United Nations agencies such as the United Nations Environment Programme (UNEP) and the Food and Agriculture Organization, multilateral financial institutions such as the World Bank and International Monetary Fund (IMF), and even the World Trade Organization (WTO), formerly the **General Agreement on Tariffs and Trade** (GATT), make decisions that have impacts on environmental problems. These institutions are the targets of lobbying and pressure by both states and nonstate actors, including nongovernmental organizations (NGOs) and multinational actors.

States have different combinations of internal economic and political forces that influence their policies toward environmental issues. The actual costs and risks of environmental degradation, moreover, are never distributed equally among all states, so some are less motivated than others to participate in international efforts to reduce environmental threats. Nor do states have the same perceptions of equitable solutions to environmental issues. Yet despite these disparate interests, states must strive for consensus, at least among those states that significantly contribute to and are significantly affected by a given environmental problem.

One of the distinctive features of global environmental politics is the importance of veto power. In every global environmental issue there is one state or a group of states whose cooperation is so essential to a successful agreement for coping with the problem that it has the potential to block strong international action. When such states oppose such an agreement or try to weaken it they become **veto** or **blocking states** and form **veto coalitions.**

On the issue of a whaling moratorium, for example, four states, led by Japan, accounted for three-fourths of the whaling catch worldwide, so they could make or break a global regime to save the whales. Similarly, the United States, which accounts for more than 20 percent of energy-related carbon emissions worldwide, was able in 1992 to block international agreement on targets and timetables for controlling such emissions in the climate convention. The role of veto coalitions is central to the dynamics of bargaining and negotiation in global environmental politics.

Because of the importance of veto power, even economically powerful states cannot count on being able to impose a global environmental agreement on a much less powerful state if the latter is both strongly opposed to it and critical to the agreement's success. For example, the highly industrialized countries could not pressure Brazil, Indonesia, Malaysia, and other tropical forest countries to accept any binding agreement on the world's forests during the negotiations on the 1992 Earth Summit. Moreover, weaker states can use their veto power to demand compensation and other forms of favorable treatment in global environmental negotiations.

A second characteristic of global environmental politics is that the political dynamics of issues often reflect the roles of state actors in international trade in a particular product. The issue of international hazardous waste trading, for instance, is defined by the relationship between industrialized countries that are exporting the waste and developing countries that are potential importers. The issue of international trade in endangered species is defined by the roles of the developing countries that export the illegal wildlife products and the major economies that import them. On tropical deforestation, trade relations between tropical timber exporters and consuming nations are critical to the dynamics of the issue.

In each of these issues, the roles and relative bargaining influences tend to be defined by a country's position in international trade in the product. In some cases, it is the producing-exporting countries that have the veto power; in others, it is the importing countries. In one case—tropical deforestation—both producers and importers have roughly equal veto power, and with few exceptions neither major exporting states nor major importing states have had any interest in limiting their trade in tropical timber.

But industrialized states and developing states do not have equal veto power over the outcomes of global environmental regimes. Although a relatively few developing states may have the ability to either prevent an agreement from being reached or to bargain for special treatment on some environmental issues, the major economic powers have the ability to do that on every environmental issue.

A third characteristic of global environmental politics is that economic power can affect the positions of states and even the outcome of bargaining on international agreements in some circumstances, whereas military power does not constitute a useful asset for influencing such outcomes. The ability of a country to give or withhold economic benefits such as access to markets or economic assistance can persuade states dependent on those benefits to go along with that power's policy, provided that those benefits are more important than the issue at stake in the negotiations. Thus Japan and Korea have accepted international agreements on driftnetting and whaling because they feared the loss of fishing benefits from the United States. And Japan succeeded in ensuring the support of some small nonwhaling nations for its pro-whaling position by offering assistance to their fishing industries.

Military power has not had any impact on the outcome of global environmental issues. Global environmental politics do not give rise to a **hegemonic power** in the traditional sense of a state with the ability to use military power to coerce other states into accepting the hegemon's position. There is no positive correlation between dominant military power and leadership on global environmental issues—and there may be a negative correlation between the two in that high levels of military spending divert financial resources from environmental issues. Moreover, it is almost universally accepted that global environmental threats can be successfully addressed only through the active cooperation of the key actors. Using military force to enforce an environmental agreement would be an impractical option even if it were politically acceptable.

The fourth characteristic of the politics surrounding global environmental issues is that the outcomes of multilateral bargaining processes usually result in cooperation to curb environmental threats, despite the obstacles of veto power and sovereignty. The overarching international political system within which global environmental issues are negotiated is a decentralized system in which sovereign states are free to act on their own definition of national interest. But during the past decade ever larger numbers of states have been able to reach agreement to address global environmental problems, sometimes giving up significant freedom of action in the process. The ways in which sovereign states with divergent interests are able to act collectively is one of the major themes of this book.

The fifth characteristic of environmental politics is the importance of public opinion and nonprofit NGOs, especially environmental NGOs, that are both national and international in scope. Environmental issues, like human rights issues before them, have mobilized the active political interest of large numbers of citizens in key countries, inducing shifts in policy that helped turn the tide in a number of environmental issues. Public opinion, channeled through electoral politics and NGOs, has had a substantial, if not decisive, influence on the outcomes of global bargaining on whaling, Antarctic minerals, and ozone depletion and could be a key factor in negotiations to strengthen the climate change treaty. Public opinion has not played comparable roles in the security and economic issue areas, which tend to be much more heavily dominated by bureaucratic or economic elites.

INTERNATIONAL REGIMES
IN ENVIRONMENTAL POLITICS

The Concept of International Regimes

One concept used to compare international politics across issues areas is **international regimes.** The concept of international regime has been defined in two very different ways. According to the first definition, it is a set of norms, rules, or decisionmaking procedures, whether implicit or explicit, that produces some convergence in the actors' expectations in a particular issue area. In this broad definition, it may be applied to a wide range of international arrangements, from the coordination of monetary relations to superpower security relations. This way of conceiving regimes has been strongly criticized for including arrangements that are merely agreements to disagree and have no predictability or stability.[28] Although a set of norms or rules governing international behavior may exist in some issue areas in the absence of a formal international agreement, it is difficult to identify norms or rules in the global environmental area that are not defined by an explicit agreement.

The second definition of regime—and the one used in this book—is a system of norms and rules that are specified by a multilateral agreement among the relevant states to regulate national actions on a specific issue or set of interrelated issues. Most regimes take the form of a binding agreement or legal instrument. On global environmental problems, the most common kind of legal instrument is the **convention,** which may contain all the binding obligations expected to be negotiated or may be followed by a more detailed legal instrument elaborating on its norms and rules.

If a convention is negotiated in anticipation of one or more later elaborating texts, it is called a **framework convention.** It is intended to establish a set of principles, norms, and goals and formal mechanisms for cooperation on the issue (including a regular conference of the parties [COP] to make policy and implementation decisions), rather than to impose major binding obligations on the parties. A framework convention is followed by the negotiation of one or more **protocols,** which spell out more specific obligations on the parties on the overall issue in question or on a narrower subissue. The negotiations on a framework convention and protocols may take several years, as they did in the cases of transboundary acid rain and ozone depletion.

A nonbinding agreement could also be viewed as a regime to the extent that it establishes norms that influence state behavior. In global environmental politics, nonbinding codes of conduct and guidelines for global environmental problems such as pesticide trade and hazardous waste trade (prior to the Basel Convention), which are referred to as **soft law,** could be considered as regimes with varying degrees of effectiveness. And the Agenda 21 plan of action adopted at the 1992 United Nations Conference on Environment and Development also could be considered an "umbrella regime" for worldwide sustainable development, defining norms of behavior on a wide range of environment and development issues. Although such nonbinding agreements do influence state behavior to some extent, regimes based on legal instruments are usually far more effective. That is why some countries become dissatisfied with a given nonbinding code of conduct or other soft-law agreement and insist that it should be turned into a legally binding agreement.

An Overview of Global Environmental Regimes

Thus far, global environmental regimes have been negotiated on a wide variety of projects from whale protection to climate change to desertification. These regimes vary widely in their effectiveness, from weak to quite strong. The regime for whales grew out of the International Convention for the Regulation of Whaling (1946), which was not originally intended to be a regime for conserving whales but grew into a ban on whaling in 1985. The regime for marine oil pollution was originally the International Convention for the Prevention of Pollution of the Sea by Oil (1954), which was limited to a zone within 50 miles (80 kilometers) of the nearest coast, allowed significant deliberate oil spillage, and had no reliable system of enforcement.[29] It was so ineffective that it was replaced by the International Convention for the Prevention of Pollution from Ships (1973), also known as the MARPOL Convention. The latter limited oil discharges at sea, prohibited them in certain sensitive zones, and set minimum distances from land for discharge of various pollutants. It was so strongly opposed by shipping interests in crucial maritime states that it did not enter into force until a decade later.

The Convention on the Prevention of Marine Pollution by Dumping of Wastes and Other Matter, or London Dumping Convention (1972), established a regime to prohibit the dumping of some substances, including high-level radioactive wastes, and to require permits for others. It was the first marine-pollution agreement to accept the right of coastal states to enforce prohibitions against pollution. It became an important forum for negotiating further controls over ocean dumping.

Until the 1970s virtually all international treaties relating to wildlife conservation were lacking in binding legal commitments and were ineffective in protecting migratory birds and other species. The first global convention on wildlife conservation with both strong legal commitments and an enforcement mechanism was the Convention on International Trade in Endangered Species, or CITES (1973). It set up a system of trade sanctions and a worldwide reporting network to curb the traffic in endangered species, but it contained loopholes allowing states with interests in a particular species to opt out of the controls on it.

The original regime to regulate acid rain that crosses boundaries before falling was the Convention on Long-Range Transboundary Air Pollution (1979), a framework convention that did not commit the signatories to specific reductions in their emissions of the compounds. Later, however, the regime was strengthened by adding the Helsinki Protocol (1985) to reduce sulphur dioxide emissions and the Sofia Protocol (1988) to freeze emissions of nitrogen oxide at 1987 levels.

Similarly, the regime for the ozone layer was initially a framework convention, the Vienna Convention for the Protection of the Ozone Layer (1985). It did not commit the parties to reduce the consumption of ozone-depleting chemicals. The Montreal Protocol (1987) represented the first real step toward protecting the ozone layer by requiring reductions in the consumption of CFCs, and in 1990 the regime was further strengthened by an amendment to the Montreal Protocol that phases out CFCs and other ozone-depleting substances by 2000. The ozone-protection regime is considered the most effective of all global environmental regimes to date.

The agreement establishing a regime on transboundary shipments of hazardous wastes is the Basel Convention on the Control of Transboundary Movements of Hazardous Wastes and Their Disposal (1989), which does not prohibit the trade but establishes conditions on it. But dissatisfaction with the agreement on the part of developing countries, especially in Africa, resulted in an agreement by the COP of the Basel Convention on a complete ban on waste exports. The international regime for protection of the Antarctic environment, the Protocol on

Environmental Protection to the Antarctic Treaty (1991), prohibits mining the Antarctic's mineral resources for at least fifty years.

A regime for biodiversity conservation was established with the signing of the Convention on Biological Diversity (1992). The biodiversity convention does not obligate signatories to any measurable conservation objectives, although it requires development of national strategies for conservation of biodiversity. Similarly, the regime for climate change, the Framework Convention on Climate Change (1992), does not impose targets and timetables for emissions of greenhouse gases but does obligate the signatories to prepare national action plans for controlling their emissions. And the International Convention to Combat Desertification (1994), establishing a regime for the problem of desertification—the destruction of formerly productive lands' biological potential, reducing them to desertlike conditions—calls for countries to draw up integrated national programs in consultation with local communities.

Theoretical Approaches to International Regimes

Several major theoretical approaches have been used to explain why international regimes in any issue area come into existence and why they change.[30] These include the structural, game theoretic, institutional bargaining, and epistemic communities approaches. Each of them may help to explain one or more international regimes, but each fails to account for all the regimes described and analyzed in this study. The structural or hegemonic power approach holds that the primary factor determining regime formation and change is the relative strength of the nation-state actors involved in a particular issue and that "stronger states in the issue system will dominate the weaker ones and determine the rules of the game."[31] This approach suggests that strong international regimes are a function of the existence of a hegemonic state that can exercise leadership over weaker states and that the absence of such a hegemonic state is likely to frustrate regime formation.

The structural approach can be viewed in two ways—one stressing coercive power, the other focusing on "public goods." In the coercive power variant, regimes are set up by hegemonic states that use their military and economic leverage over other states to bring them into regimes, as the United States did in setting up trade and monetary regimes in the period immediately after World War II.[32] The second variant views the same postwar regimes as the result of a hegemonic power adopting policies that create public goods—benefits open to all states who want to participate, such as export markets in the United States and the dollar as a stable currency for international payments.

However useful the structural approach has been to explain the post–World War II global economic systems, it cannot explain why global environmental regimes have been negotiated in the 1980s. The international regimes negotiated since then—including environmental regimes—have come about despite the fact that the role of the United States, which had been the hegemon in the past, has been constrained by two factors: the rise of competing economic powers in Japan and Western Europe and, from 1981 to 1993, a U.S. ideological hostility toward international environmental regulation. The environmental regimes that have been successfully negotiated have depended on wide consensus among a number of states, not on imposition by the United States.[33]

Another approach to regime creation is based on game theory and utilitarian models of bargaining. It focuses on such issues as the number of parties in the negotiations. This approach suggests that small groups of states are more likely to be able to successfully negotiate an international regime than a large number because each player can more readily understand the bargaining strategies of other players. On the basis of this approach, Fen Osler Hampson analyzed the process of regime creation as an effort by a small coalition of states to form a regime by exercising leadership over a much larger number of national actors.[34]

Because of the importance of veto power in global environmental politics, however, relatively small groups of states are no more likely to be able to form regimes than much larger ones. If veto states are included among a small group, they will be just as prone to opposition as they would have been in a large group of states. If veto states are left outside the small group, they will still be in a position to frustrate regime formation when it is enlarged. The Group of Seven, according to this approach, would be the ideal forum in which the highly industrialized countries could work out the essentials of a global climate-change agreement and then try to bring in other countries. But opposition by a single state (the United States) prevented such a result. This small-group model is further weakened by the fact that, in some cases (whaling and ocean dumping of radioactive wastes), enlarging the number of actors involved in past bargaining has helped to bring about stricter environmental regimes.

A third approach, which has been called the institutional bargaining model of regime creation, hypothesizes that regime formation can be successful only if state actors are unclear about how their interests would be affected by any proposed international regime.[35] The global environmental negotiations that have resulted in the formation of regimes suggest, however, that lack of clarity about the interests of the actors is seldom, if ever, the factor that makes regimes possible. As will be shown in Chapter 3, it is not imperfect information about the consequences of the regime but other factors that have induced veto states to make concessions necessary to establish or strengthen regimes.

The fourth approach is the epistemic communities model, which emphasizes international learning, primarily on the basis of scientific research on a given problem, as a factor influencing the evolution of regimes.[36] This approach, advanced specifically to explain both adherence to and compliance with the Mediterranean Action Plan, identifies intraelite shifts within governments as the critical factor in the convergence of state policies in support of a stronger regime. The shifts empowered technical and scientific specialists allied with officials of international organizations. These elites thus formed transnational epistemic communities, that is, communities of experts sharing common values and approaches to policy problems.

The importance of scientific evidence and scientific expertise in the politics of some key global environmental issues cannot be ignored. Global warming and ozone depletion, involving threats that cannot be detected, much less understood, without scientific research have been defined to an extent by the judgments of scientists. A significant degree of scientific consensus has sometimes been a minimum condition for serious international action on an issue. A 1985 agreement to reduce sulfur dioxide emissions by 30 percent of 1980 levels was made possible by mounting scientific evidence of the damaging effects on European forests, especially those of West Germany. The impetus for an agreement to phase out CFCs in 1990 was scientific evidence that the ozone layer was much thinner than had previously been thought. The formal international consideration of the climate change issue beginning in 1988 was made possible by a wide consensus among climatologists and scientists in related fields that the threat of greenhouse warming is indeed real.

But although scientific elites may play a supportive and enabling role in some environmental negotiations, on other issues they remain divided or even captured by particular government or private interests. And on some issues, such as the whaling ban, hazardous waste trade, the Antarctic, biodiversity loss, and ocean dumping of radioactive wastes, scientists have contributed little to regime formation and/or strengthening. In those cases, either scientific elites were not particularly influential in the policymaking process or scientific findings were explicitly rejected as the basis for decision by some key actors.[37]

The case studies presented in Chapter 3 suggest that theoretical approaches based solely on a **unitary actor model** (one suggesting that state actors can be treated as though they are a single entity with a single, internally consistent set of values and attitudes), ignoring the roles of domestic sociopolitical structures and processes, are likely to be poor bases for analyzing and predicting the outcomes of global environmental bargaining.

Negotiating positions usually reflect domestic sociopolitical balances and may change dramatically because of a shift in those balances. Although the structure of an issue in terms of economic interests may indicate which states are most likely to join a veto coalition, it is often domestic political pressures that tip the balance toward regime creation. A theoretical explanation for global environmental regime formation or change, therefore, must incorporate the variable of state actors' domestic politics.

A theoretical explanation for the formation of global environmental regimes must also leave room for the importance of the rules of the negotiating forum and the linkages between the negotiations on regimes and the wider relationships among the negotiating parties. The legal structure of the negotiating forum—the "rules of the game" regarding who may participate and how authoritative decisions are to be made—are particularly important when the negotiations take place within an already established treaty or organization. The cases of whaling and Antarctica both illustrate how these rules can be crucial determinants to the outcomes of the negotiations.

Economic and political ties among key state actors can also sway a veto state to compromise or defect. Particularly when the global environmental regime under negotiation does not involve issues that are central to the economy of the states who could block agreement, the formation or strengthening of a regime is sometimes made possible by the potential veto state's concern about how a veto would affect relations with states that are important for economic or political reasons.

Building a theoretical approach that accounts for actual historical patterns of regime formation and regime strengthening and can predict most outcomes will require advancing a series of testable hypotheses encompassing multiple variables rather than relying on a single-variable approach. Until such explicit hypotheses are generated and tested, the study of regime formation will focus primarily on identifying some common patterns through case studies.

PARADIGM SHIFT AND ENVIRONMENTAL POLITICS

In any issue area, public policy is shaped not only by impersonal forces, such as technological innovation and economic growth, but also by people's perception of reality. In times of relative social stability, there is a dominant social **paradigm,** a set of beliefs, ideas, and values from which public policies and whole systems of behavior flow logically.[38] A view of the world emerges as the dominant social paradigm within a society because it has been the most useful way of thinking about and solving certain problems and is transmitted across social sectors and generations by various socialization processes. Every dominant paradigm is ultimately challenged, however, as its anomalies—the contradictions between its assumptions and observed reality—multiply and its usefulness wanes. Finally, it gives way to a new paradigm in a process called a paradigm shift.

The Dominant Social Paradigm

Because economic policy and environmental policy are so intertwined, the social paradigm that has dominated public understanding of environmental management during the period of rapid global economic growth has been essentially a system of beliefs about economics. It has been referred to as the **exclusionist paradigm** because it excludes human beings from the laws of nature. It has also been called "frontier economics," suggesting the sense of unlimited resources that characterizes a society with an open frontier.[39]

In capitalist societies this dominant social paradigm has been based primarily on the assumptions of **neoclassical economics:** first, that the free market will always maximize social welfare, and second, that there is not only an infinite supply of natural resources but also of "sinks" for disposing of the wastes from exploiting those resources—provided that the free market is operating. Humans will not deplete any resource, according to this world view, as long as technology is given free rein and prices are allowed to fluctuate enough to stimulate the search for substitutes, so absolute scarcity can be postponed to the indefinite future.[40] Waste disposal is viewed as a problem to be cleaned up after the fact but not at the cost of interference with market decisions.[41] Because conventional economic theory is concerned only with the allocation of scarce resources, and nature is not considered a constraining factor, this paradigm considers the environment to be irrelevant to economics. (Despite a different economic and political ideology, the Soviet Union and other communist states also shared this assumption.) The traditional legal principles of unrestricted freedom of the seas and open access to common resources such as the oceans and their living resources buttressed the exclusionist paradigm and weakened the impulse toward international cooperation for environmental protection.

Beginning in the early 1960s the dominant paradigm came under steadily mounting attack, starting in the United States, where it had its most articulate advocates, and then spreading to Europe and other regions. The publication in 1962 of Rachel Carson's *Silent Spring*, which documented the dangers to human health from synthetic pesticides, was the beginning of an explosion in popular literature reflecting the new scientific knowledge about invisible threats to the environment: radiation, heavy metal toxic wastes, chlorinated hydrocarbons in the water, and others. Such research and writing helped raise awareness that public policies based on the exclusionist paradigm carry high costs to societies. The first mass movement for environmental protection, focused on domestic issues, began to develop in the United States. Parallel changes in public concern about air, soil, and water pollution also occurred in other noncommunist industrialized countries. One result of the burst of environmental activism was the passage of the National Environmental Policy Act of 1969 (NEPA), which directed federal agencies to support international cooperation in "anticipating and preventing a decline in the quality of mankind's world environment."[42]

As a result of a 1967 Swedish initiative supported by the United States, the first worldwide environmental conference in history, the United Nations Conference on the Human Environment, was convened in Stockholm in 1972. The **Stockholm conference,** attended by 114 states (not including the Soviet bloc states), approved a declaration containing twenty-six broad principles on the management of the global environment and an action plan, with 109 recommendations for international cooperation on the environment. On the recommendation of the conference, the U.N. General Assembly in December 1972 created the United Nations Environment Programme to provide a focal point for environmental action and coordination of environmentally related activities within the U.N. system.

The Rise of an Alternative Social Paradigm

The rapid rise of environmental consciousness and pressure groups in the 1960s and early 1970s was not yet accompanied by an alternative set of assumptions about both physical and social reality that could become a competing world view. The essential assumptions of classical economics remained largely intact. Confronted with evidence that existing patterns of exploitation of resources could cause irreversible damage, proponents of classical economics continued to maintain that such exploitation was still economically rational.[43]

During the 1970s and 1980s, however, an alternative paradigm challenging the assumptions of frontier economics began to take shape. Two of the intellectual forerunners of this paradigm were the *Limits to Growth* study by the Club of Rome, published in 1972, and the *Global 2000 Report to the President* released by the U.S. Council of Environmental Quality and the Department of State in 1980.[44] Both studies applied global-systems computer modeling to the projected interactions among future trends in population, economic growth, and natural resources. They forecast the depletion of natural resources and the degradation of ecosystems. Because each of the studies suggested that economic development and population growth were on a path that would eventually strain the earth's "carrying capacity" (the total population that the earth's natural systems can support without undergoing degradation), the viewpoint underlying the studies was generally referred to as the limits-to-growth perspective.

These studies were widely criticized by defenders of the dominant paradigm, such as Herman Kahn and Julian Simon, for projecting the depletion of nonrenewable resources without taking into account technological changes and market responses. These critics argued that overpopulation would not become a problem because people are the world's "ultimate resource," and they characterized the authors of these studies that were based on global-systems models as "no-growth elitists" who would freeze the underdeveloped countries out of the benefits of economic growth. They argued that human ingenuity would enable humanity to leap over the alleged limits to growth through new and better technologies.[45]

The development of an alternative paradigm regarding the world society and environment was set back in the United States in the early 1980s, as the Reagan administration enthusiastically embraced the exclusionist paradigm. But meanwhile, knowledge of ecological principles and their relationship to economic development issues was spreading across the globe and the web of specialists on these linkages was thickening. A global community of practitioners and scholars was emerging, allied by the belief that economic policies based on the dominant paradigm had to be replaced by ecologically sound policies.

By the early to mid-1980s, **sustainable development** was emerging as the catchword of an alternative paradigm. It was being heard with increasing frequency in conferences involving NGOs and government officials in the United States and abroad.[46] The publication in 1987 of *Our Common Future*, the Reports of the World Commission on Environment and Development (better known as the Brundtland Report after the commission's chair, Norwegian prime minister Gro Harlem Brundtland) popularized the term "sustainable development" and gave the new paradigm momentum in replacing the dominant paradigm.[47] Drawing on and synthesizing the views and research of hundreds of people across the globe, that report codified some of the central beliefs of the alternative paradigm.

The Brundtland Report defined sustainable development as development that is "consistent with future as well as present needs." Its central themes criticized the dominant paradigm for failure to reconcile those needs. It asserted that the earth's natural systems have finite capabilities to support human production and consumption and that the continuation of existing economic policies risks irreversible damage to natural systems on which all life depends.

The sustainable development paradigm emphasizes the need to redefine the term "development." It posits that economic growth cannot continue to take place at the expense of the earth's natural capital (its stock of renewable and nonrenewable resources) and vital natural support systems such as the ozone layer and climate system. Instead, the world economy must learn to live off its "interest." That means radically more efficient energy use, i.e., reducing the amount of energy used per unit of gross national product (GNP) and shifting from fossil fuels to greater reliance on renewable energy sources over the next several decades. It also implies a rapid transition to sustainable systems of renewable natural resource management and stabilizing world population at the lowest possible level.[48] This viewpoint also suggests, although not always explicitly, the need to impose some limits on total worldwide consumption.

The sustainable development paradigm assumes the need for greater equity not only between wealthy and poor nations but also within societies and between generations (**intergenerational equity**). Highly industrialized countries such as the United States, which now use a disproportionate share of the world's environmental resources, are seen as pursuing economic growth that is inherently unsustainable, as are societies in which the distribution of land and other resources is grossly unequal. Sustainable development further holds that future generations have an equal right to use the planet's resources.[49] The paradigm recognizes that developing countries must meet the basic needs of the poor in ways that do not deplete the countries' natural resources, and it also points to a need to reexamine basic attitudes and values in industrialized countries regarding the unnecessary and wasteful aspects of their material abundance.[50]

One of the main anomalies of the classical economic paradigm is its measure of macroeconomic growth, that is, gross national product. Advocates of sustainable development have noted that GNP fails to reflect the real physical capability of an economy to provide material wealth in the future or to take into account the relative well-being of the society in general. Thus, a country could systematically deplete its natural resources, erode its soils, and pollute its waters without that loss of real wealth ever showing up in its income accounts. Because of the rise of the new paradigm, some economists began in the second half of the 1980s to study how to correct this anomaly in conventional accounting and to advocate **environmental accounting** in all governments and international organizations.[51] Critics have proposed alternatives to GNP, such as "real net national product," "sustainable social net national product," or "index of sustainable economic welfare," that include changes in environmental resources as well as other indicators that measure human welfare. Of particular importance is the United Nations Development Programme's (UNDP) annual *Human Development Report*, which uses "human indicators" to rate the quality of life in all countries by other than economic measures.[52]

The new paradigm points to the failure of markets to encourage the sustainable use of natural resources. Prices should reflect the real costs to society of producing and consuming a given resource, but conventional free-market economic policies systematically underprice or ignore natural resources.[53] Public policies that do not correct for such market failure encourage overconsumption and thus the more rapid depletion of renewable resources and the degradation of **environmental services.** (Environmental services are the conserving or restorative functions of nature, e.g., the conversion of carbon dioxide to oxygen by plants and the cleansing of water by wetlands.) Raising the prices of resources through taxation to make them reflect real social and environmental costs is the favored means of showing the rates of consumption of energy and tropical timber. Such **green taxes** are one tool by which the "polluter pays" principle, endorsed in the Earth Summit's Declaration of Principles, may be implemented. Placing an upper limit on consumption is another method.[54]

The process of paradigm shift has already begun. The sustainable development paradigm has begun to displace the exclusionist paradigm in some parts of the multilateral financial institutions, in some state bureaucracies, and in some parliamentary committees dealing with the environment and development. For instance, publications of the Asian Development Bank, the Inter-American Development Bank, and the Organization of American States (OAS) all impugn mistaken unsustainable development paths of the past and recommend new sustainable development strategies.[55] Within most of the powerful institutions in the United States and elsewhere in the industrialized world, however, the assumptions of the exclusionist paradigm still influence policymaking. Corporations, government ministries dealing with trade and finance, the leaders of some political parties, and some top officials of the World Bank and other multilateral institutions have been slow to change.

The single most important indication of a worldwide paradigm shift was the United Nations Conference on Environment and Development, held in Rio de Janeiro in June 1992. One hundred seventy-two governments and thousands of nongovernmental organizations around the world participated in two years of discussions on domestic environmental and poverty problems and global environment issues, especially questions of North-South inequities and responsibility. Also completed and signed at Rio were important treaties on climate change and biodiversity. During this two-year exercise, countries were forced to start thinking through the implications of integrating sustainable development goals into the full range of their economic development policies. In many countries, domestic conflicts and debates surfaced on a wide range of issues related to socioeconomic equity and sustainability. UNCED accelerated the paradigm shift described in this chapter and may some day appear to be a watershed in that process.

An Alternative Security Paradigm

Paralleling the shift from the exclusionist economic paradigm to the sustainable development paradigm, an alternative paradigm has taken shape to challenge the traditional paradigm regarding national and global security. The traditional security paradigm assumed that security is based essentially on political-military power and that the primary security threats to states and peoples come from other states who are competing for power. It also assumed that such threats to the existence or autonomy of states must be the supreme concern of states.

In the 1980s, however, a new paradigm of national and international security emerged that challenged traditional notions of security. Called "comprehensive security" or "common security," the alternative security paradigm is based on the belief that no country can increase its own security without at the same time increasing the security of other countries. It assumes that the main threats to global security come not from individual states but from global problems shared by the entire international community, such as the threat of nuclear war and global environmental degradation. The common security paradigm views traditional military security policies, regardless of the state adopting them, as a serious obstacle to meeting these common global threats. The Palme Commission, composed of senior political leaders from both the United States and the Soviet Union and others from developed and developing nations, articulated this new concept of security in 1982 and 1989 reports. It argued that the abolition of or large reduction in weapons of mass destruction and conventional disarmament is necessary to provide momentum in progress on economic and social development and environmental conservation.[56]

The concept of comprehensive security, as further elaborated by a group of experts convened by the United Nations Environment Programme and by other specialists on international security and environmental problems, holds that "environmental security" is one of the two fundamental aspects of global security, along with avoidance of nuclear war. According to this view of security, threats to global life systems such as **global warming**, ozone depletion, and the loss of tropical forests and marine habitats are just as important to the future of humankind as the threat of nuclear catastrophe.[57]

As the cold war ebbed and finally ended, the power of the traditional security paradigm was diminished. Former Soviet premier Mikhail Gorbachev's dramatic reform of Soviet foreign and security policy helped legitimize a common security paradigm that put environmental sec₁ at the center of global security. Gorbachev was the first leader of a major power to accept the new concept of common security, arguing that the traditional notion of national security based primarily on military power is "totally obsolete."[58]

Even as the cold war waned, the United States, Britain, and France remained strongholds of the traditional security paradigm, resisting any linkage between global environment and national security in votes in the U.N. General Assembly.[59] But the collapse of the Soviet Union and its replacement by a transitional, quasi-democratic Russian government left the major powers in the world for the first time without any plausible significant enemy, and thus without a "strategic imperative" or incentive to compete for political-military power.[60]

The Clinton administration, the first to be elected after the end of the cold war, has begun to integrate the concepts of sustainable development and environmental security into its national security thinking. The administration's 1994 document on national security asserts that increasing competition for dwindling renewable resources "is already a very real risk to regional stability around the world" and that worldwide environmental degradation "will ultimately block economic growth." And President Bill Clinton himself publicly expressed views reflecting the shift to a new security paradigm in which environmental and sustainable development concerns are central.

Whereas many scientists, academics, and professionals in the fields of international development and the environment generally share the assumptions of the common security paradigm, most foreign affairs professionals tend to continue to view security as a matter of potentially violent conflict. The shift to a new global security paradigm will certainly take many years.

CONCLUSION

Global environmental politics involve interactions among states and nonstate actors transcending a single region regarding international decisions that affect the environment and natural resources. The emergence of this issue area in world politics is a reflection of the growing awareness of the cumulative stresses on the earth's resources and life-support systems from economic activities during the twentieth century.

Much of global environmental politics focuses on efforts to negotiate multilateral agreements for cooperation to protect the environment and natural resources. These agreements constitute global environmental regimes of varying effectiveness that govern state behavior in regard to the environmental problem in question.

Divergences of environmental interests as defined by states themselves make the achievement of unanimity among the parties responsible and directly affected by an environmental problem a political and diplomatic challenge. One of the primary problems of global environmental politics is the ability of one or more states to block or weaken multilateral agreements and how to overcome such blockage. For a regime to be formed, veto states and coalitions must be persuaded to abandon their opposition to a proposed regime or at least compromise with states supporting it.

One of the obstacles to effective international action for environmental conservation in the past has been a dominant social paradigm that justifies unlimited exploitation of nature. Despite the weakening of that paradigm and the widespread adherence to the sustainable development paradigm in some sectors of societies, paradigm shift may take many years to complete because of its dominance in powerful political and economic institutions.

Theoretical approaches that have been advanced to explain the formation of international regimes generally include the structural, game theoretic, institutional bargaining, and epistemic community models. These approaches fail to account for most global environmental regimes. To explain why environmental regimes are formed and strengthened, a theoretical approach will have to deal with the central problem of veto coalitions and why they are or are not overcome in regime negotiations. It will have to avoid relying solely on the unitary actor model and encompass domestic political forces, the structure of the negotiating forum, and the role of other international political concerns.

TWO

□ □ □

Actors in the
Environmental Arena

State actors are the final determinants of the outcomes of global environmental issues. States negotiate the international legal instruments creating global environmental regimes as well as adopting international trade and financial policies that directly and indirectly affect the environment. States also decide which issues are considered by the global community both directly (by arguing for international action on an issue) and indirectly (through their membership in the governing councils of international organizations). And donor states influence environmental policies through their bilateral aid programs and donations to multilateral banks.

But nonstate actors also exert major and increasing influence on global environmental politics.[1] International organizations help to set the global environmental agenda, initiate and mediate the process of regime formation, and cooperate with developing countries on projects and programs directly affecting the environment. Nongovernmental organizations also participate in setting the agenda, influencing negotiations on regime formation, and shaping the environmental policies of donor agencies toward developing countries. Multinational corporations both influence the bargaining over regime creation and carry out actions that directly affect the global environment.

NATION-STATE ACTORS:
ROLES AND INTERESTS

The most important actions by state actors in global environmental politics are those relating to the process of regime formation. In the negotiations on an environmental regime, a state actor may play one of four possible roles: **lead state, supporting state, swing state,** or veto or blocking state. A lead state has a strong commitment to effective international action on the issue, moves the process of negotiations forward by proposing its own negotiating formula as the basis for an agreement, and attempts to get the support of other state actors.

A supporting state speaks in favor of the proposal of a lead state in negotiations. A swing state may demand significant concessions to its interests as a price for going along with an agreement. A veto or blocking state either opposes a proposed environmental regime outright or tries to weaken it to the point that it cannot be effective.

States may shift from what appears to be a veto role to a swing role, since threatening a veto is sometimes the best means of enhancing bargaining leverage. The Indian delegation to the London conference of the parties to the Montreal Protocol in June 1990 at first seemed to be rejecting any agreement that would bind India to phase out CFCs in 2010 but eventually settled for a compromise that could provide financial assistance for Indian companies to purchase substitute technology. In other cases, however, a veto role may give way to a swing role because of domestic or international pressures. The United States seemed prepared to be a veto state at the same conference because of its vociferous opposition to a new funding mechanism for the Montreal Protocol but changed its stance only days before the conference under pressure from business interests and major foreign allies. Even so, it played the role of swing state by insisting on a slower timetable for a phaseout than a number of other industrialized countries were proposing.

There may be more than one lead state on a given issue. Sweden and Norway were allied from the beginning in pushing for a long-range transboundary air pollution agreement, for example. But often one state steps forward to advance a policy that puts it clearly in the lead, as did Australia on the Antarctica issue and West Germany on the climate change issue in 1990. As issues go through several stages, the role of lead state may shift from one state or combination of states to another. In the negotiation of the Vienna Convention on the ozone layer in 1985, Finland and Sweden took the lead by submitting their own draft convention and heavily influencing the draft put before the conference. In 1986, the United States stepped into the lead role by proposing an eventual 95-percent reduction in CFCs, and by 1989–1990 several OECD (Organization for Economic Cooperation and Development) states had become the lead states by working for a phaseout before 2000.

Lead states have a wide range of methods for influencing other state actors on a global environmental issue. A lead state may

□ produce and call attention to research that defines the problem and demonstrates its urgency, as when Swedish research showed the serious damage done by acid rain;
□ seek to educate public opinion in target states, as does Canada when it supplies U.S. tourists with pamphlets on acidification of its forests and waters or instructs its Washington embassy to cooperate with like-minded U.S. environmental organizations;
□ take unilateral action on an issue and thus lead by example, as in the case of U.S. regulation of aerosols containing CFCs in 1979;
□ use its diplomatic clout to get an international organization to identify the issues as a priority, as when the United States and Canada got the OECD to take up the ozone layer and CFCs;
□ rely on the worldwide network of NGOs to support its position in other countries and at international conferences, as Australia did in its effort to derail the Antarctic minerals treaty;
□ make a diplomatic demarche to a state that is threatening a veto role, as the United States did with Japan on African elephant ivory;
□ threaten to use trade sanctions against veto states;
□ pledge to commit financial resources to the problem.

Although scientific-technological capabilities and economic power cannot assure that a lead state will prevail on an environmental issue, they constitute valuable assets for helping to create a regime. When a big power like the United States has taken a lead role through scientific research, unilateral action, and diplomatic initiative as it did on the issue of ozone protection in the 1970s and again in the mid-1980s, it helps to sway states that do not otherwise have clearly defined interests on the issue.

Whether a state plays a lead, supporting, swing, or veto role in regard to a particular global environmental issue depends primarily on domestic political factors and on the relative costs and benefits of the proposed regime. A third variable, which has been important in some cases, is anticipation of international political consequences, including increased prestige or damage to the country's image worldwide.

Domestic Political Factors

A state's definition of interest and choice of role on global environmental issues turn largely on domestic economic and political interests and domestic ideological currents. Whether a state actor opposes, supports, or leads on an issue depends first on the relative strength and influence of powerful economic and bureaucratic forces and of domestic environmen-

Anti-Norway Feeling Increases

Jeff Danziger in *The Christian Science Monitor* ©1993 TCSPS.

tal constituencies. Ideological factors related to broader domestic political themes also play a prominent role in the definition of interests in some cases.

Domestic economic interests are particularly prominent in promoting veto roles. In Japan, for example, major trading companies have generally received government support for their interests in whaling because of close ties between those companies and the former ruling Liberal Democratic Party.[2] Norway's fishery industry, which claims to have suffered declining fish catches because of the international protection of whales, has prevailed on Prime Minister Gro Harlem Brundtland to defend Norwegian whaling in the face of criticism from European Community (EC) countries.[3] Norway, Japan, and Greece have all tended to be swing or blocking actors on questions of marine pollution from oil tankers because of the economic importance of their shipping industries. Germany, Italy, the Netherlands, and Sweden, all of which have smaller shipping industries, have been more flexible in negotiations on pollution from ships.[4]

In some cases a state's veto role reflects the interests of a dominant socioeconomic class. Brazil's hostility toward any international efforts to slow deforestation in tropical forests, for example, has been determined by the interests of its agroindustrial class. The policy of colonization of the Amazonian rainforest by millions of poor migrants and the conversion of large areas of the rainforest to ranching and commercial logging that was launched in the 1960s primarily benefited the country's agroindustrial elite. That policy provided a convenient solution to agrarian tensions caused in large part by inequitable land tenure and offered generous tax incentives to the elite for investing in cattle ranches and timber industries in the Amazon.[5]

Government bureaucracies with institutional interests that are in direct conflict with global action on behalf of the environment are often critical factors in swing and blocking roles. In the 1980s, the U.S. Department of Energy, the Department of Interior, and the Treasury Department opposed U.S. support for strong environmental protection in the Antarctic when it appeared to impede the potential development of energy resources.[6] The major obstacles to the United Kingdom's agreeing to an acid rain agreement through the mid-1980s were two public bodies, the National Coal Board and the Central Electricity Generating Board, which did everything possible to avoid having to reduce sulfur dioxide emissions.[7] Similarly, the public power sectors in countries such as India and Brazil, which derive enormous political and economic power from their investment in large conventional power-station projects, could be major influences on their government's policies on negotiating a protocol for limiting greenhouse-gas emissions in the future.

The ability of dominant elites and bureaucratic interests to resist restrictions on their despoiling of the environment is enhanced by authoritarian political regimes that can simply suppress any opposition to their policies. The military regime that ruled Brazil from 1964 to 1985 had virtually unlimited power to determine how natural resources were exploited, permitting no opposition to its campaign to open the Amazonian rainforests to agriculture and other large-scale commercial activities. But under an elected government, with NGOs and media freer to criticize it, the government was less hostile toward international agreement to slow deforestation.

Where other motives for a lead role on a global environmental issue are present, such a role becomes far more likely if there is little or no domestic opposition to it. The United States could easily take the lead role on the issue of whaling in the 1970s and 1980s, for example, because the U.S. whaling industry had already been eliminated. Similarly, the absence of any significant bureaucratic or business interest opposing a ban on imports of African elephant ivory products made it easy for the United States to assume a lead role on that issue.

The existence of a strong environmental movement can be a decisive factor in a state's definition of its interest on an issue, especially if it is a potential swing vote in parliamentary elections. The sudden emergence of West German and French bids for leadership roles on environmental issues in 1989 reflected in large part the upsurge of public support for strong environmental protection policies in Western Europe. The West German Greens had already won 8.2 percent of the vote in the 1984 European Parliament elections, and by 1985 the Green Party, backed by popular environmental sentiment, was already a strong force in the German parliament.[8] Before the 1989 European Parliament election, polls indicated a new surge in environmentalist sentiment in West Germany and France. As a result both West Germany and France in early 1989 became part of a lead coalition of states proposing negotiations on a framework convention on climate change to stabilize carbon dioxide emissions not later than 2000, and France shifted to support of Australia's proposal for a "world park" in Antarctica. Germany, the Netherlands, and Denmark have continued to be lead states on climate change in part because they have the largest and most active environmental movements in Europe.[9] The German environmental movement's clout helped overcome the influence of the powerful German coal industry.

Australia's leadership on issues of nuclear-waste dumping in the Pacific and rejection of the Antarctic minerals treaty in favor of a comprehensive environmental protection convention for the continent was also driven in part by the rise of Australia's environmental movement as a crucial factor in Australian elections. In 1987, the Labor Party's electoral victory was attributed to a "green vote" after environmental groups called on their supporters to vote for labor candidates.[10] And the Netherlands' role as the only state within the EC to support the proposal for a global climate fund reflects a particularly strong and active environmental movement, as well as the country's political tradition of popular involvement in policy issues.

A strong environmental movement does not guarantee that the state actor will play a lead or supporting role on an issue. The U.S. environmental movement is the largest and best organized in the world, but it was unable in the late 1980s and early 1990s to sway U.S. policy in the negotiation of climate and hazardous waste trade regimes, in part because powerful interests were arrayed against it and it had not been able to influence the outcomes of congressional or presidential elections.

Conversely, the absence of a strong environmental movement makes it more likely that a state will play a swing or blocking role on an international environmental issue. For example, Japanese NGOs are relatively underdeveloped in comparison with those in North America and Western Europe, and the Japanese political system makes it difficult for private interest groups without high-level political links to influence policy. So the Japanese government felt little or no domestic pressure to support regimes on African elephants, whaling, and drift-net fishing.

A final domestic political factor that has occasionally shaped a country's definition of its interest in an environmental regime is the ideology or belief system of the policymaker. Despite the fact that the United States exported very little of its hazardous waste, in the UNCED negotiations the Bush administration led the veto coalition against a ban on hazardous waste exports to developing countries because of its strong hostility to the intervention of states in national and international markets. The Bush administration also vetoed a proposal in the UNCED negotiations for targets to be set by each industrialized state for per capita energy use, regarding it as an unwarranted interference by the state in consumer preferences.[11]

Differential Costs and Benefits of Environmental Regimes

A second group of variables that shape the definition of national interest in a global environmental issue includes the degree of cost and risk that the environmental threat poses to a country as well as the costs and opportunities associated with the proposed regime.

Exceptional vulnerability to the consequences of environmental problems has driven countries to support or even take the lead on strong global action. Thirty-two small island states that are especially vulnerable to sea-level rise because of global warming formed the Association of Small Island States (AOSIS) in November 1990 to lobby the climate treaty negotiations for action to limit carbon dioxide emissions from the industrialized countries. States with densely populated coastal plains, such as Bangladesh, Egypt, and the Netherlands are also likely to face particularly severe disruptions from storm surges, hurricanes, and typhoons due to climate change and can be expected to support an effective global regime for climate.

Australia's support for strong climate-change agreements is linked with its concentration of population centers in low-lying coastal regions and large areas of semiarid, marginal land that could easily become desertified with global warming. Its location in the South Pacific near a small number of small, low-lying islands is also a factor. Australian officials fear that several hundred thousand refugees from Pacific islands inundated by sea-level rise would seek refuge in Australia.[12] Australia has been motivated to strongly support protection of the ozone layer because ultraviolet readings in that country are 20 percent above normal and the rate of skin cancer is already the world's highest.[13]

Sweden and Norway, which led the fight for a Long-Range Transboundary Air Pollution Convention in the 1970s, have been the major recipients of sulfur dioxide from other European countries and also have acid-sensitive soils and lakes. The damage from acid rain therefore appeared earlier and was more serious in those Nordic countries than in the

United Kingdom or West Germany. Similarly, Canada has a higher proportion of soil that is vulnerable to acid deposition than does the United States and receives far more sulfur dioxide from U.S. factories than it sends across the border, so it has pushed the United States for stronger action on the issue.

The negotiation of the Montreal Protocol provides several examples of states whose roles were linked with economic interests. UNEP executive director Mostafa Tolba is reported to have observed, "The difficulties in negotiating the Montreal Protocol had nothing to do with whether the environment was damaged or not. . . . It was all who was going to get the edge over whom."[14] Because of an earlier unilateral ban on aerosols using ozone-depleting chemicals, the United States was ahead of members of the European Community and Japan in finding substitutes for CFCs in aerosol cans. So it joined Canada and the Nordic states in supporting such a ban. Western Europe and Japan rejected a ban on aerosols in the early 1980s because they did not yet have technological alternatives. The Soviet Union initially resisted the idea of a CFC phaseout in 1986–1987, fearing it would be unable to develop new technologies to replace CFCs. China and India, who were minor producers at the time but were already gearing up for major production increases, also feared that the transition to ozone-safe chemicals would be too costly without noncommercial access to alternative technologies. Moreover, India's chemical industry planned to export half its projected CFC production to the Middle East and Asia.

A climate change agreement requiring reductions in carbon emissions would be easier and/or cheaper for some countries to implement than others. France lacks self-sufficiency in fossil fuels, has a low concentration of heavy industry and an extremely modern industrial sector with high energy efficiency, and relies on nuclear power for more than two-thirds of its electricity, with relatively little popular dissent. So it has one of the lowest rates of carbon emissions per capita in the OECD. Furthermore, a global warming convention might boost French exports of nuclear power. Similarly, Japan, which must import virtually all of its oil, is also heavily dependent on nuclear power and is a major exporter of energy-efficient technologies because of its adjustment to the oil price hikes of the 1970s. A stronger climate convention would present promising new opportunities to market its energy-efficient technologies abroad.

The United Kingdom, which relies heavily on indigenous fossil fuels for energy, has been the main opponent in Europe of a carbon tax. Germany is also dependent on coal for energy, has no natural gas of its own, and has faced strong opposition to nuclear power. However, Germany does have high levels of electricity from cogeneration, and it can achieve very large reductions in carbon emissions by bringing the energy-inefficient East German industrial sector up to West Germany's higher standards. Germany has been the leader on carbon taxes in the EU.

China and India may adopt veto or swing roles in future negotiations on greenhouse-gas emissions. China, with one-third of the proven coal reserves in the world, relied on coal for 77 percent of all primary energy in 1985 and plans to increase that reliance in the future. India also plans to vastly increase its consumption of coal in future decades.[15] So China and India can be expected to bargain for favorable terms of access to energy-efficient technology so that they can enjoy the same amount of energy services with fewer carbon emissions.

International Political-Diplomatic Considerations

A state's definition of its interest is sometimes influenced as well by anticipated benefits or costs of lead or veto roles to the state's international relations. A state may hope to gain international prestige by assuming a lead role. Or it may decide against a veto role in order to avoid international opprobrium or damage to its relations with other countries for whom the issue is of significantly greater concern.

Concern for national prestige—a state's reputation or status in the international community—was once confined to the issue area of international security. But by the early 1990s a few states had begun to regard leadership on the global environment as a means of enhancing their international status. Both the United States and Germany made bids for leadership on a possible world forest convention in 1990–1991, in large part because both anticipated that such leadership would enhance their environmental image around the world. The European Community had aspirations for a lead role on climate change and in the Rio conference in order to signify its emergence as a global power. In 1994, EU environment commissioner Yannis Paleokrassas hailed the prospect of a regionwide carbon tax, which would give the EU a lead role on climate change and lead to "the resumption of world environmental and fiscal leadership by the European Union," thus suggesting that it would gain a new kind of international prestige.[16]

At the 1992 Earth Summit in Rio de Janeiro, the image of the United States was seriously tarnished because it stood alone in rejecting the biodiversity agreement. Germany and Japan, among other countries, shared the unhappiness of the United States with some provisions of the biodiversity convention but shunned a veto role, fearing damage to their prestige. In a telling display of anger, a Bush administration official charged that Germany and Japan had departed from the U.S. position on the convention in part to demonstrate their new status as emerging world powers.[17]

A state's concern about how a veto role might affect its image is some-times focused on a particular country or group of countries. In the case of the international trade in hazardous wastes, France and the United Kingdom were swayed by the desire to maintain close ties with former colonies to modify their veto of a hazardous waste trade ban in 1989. And Japan avoided a veto role on banning African elephant ivory in 1989 largely because it feared damage to its relations with its most important trading partners, the United States and Europe.

Subnational Actors

National governments, despite their assertion of exclusive rights to act in international relations, are no longer the only governmental actors in global environmental politics. In recent years cities, states, and provinces have shown increased interest in adopting their own environmental and energy policies that could have a major impact on global environmental problems, especially global warming.

Large cities are major producers of greenhouse gases because of their heavy concentrations of transportation, which is the single biggest source of carbon dioxide emissions. So urban policies, if effective, could substan-tially reduce greenhouse-gas emissions. The governments of fourteen ma-jor cities in North America, Europe, and the Middle East joined in the Urban CO_2 Reduction Project in 1990 in order to develop strategies for re-ducing greenhouse-gas emissions at the local level. In November 1993, Portland, Oregon, became the first U.S. city to formally adopt a compre-hensive global warming strategy. It declared a goal of reducing its carbon dioxide emissions 20 percent below 1988 levels by the year 2010, primar-ily by reducing automobile travel and encouraging less polluting trans-port.[18] In the Netherlands, fifty-four municipalities formed a Climate Alliance aimed at developing their own local greenhouse policies.[19] In preparation for UNCED, mayors from around the world organized fo-rums to prepare proposals for Agenda 21, including recommendations on transportation. Since Rio they have continued to promote their own proj-ects for sustainable development.[20]

Federal states could have even greater impact on global warming by adopting similar plans. Californians claim their state is the seventh largest economy in the world. If California were to decide on an ambi-tious strategy for reducing greenhouse gases, it would be as important as most members of the **Group of Seven** industrialized nations (the United States, Canada, the United Kingdom, Japan, Germany, France, and Italy) in influencing the success of a global regime for global warming. In fact, such a plan was proposed as part of the Proposition 128 environmental initiative that was on the ballot in California in 1990. The initiative, which would have approved a plan to reduce the state's emissions of carbon dioxide by 20 percent by the year 2000 and 40 percent by 2010, was defeated but got a respectable 37 percent of the vote.[21]

Municipal and state governments are not likely to usurp national government functions in regime strengthening. But they may reinforce and supplement the decisions of national governments on the regime on climate change, especially as the world becomes increasingly urbanized.

INTERNATIONAL ORGANIZATIONS AS ACTORS

The influence of international organizations (IOs) on global environmental politics has greatly increased since 1972. Also referred to as international governmental organizations (IGOs), IOs are formed by member states either for multiple purposes, as in the case of the United Nations or various regional associations, such as the Organization of American States, or for more specific purposes, as in the case of the specialized agencies of the United Nations, such as the Food and Agriculture Organization and the World Health Organization (WHO). IOs range in size and resources from the World Bank, which has a staff of over 6,000 and lends billions of dollars annually, to the UNEP with its annual budget of only $60 million and a professional staff of 240. These organizations are staffed by officials from many nations who tend to share common approaches to functional problems. Although they are ultimately accountable to governing bodies made up of the representatives of their member states, staff can take initiatives and influence the outcomes of global issues. The professional skills of these bureaucrats can be an important factor in environmental negotiations, as was obvious in the resourcefulness of the UNCED secretariat. IO bureaucracies have widely varying degrees of independence: Those at UNEP and the FAO must take their cues from their governing councils on setting agendas, sponsoring negotiations, and implementing development and environment programs; at the World Bank, which is dependent on major donor countries for its funds, the staff nevertheless has wide discretion in planning and executing projects.

An IO may influence the outcomes of global environmental issues in the following four ways:

☐ It may set the agenda for global action, determining which issues will be dealt with by the international community.
☐ It may convene and influence negotiations on global environmental regimes.
☐ It may develop normative codes of conduct (soft law) on various environmental issues.

☐ It may influence state policies on issues that are not under international negotiation.

No IO influences global environmental politics by performing all of the above functions; IOs tend to specialize in one or more political functions, although one function may, in fact, indirectly influence another.

Setting Agendas and Influencing Regime Formation

The agenda-setting function in global environmental politics has been dominated by UNEP because of its unique mandate, growing out of the 1972 Stockholm conference, to be a catalyst and coordinator of environmental activities and focal point for such activities within the UN system. Through the decisions of its Governing Council, composed of fifty-eight U.N. member governments elected by the General Assembly, UNEP has regularly identified the critical global environmental threats requiring international cooperation. In 1976, for example, UNEP's Governing Council chose ozone depletion as one of five priority problems, and consequently UNEP convened a meeting of experts in Washington, D.C., that adopted the World Plan of Action on the Ozone Layer in 1977—five years before negotiations on a global agreement began.

UNEP has played a similar role in initiating negotiations on biological diversity and climate change. It cosponsored with the Rockefeller Brothers Fund the Villach and Bellagio workshops that helped create scientific consensus and raised worldwide consciousness about the threat of greenhouse warming. Along with the World Meteorological Organization (WMO), it sponsored the Intergovernmental Panel on Climate Change to study scientific and policy issues in preparation for negotiations on a global convention on climate change. UNEP convened international negotiations on most of the major environmental conventions of the past two decades: the Vienna Convention for the Protection of the Ozone Layer (1985), the Montreal Protocol on Substances that Deplete the Ozone Layer (1987), the Basel Convention on the Control of Transboundary Movements of Hazardous Wastes and Their Disposal (1989), and the U.N. Convention on Biological Diversity (1992).

UNEP also has sought to shape the global environmental agenda by monitoring and assessing the state of the environment and disseminating the information to governments and nongovernmental organizations. UNEP's Earthwatch program includes a series of systems directly under UNEP's control as well as a loose network of U.N. agencies that also carry out global environmental monitoring. But although monitoring and assessment is essential to stimulating international cooperation on environmental threats, donor countries have not supported those activities adequately. As a result, serious gaps remain in the data, such as the lack of accurate remote sensing images of Indonesia's tropical forests.[22] And many developing countries have regarded this program as a way for industrialized countries to "spy" on them—especially in regard to deforestation—and have reduced funding for it in the UNEP Governing Council since 1993.[23]

Former UNEP executive director Mostafa Tolba has influenced environmental diplomacy through direct participation in the negotiations. During the negotiations on the Montreal Protocol he lobbied hard for a complete phaseout of CFCs in informal talks with the chiefs of EC delegations.[24] At the London conference of the parties in 1990, he convened informal meetings with twenty-five environmental ministers to work out a compromise on the contentious issue of linking protocol obligations with **technology transfer** (the transfer of scientific and technological knowledge, patents, or equipment, usually from the most industrialized nations to the less developed ones). He also urged a compromise to bridge the gap between U.S. and Western European timetables for a CFC phaseout.

Tolba sometimes openly championed the developing countries against the highly industrialized countries. At Basel in 1989, for instance, he fought for a ban on shipping hazardous wastes to or from noncontracting parties and for a requirement that exporters check disposal sites at their own expense. Opposed by the waste-exporting states, Tolba and the developing countries lost on both issues.[25]

Despite his siding with them on the emotional waste trade issue, the developing countries began to lose confidence in Tolba and UNEP by 1990. They felt he was not sufficiently committed to their agenda and put too much emphasis on climate change, ozone depletion, and loss of biodiversity, which they considered "Northern" issues. When UNCED was being organized in the United Nations General Assembly (UNGA), the **Group of 77** (a coalition of developing countries pressing for North-South economic reform since the 1970s) sought emphasis on environmental problems of primary concern to developing nations—drinking water and sanitation, urban pollution, desertification, and so on. It succeeded in naming the twentieth anniversary of the Stockholm environmental conference the 1992 U.N. Conference on Environment *and Development* and assigned organizing responsibility to the U.N. secretariat rather than to UNEP. At the same time, the UNGA took the climate negotiations out of the hands of UNEP and WMO and gave them to an ad hoc U.N. body, the Intergovernmental Negotiating Committee (INC), which reported directly to the General Assembly.

And after the Earth Summit conference in 1992, the UNGA established the United Nations Commission on Sustainable Development (UNCSD) to monitor and coordinate implementation of Agenda 21, further reducing UNEP's role in agenda-setting for global environmental politics. The

UNCSD has fifty-three members elected on a carefully balanced political and geographical quota system and is charged with monitoring progress in implementing Agenda 21 commitments. It will review sectoral issues in clusters over a four-year cycle and cross-sectional issues (financing, technology, education, and capacity building) every year. Although it has a small secretariat, UNCSD has not been able to push governments to take any major new initiatives in its first three annual meetings.

Another way that international organizations influence global environmental politics is to facilitate the negotiations of common norms or rules of conduct that do not have binding legal effect on the participating states. A variety of creative nontreaty measures, often called soft law, have been developed to influence state behavior on environmental issues, including codes of conduct, declarations of principle, global action plans, and other international agreements that create new norms and expectations without the binding status of treaties.[26]

These nonbinding agreements are negotiated by groups of experts representing their governments convened by one of the IOs. Most U.N. agencies have contributed to this process, but UNEP has done the most to promote it. In the case of UNEP's guidelines for the management of hazardous waste, for instance, an ad hoc working group of experts helped draft guidelines in 1984. In 1987, the same process produced a set of guidelines and principles aimed at making the worldwide pesticide trade more responsive regarding threats to environmental health. Other examples include the 1980 International Program on Chemical Safety and the 1985 Action Plan for Biosphere Reserves—each of which has become the recognized standard in the field.

The FAO has drafted guidelines on the environmental criteria for the registration of pesticides (1985) and the International Code of Conduct on the Distribution and Use of Pesticides (1986). A set of criteria for food regulations, the Codex Alimentarius, also developed under FAO aegis, could be used in a trade dispute to have a national environmental health standard declared an illegitimate barrier to trade.

Soft-law agreements are often a good way to avoid the lengthy process of negotiating binding agreements. They do not require enforcement mechanisms and can sometimes depend on the adherence of networks of bureaucrats who share similar views of the problem. But in cases where soft-law regimes are adopted only because key parties are unwilling to go beyond nonbinding guidelines, the norms agreed on may be less stringent and the compliance may be haphazard at best. The FAO Code of Conduct on pesticide trade, negotiated from 1982 to 1985, and the Cairo guidelines on international hazardous waste trade are examples of this pattern.

Soft law may be turned into binding international law in two ways: Principles included in a soft-law agreement may become so widely regarded as the appropriate norms for a problem that they are ultimately absorbed into treaty law; or political pressures may arise from those dissatisfied with spotty adherence to soft-law norms to turn a nonbinding agreement into a binding one.

Influencing National Development Policies

A fourth way that IOs affect global environmental politics is to influence the environmental and development policies of individual states outside the context of regime negotiations. National policy decisions on such issues as what goals should be set for population growth rates, how much of the government budget should be allocated to human resource development, how to manage forests, how to generate and use energy supplies, and how to increase agricultural production determine how sustainable the national economies and societies will be. IOs influence such policies, and thus the sustainability of societies, in several ways:

□ They provide financing for development projects, as well as advice and technical assistance that help shape the country's development strategy.

□ They undertake research aimed at persuading state officials to adopt certain policies.

□ They focus normative pressure on states regarding sustainable development policy issues.

The FAO has been one of the most powerful international organizations within the U.N. system with respect to environmental issues. It has had a major impact on the policies of the developing world—much of which critics charge has been negative—through its promotion of commercial exploitation of forests and export crops, large-scale irrigation projects, and heavy use of chemical inputs.[27] As the lead agency in the Tropical Forest Action Plan (TFAP), which was supposed to help reduce the rate of tropical deforestation through increased investments in forests, the FAO steered most of the new investments into commercial development of tropical timber rather than toward conservation or sustainable use. Its main constituency in regard to forest issues was the government forestry departments, whose interests were to promote vigorously the sale of timber resources.[28] NGOs monitoring the TFAP wanted a new structure that would take the program out of the FAO's Forestry Department, but the FAO director-general resisted the suggestion.[29]

On a much smaller scale, FAO has also used research to promote sustainable alternatives to the conventional agricultural development model. FAO's program on integrated pest control in South and Southeast Asia, launched in the early 1980s, helped spread integrated pest management

(IPM) techniques to farmers in several Asian countries. The research done by the FAO showing the superiority of natural pest control strategies over reliance on chemical pesticides helped convince key Indonesian government officials in 1986 to adopt IPM as an alternative to heavy reliance on pesticides and to train Indonesian farmers to make their own informed decisions about pest management.[30]

In the early 1990s, the organization was restructured for the first time for the purpose of integrating sustainability into its programs and activities.[31] And in 1993, the FAO received a new mandate from its governing body to focus more on the consequences of the earth's shrinking natural resource base, sustainable agricultural and rural development, and food security through protection of plant, animal, and marine resources. How dramatically the new structure and mandate of the FAO will change its operations remains to be seen.

UNDP, with a 1993 budget of $1.4 billion annually, a staff of 6,600, and liaison offices in 132 countries, is the largest single source of multilateral grant development assistance. Moreover, it has projects in every developing country, allocating its funds for five-year periods according to a formula based primarily on population and per capita GNP, and is the only U.N. agency with resident representatives in each member country. Prior to the preparations for UNCED, however, UNDP gave little attention to the environment or sustainable development as a mission and lacked the expertise to provide environmentally sound technical advice to developing countries. With the prospect of new funds specifically for global environmental problems, UNDP became a major actor in global environmental matters. It is one of the three implementing agencies of the GEF and is the lead U.N. agency in building the capacity of developing-country governments for sustainable development.

IOs may influence state policy by focusing normative pressures on states regarding the environment and sustainable development even when no formal international agreement exists on the norm.[32] UNDP has gone the farthest of any U.N. agency in this regard, asserting the allocation of a minimum level of resources for human resource development (health, population, and education) by both donor countries and developing-country governments as a norm in the context of what it calls "sustainable human development." Through its annual *Human Development Report*, which ranks nations on the basis of their provision of these social services, UNDP pressures developing countries to devote more of their budgets to these social sectors. Under its new administrator, Gus Speth, a prominent American environmentalist, UNDP also began to inject norms into U.N.-related international forums, including preparatory meetings for the World Summit for Social Development. UNDP's normative advocacy has made some developing countries uncomfortable.[33]

Multilateral Financial Institutions as Actors

In terms of direct impact on the development and environmental policies of developing states, the most powerful IOs are the multilateral financial institutions, including the World Bank, the International Monetary Fund, and the regional banks, because of the amount of financial resources that they transfer to developing countries each year in support of particular development strategies and economic policies. The World Bank provided $10.3 billion in 1993–1994 in loans to environmentally sensitive sectors (energy and power, transportation, and agriculture),[34] and they leverage much more lending and investment from other international sources. Within these IOs, in which voting is weighted according to the size of a country's contributions, the donor countries are the dominant players. The United States has the preponderance of power in the World Bank and the Inter-American Development Bank (IDB); Japan, in the Asian Development Bank.

The World Bank's influence on the policies of its borrowers has been viewed by environmental activists as contributing to unsustainable development. The Bank has been driven by the need to lend large amounts of money each year; by a bias toward large-scale, capital-intensive, and centralized projects; and by its practice of assessing projects on the basis of a quantifiable rate of return while discounting longer-term, unquantifiable social and environmental costs. In the 1970s and 1980s, the Bank supported rainforest colonization schemes in Brazil and Indonesia, cattle-ranching projects in Central and South America, and tobacco projects in Africa that contributed to accelerated deforestation and a cattle development project in Botswana that contributed to desertification.[35] And it supported fossil-fueled power plants, whose CO_2 emissions contribute heavily to global warming.

In response to persistent, well-orchestrated pressure from NGOs and U.S. Congress criticism of such egregious loans, the World Bank began a process of evolution in the mid-1980s toward greater sensitivity to the environmental implications of its lending. It refused to provide new support for some of the worst projects in Brazil and Indonesia, created an Environment Department, began to build an environmental staff and to finance more explicitly environmental programs. But the Bank's loan portfolio scarcely changed.

Under pressure to help reduce the threats of global warming and tropical deforestation, the Bank announced a new energy strategy in 1989. But it was difficult for the Bank to shift to renewable energy loans because that would require moving from a few large-scale projects to many small-scale projects and because loan officers are reluctant to push environmental initiatives on unwilling governments. Its loans to reduce greenhouse-gas emissions continued to be swamped by energy and power loans that reinforced reliance on fossil fuels.[36] Indeed, energy lending typifies the Bank's difficulty in making sustainable development an operational concept. In 1992, for instance, the Bank gave China a $2 million loan to reduce greenhouse-gas emissions. At the same time, the Bank proposed $630 million in loans to the Chinese for fossil fuel development.[37] A 1992 energy-policy paper emphasizing greater attention for energy efficiency and renewables signaled a change to more environmentally beneficial energy strategies, but two years later environmentalists could detect little actual change in the Bank's energy-loan portfolio.[38] It did adopt a new policy that precluded support for commercial logging in primary tropical forests, however.

The Bank has continued to adjust its policies and organizations as the sustainable development paradigm has gained greater legitimacy internationally. A 1993 reorganization of the Bank created a vice-presidency for sustainable development, but the new position did not have authority over the powerful energy and industrial departments.

Structural adjustment lending by the World Bank and the International Monetary Fund (IMF) also strongly influences the policies of developing countries on key issues of sustainability. Structural adjustment loans by both institutions have required borrowing governments to take stringent measures not only to reduce domestic demand through removing subsidies and other government budget cuts but to devaluate currencies, tighten credit, and reduce imports while increasing exports in order to achieve positive trade balances and pay off debts. One of the objectives of structural adjustment lending is to shift resources from domestic consumption to the export sector. Some environmental and development organizations, academic researchers, and the Inter-American Development Bank have cited evidence that the consequences of these policies (such as greater industrial unemployment and fewer primary health care services) have worsened the plight of the poor, causing increased movement of the population onto marginal lands and creating pressures for more rapid logging of forests and more intensive cultivation of crops for export—all at the expense of the natural resource base.[39] Other analysts found no clear pattern of adverse enviromental impacts from adjustment lending but recommended that poverty alleviation and sustainable management of natural resources be explicit objectives of adjustment lending.[40] IMF and World Bank officials have argued that the elimination of economic distortions such as overvalued exchange rates, artificially low agricultural prices, and subsidies on food, energy, and agricultural inputs actually hurt the poorest segments of society and create perverse incentives for activities that degrade the environment.[41] The Bank has, in effect, admitted that its structural adjustment loans can have negative environmental impacts. In June 1992, the Bank's own Operations Evaluation Department, reporting on the Bank's adjustment loans, remarked that none of the projects being evaluated had an environmental component and noted the need for environmental impact assessments on adjustment lending.[42]

The IMF has been far slower than the World Bank and regional banks to acknowledge the need to take environmental considerations explicitly into account in its lending operations, defining its role as limited to helping countries achieve balance of payments and pay off their international debts. Only in 1991 did the IMF executive board consider for the first time the extent to which the IMF should "address environmental issues." It decided that the IMF should avoid policies that might harm the environment but that it should not do any research or build up its own expertise on possible environmental consequences of its policies.[43] As recently as May 1993, an IMF official, meeting for the first time with NGOs, suggested that the IMF must pursue its macroeconomic objectives "separate" from issues of sustainable development.[44]

In summary, though the World Bank and regional multilateral development banks (MDBs) have made some significant policy changes, neither they nor the IMF has internalized the goal of sustainable development. Neither have these organizations made organizational changes or established staff incentives that might significantly change their lending patterns and contribute to the paradigm shift. Indeed, at present the **Bretton Woods institutions** in some respects remain an obstacle to progress toward a new paradigm.

Regional and Other Multistate Organizations as Actors

In recent years, regional groupings of states have played an increasing role in environmental politics. Some, such as the regional fishing organizations, are specific functional groups that have taken on environmental responsibilities out of necessity. Others have a broad political or economic agenda but have taken on significant environmental functions. The European Union is the most advanced of the latter group in that it is the only such regional organization whose decisions obligate its members. It is often represented by its own delegation in negotiations, though only its individual member states can sign and ratify international agreements.[45]

A second example is the Organization of American States (OAS). In a move to revitalize the organization after the cold war, some member states have urged an OAS role on "new issues," which include regional environmental concerns. The OAS has established the Permanent Commission on the Environment and is bidding to undertake the regional implementation of the biodiversity treaty and to get involved in trade and environment issues via development of regional standards.[46]

The Organization of African Unity (OAU) has also undertaken several regional environmental initiatives. It is trying to demonstrate regionally appropriate sustainable development strategies, and it organized strong opposition to importation of all hazardous wastes into its region. It hosted the Bamako Convention on trade in hazardous wastes and argued consistently for a worldwide ban under the Basel Convention. The OAU submitted a number of proposals that were incorporated into the desertification treaty, completed in 1994. A subregional organization, the Southern African Development Coordination Conference, has developed joint research and training projects and policies for sustainable development but has not so far acted as a body on global environmental issues such as climate change.[47]

Since UNCED a new type of regional organization, created for explicit environmental purposes, has appeared. The Central American Commission on Environment and Development (CCAD is its Spanish acronym) was organized for regional cooperation on development. It developed a Central American agenda in preparation for UNCED and a common position on hazardous waste and has proposed an Alliance for Sustainable Development that will try to coordinate policy, especially requests for assistance from the United States and the Inter-American Development Bank.[48] The CCAD has negotiated a regional forestry treaty and is building regional environmental institutions.

As a direct outcome of their experience with UNCED, especially their shared concern about sea-level rise, the small island states of the world have formed the Small Island Developing States (SIDS) to collectively examine how they can best pursue sustainable development. Membership in SIDS is from the Caribbean, South Pacific, and Indian Ocean. Two carefully orchestrated technical meetings led to a high-level policy meeting held in Barbados in April-May 1994, under U.N. auspices. The conference produced an action plan that recognizes the unique development problems facing island states and got commitments for international funding. SIDS can also be expected to continue trying to strengthen the climate treaty.[49]

NONGOVERNMENTAL ORGANIZATIONS AS ACTORS

The emergence of the global environment as a major issue in world politics has coincided with the rise of nongovernmental organizations (NGOs) as a major new force in the politics of the environment. Although business organizations are included in the United Nation's definition of an NGO,[50] the term is used here to mean a private, nonprofit organization that is not beholden either to government or to a profit-making organization. Although no one knows how many NGOs worldwide undertake activities aimed at affecting global environmental issues, at least 4,000 NGOs are included in one environmental organization's database.[51]

NGO influence on global environmental politics has been based on one or more of three factors: first, NGOs' expert knowledge and innovative thinking about global environmental issues, acquired from specializing in issues under negotiation; second, their dedication to goals that transcend narrow national or sectoral interests; and third, their representation of substantial constituencies within their own countries that command attention and that sometimes influence tight electoral contests.

In the industrialized countries, most NGOs that are active in global environmental politics fall into one of three categories: organizations that are affiliated with international NGOs (INGOs), which are NGOs with branches in a number of countries; large, national organizations focused primarily on domestic environmental issues; and think tanks, or research institutes whose influence comes primarily from publishing studies and issuing proposals for action.

INGOs may be a loose federation of national affiliates or a more centralized structure. Friends of the Earth International (FOEI), based in Amsterdam, is a confederation of fifty-three national, independent affiliates, half of which are in developing countries. At an annual meeting, delegates democratically set priorities and select five or more campaigns on which they cooperate each year. Greenpeace is the fastest-growing INGO, with more than 3.3 million members in twenty countries. Its international activities are tightly organized from a well-staffed headquarters (also in Amsterdam) and guided by issues and strategies determined at an annual meeting.

The Switzerland-based World Wildlife Fund (WWF)—also known in Europe as the Worldwide Fund for Nature—has twenty-eight national organizations, of which the U.S. affiliate is much the largest, and a total of 4.7 million members, mostly in the industrialized countries. Its focus traditionally has been the protection of wildlife, but recently it has also been involved in policy issues such as trade and structural adjustment. In recent years, the U.S. affiliate has established extensive development and conservation projects in Latin America and Asia, which gives the organization international credibility and valuable links with local groups around the world. The European Environmental Bureau (EEB), organized in 1974, is now a confederation of 120 national-level environmental organizations with a combined membership of 20 million in the twelve states of the European Union. The EEB works on issues within the EU as well as on EU policies toward global environmental issues and has direct access to the European Commission, which also contributes financially to its work. It includes the full range of European NGOs, and its style of operation is moderate rather than confrontational. Affiliates of all the INGOs make extensive use of fax and e-mail, greatly improving their ability to act expeditiously in concert on key issues.

In the second category of NGOs are the big U.S. environmental organizations, all of which have developed international programs in the past twelve years. Some, such as the Sierra Club, the National Audubon Society, and the National Wildlife Federation (NWF), were formed in the late nineteenth and early twentieth centuries around conservation issues. Other organizations with a broad national agenda, including the Environmental Defense Fund (EDF) and the Natural Resources Defense Council (NRDC), which have used legal, economic, and regulatory processes to affect national policy and have become very important actors on international atmospheric and climate issues, arose in the early 1970s. Along with FOE/USA, they have played effective roles in the negotiations on climate and ozone and have also helped reshape the policies of the multilateral development banks. Still other organizations with more specific agendas have become internationally active on their issues: Defenders of Wildlife and the Humane Society on marine-mammal issues. Total membership in these national environmental organizations increased in the 1980s to an estimated 13 million and leveled off in the early 1990s.

Environmental think tanks, normally funded by private donations or contracts, rely primarily on their technical expertise and research programs to influence global environmental policy. Examples are the Worldwatch Institute, whose publications have often identified new problems and suggested alternative approaches to international issues, and the World Resources Institute (WRI), which publishes reports on the global environment and policy studies on specific issues, often aimed at particular international conferences such as Intergovernmental Panel on Climate Change (IPCC) meetings and UNCED. The International Institute for Environment and Development (IIED) in London and Buenos Aires drew early attention to the environment/poverty connection in developing countries. In a few countries, government-funded but nevertheless independent institutes seek to directly influence the policies of their own governments and of international negotiations. The International Institute for Sustainable Development of Canada and the Stockholm Environment Institute of Sweden have played such roles. All of these organizations collaborate with colleagues in other countries.

Environmental NGOs in developing countries tend to be as much concerned with poverty and other development issues as with strictly environmental issues. They tend to stress issues such as land use, forest management and fishing rights, and redistribution of power over natural resources, rather than ozone and global warming.[52] But there are many exceptions, such as the Chilean and Argentinean NGOs' interest in the ozone layer. Developing-country NGOs often have become involved in international policy issues through opposition to multilateral-bank projects and government policies that displace villages or threaten rainforests, and they tend to regard transnational corporations as enemies of the environment. Inherently critical of their governments on most domestic policies, NGO members who are committed to environmental protection often have been harassed, subjected to political repression, and jailed. In some countries, however, they have acquired political legitimacy and even a measure of influence on national environmental policy issues. In many countries, the widespread, effective, visible participation of NGOs in the UNCED process added to their stature at home.

Developing-country NGOs often form national-level coalitions, such as the Brazilian NGO Forum, which had over 1,000 organizations affiliated with it at the time of UNCED; the Indonesian Environmental Forum (WALHI), which unites more than 450 environmental organizations countrywide; and the Kenya Environmental Non-Governmental Organization (KENGO), founded in 1982, which now includes sixty-eight environmental groups and has ties with groups in twenty-two other African countries. Indigenous minorities in the five Amazon-basin countries have begun to organize their own national-level coalitions, which in turn have formed a coordinating body (called COICA, for its Spanish name) to lobby for a voice in all Amazon development projects affecting them. Indeed, UNCED recognition of indigenous groups in Chapter 26 of Agenda 21, and their highly visible participation at the Rio conference, have given a boost to the rights of indigenous peoples and given them a modest influence on international environmental negotiations.

Broad international coalitions of NGOs working on a specific environmental issue have also become a means of increasing NGO influence. The Antarctic and Southern Oceans Coalition (ASOC) is a consortium of 200 environmental organizations in thirty-three countries that lobbied against the Antarctic minerals treaty and for an Antarctic environmental protocol. The Climate Action Network, formed in November 1989, united sixty-three NGOs from twenty-two countries to press for a minimum 20-percent reduction in the 1988 level of carbon dioxide emissions by the year 2000.

North-South NGO alliances have sometimes been very effective in influencing international events. An alliance between U.S. NGOs and indigenous opponents of rainforest destruction brought worldwide attention to Brazilian policy in 1986. Together they helped stop the World Bank's Polonoreste project, an Amazonian road-building and colonization scheme, persuaded President José Sarney to halt the tax incentives for agriculture and ranching that had stimulated the Amazon land boom, and persuaded members of the U.S. Congress and officials of the Inter-American Development Bank to support extractive reserves.[53]

But relations between Northern and Southern NGOs are not always smooth. At climate change negotiations in February 1991, developing-country NGOs charged that they had not been consulted by Northern NGOs advocating steeper curtailment of CO_2 emissions—the burden of which they thought would fall on developing countries. There was a similar division in the pre-UNCED discussions of a forest treaty. In this matter, also, the Southern NGOs' position tended to parallel their governments'. There is sometimes a Southern resentment of Northern NGOs, especially at the big international conferences such as UNCED where the better prepared, better financed U.S. and European NGOs were heavily represented. Despite these tensions, however, there were many instances of close North-South cooperation in lobbying during UNCED, as well as jointly issued statements on key issues. For example, the Brazilian NGO Forum and CAPE '92, the coalition of six leading U.S. environmental organizations, issued a joint paper on financial resources and mechanisms with specific proposals on sources of funding and environmental commodity agreements.

One world organization through which NGOs influence environmental politics is the International Union for the Conservation of Nature (IUCN). It includes 810 member groups, including individual government agencies and NGOs, and it can draw on the work of six international commissions composed of 6,000 volunteer scientists and other professionals. Governed by the General Assembly of delegates from its member organizations that meets every three years, the IUCN has had a major influence on global agreements regarding wildlife conservation and species loss.

Influencing Environmental Regime Formation

NGOs influence international regimes in five ways. They may

☐ influence the global environmental agenda by defining a new issue or redefining an old one;
☐ lobby or pressure their own or other governments to accept a more advanced position toward an issue, by advancing new proposals, by carrying out consumer boycotts and educational campaigns, or by bringing lawsuits;
☐ propose entire draft texts of conventions in advance of conferences;
☐ lobby international negotiations;
☐ monitor the implementation of conventions and report to the secretariat and/or the parties.

An example of influencing the global environmental agenda is the role that WWF and Conservation International (CI) played in 1988–1989 in creating a new issue of banning commerce in African elephant ivory by publishing a report on the problem and circulating it to parties of the Convention on the International Trade in Endangered Species (CITES). In 1987, despite momentum toward an Antarctic minerals convention, the Antarctic and Southern Oceans Coalition, in which Greenpeace, Friends of the Earth, and WWF were the biggest and most active organizations, put forward a detailed proposal for an Antarctic World Park that would exclude mineral exploration. Two years later, the World Park proposal was the basis for a new policy rejecting a treaty to govern future minerals exploitation in Antarctica.

Pressing for changes in the policy of a major actor is sometimes the best means for NGOs to influence an international regime. In the case of protecting the ozone layer, the U.S. Clean Air Coalition, a group of national environmental organizations, successfully lobbied for a ban on aerosols and regulation of CFCs. They lobbied for a total phaseout of CFCs before negotiations on the Montreal Protocol began, contributing to U.S. international leadership on this issue. Similarly, three U.S. NGOs working with pro-treaty biotechnology firms were a major influence on the new Clinton administration's decision to reverse the Bush administration's position and sign the biodiversity convention in 1993.[54] Although effective consumer boycotts are rare, an NGO-organized boycott affected the whaling issue in 1988 when a hundred school districts and several fast-food and supermarket chains boycotted Icelandic fish because of Iceland's pro-whaling stand and brought a temporary halt to that country's whaling.[55]

The most important example of NGO influence on key government policies, however, was the negotiations on Antarctic minerals. A coalition of twenty Australian NGOs were instrumental in converting Australian prime minister Bob Hawke in 1989 to reject the Antarctic minerals treaty that his negotiators had just helped negotiate and adopt the Antarctic World Park in its place. And when Italy, Belgium, and other countries supported the Australian position, it was in large part due to effective lobbying by NGOs affiliated with the ASOC.[56]

A more specialized way for NGOs to influence international regimes is to write a draft convention well in advance of the negotiations. Few NGOs have the staff resources to devote to such a task, and only IUCN has succeeded in getting draft conventions to be used as the basis for negotiations. The Convention Concerning the Protection of the World Cultural and Natural Heritage, signed in 1972 in Paris, was based on a draft produced by IUCN. CITES, signed in 1973, was the result of an IUCN initiative that went through three drafts over nearly a decade.[57]

NGOs have become especially active and well organized in lobbying at international negotiating conferences. The conferences of the parties to most environmental conventions permit NGO observers, enabling NGOs to be actively involved in the proceedings. Certain NGOs specialize in the meetings of particular conventions and have acquired over the years a high level of technical and legal expertise. The Humane Society of the United States has been lobbying at meetings of the International Whaling Commission (IWC) since 1973, and Greenpeace has been active in the conference of the parties to the London Dumping Convention since the early 1980s. The Antarctic and Southern Oceans Coalition, led by Friends of the Earth/USA and Greenpeace, began attending meetings of the Antarctic Treaty Consultative Parties to lobby on Antarctic environmental issues in 1987, when those meetings were first opened up to NGO observers.

EDF, NRDC, and WRI have brought a significant level of expertise to the IPCC meetings on the climate convention. Although not a single environmental organization was present at the final negotiating session of the Vienna Convention on the ozone layer in March 1985,[58] NGOs had a strong presence at the more decisive first meeting of the parties to the Montreal Protocol in 1989. On behalf of ninety-three NGOs worldwide, they called for a total phaseout of CFCs.[59]

NGOs influence international conferences primarily by providing scientific and technical information or new arguments to delegations that are already sympathetic to their objectives. In the process leading up to the whaling moratorium, NGOs supplied factual information on violations of the whaling convention as well as scientific information not otherwise available to the delegations.[60] In some circumstances, however, NGOs may have particularly strong influence on a key delegation's positions, as happened with the biodiversity negotiations in 1991–1992, when WWF/Australia and other NGOs represented on the Australian delegation were consulted on all major issues in the convention before the delegation adopted positions.[61]

NGOs can also influence regime formation by monitoring compliance with an agreement once it goes into effect. Investigation and reporting by NGOs can bring pressure on parties that are violating provisions of an agreement. They can demonstrate the need for a more effective enforcement mechanism (or for creation of a new mechanism where none exists) or help build support for the further elaboration or strengthening of the existing regime rules.

This NGO function has been especially important with regard to CITES and whaling regimes. The international TRAFFIC network and IUCN have played a vital role in supplementing the CITES secretariat in monitoring the compliance of various countries with CITES bans on trade in endangered species.[62] Climate networks in the United States and the EC produced specific critical reviews of countries' national climate action plans even before the climate treaty came into effect. Greenpeace's aggressive reporting of hazardous wastes dumped in violation of the Basel and Bamako agreements helped create a climate in which a full ban on international shipping of such wastes to non-OECD countries was accomplished in 1994.

NGOs and International Institutions

Influencing the structure and policies of major international institutions active in global environmental politics poses a different set of challenges to NGOs. The international NGO community has taken on a wide range of global institutions, from the World Bank and the Global Environment Facility (GEF) to the International Tropical Timber Organization (ITTO) and the General Agreement on Tariffs and Trade (GATT). These institutions have different characteristics that help to explain the degree of success of NGO efforts to influence the policies and structures of each.

The most successful such NGO effort was influencing the restructuring of the Global Environment Facility, on which both Southern and Northern NGOs were in full agreement. The NGOs were highly critical of the GEF as administered by the World Bank during its 1991–1993 pilot phase. They pushed successfully for a secretariat independent of the World Bank and for project approval by a council of all treaty parties.[63]

Primarily because of the importance of the U.S. Congress in approving funding for the multilateral development banks, U.S. NGOs have been effective in forcing some changes in the lending of MDBs.[64] Between 1983 and 1987, U.S. environmental NGOs in alliance with congressional fiscal conservatives persuaded congressional appropriations subcommittees to sponsor legislation directing the U.S. executive directors of the MDBs to press for environmental reforms. As a result, by 1986, the United States began voting against particularly egregious World Bank loans, prompting Bank president Conable's 1987 commitment to greater attention to the environment.

In the late 1980s, NGO campaigning for bank reform began to focus on issues of public participation and accountability. About 100 NGOs worldwide have participated in some fashion in a campaign to get the World Bank to release to the public documents related to project assessment and implementation and to create an appeals panel to examine complaints from the public about Bank projects. The Bank responded in 1993 by establishing a three-member, independent Inspection Panel that would have the power to investigate compliants from any group that can show that it has been harmed by the Bank's failure to follow its policies or procedures.[65] The campaign also brought about a new World Bank information policy in early 1994 that met some, but not all, of the campaign's demands.

Much more difficult still for NGOs is the trade and environmental issue, to which they turned their attention only in 1990. The GATT has one single-minded goal, determined forty-five years ago, to reduce tariffs and other trade barriers. The GATT has never had provisions for NGO observers. Through their pressure on the NAFTA process, and the Uruguay Round, however, the NGOs made "trade and environment" a major international issue for the 1990s. (See Chapter 4.)

NGOs in the UNCED Process

The United Nations Conference on Environment and Development process, which began in August 1990 and concluded at the Earth Summit in Rio de Janeiro in June 1992, represented a new level of NGO participation in global environmental politics. In fact, NGOs' unusual degree of access to meetings and delegations, especially at the Preparatory Committee meetings (PrepComs), has become the standard by which subsequent U.N. conferences are judged, and NGO success at Rio helped open up subsequent U.N. conferences on human rights, population, and women to greater NGO participation. A record number of NGOs participated in the UNCED process: About 200 NGOs were accredited to the second PrepCom for UNCED in Geneva in March 1991, and nearly 500 NGOs brought some 1,200 people to the final PrepCom for UNCED in New York. About one-third of them were from developing countries, as nearly 100 developing-country NGOs were helped in financing the trip to New York by a fund established by the UNCED secretariat (which recognized the NGOs as potential allies) and supported by some governments and private foundations.[66]

The UNCED preparatory process enhanced NGO influence in other ways: NGOs in industrialized countries were encouraged to form new cross-sectoral coalitions that integrated environment and development issues. The use of electronic conferencing made it possible for the first time for NGOs involved in the UNCED process to work on common policy positions in between the PrepComs. And a number of official delegations, including those of the United States, Canada, the U.K., Sweden, Australia, and the Netherlands, included NGOs at each PrepCom. NGOs gained unprecedented access to "informal" negotiating sessions in the final PrepCom (though they still could not attend the much smaller "contact groups"), and the series of PrepComs provided many NGOs with a new level of experience in international negotiating.

But the political effectiveness of NGOs in the preparatory process was constrained by a number of factors. Most NGOs spent their time in numerous meetings organized by the NGOs themselves, and few showed interest in influencing the daily negotiations.[67] Many Southern NGOs viewed debate over text as too far removed from the issues over which they were struggling within their own countries.[68] Only larger and wealthier NGOs, mostly from the North, could maintain a presence throughout the entire two to three weeks of an entire PrepCom, and the lack of continuity in NGO participation made it very difficult to sustain a broad lobbying effort from beginning to end of a PrepCom.

The degree of NGO success in influencing the negotiations depended on the issue. On issues where negotiating instructions permitted some flexibility, NGO impact was often significant, but NGOs had little or no influence on highly sensitive issues, such as financial resources and trade, on which negotiating instructions often came straight from the office of the president or prime minister. Nor did NGOs succeed in improving the text of the nonbinding Statement of Forest Principles, despite thorough preparation and determination.

Many of the provisions of the Agenda 21 chapter on women reflected a document adopted by an NGO conference of women from eighty-three countries, incorporated into the secretariat draft by sympathetic staff.[69] NGOs probably had their greatest influence on the poverty and consumption chapters of Agenda 21, which incorporated about 90 percent of the proposals of the NGO task group on poverty and consumption via amendments offered by the EC and the CANZ (Canada, Australia, and New Zealand) group.[70] NGO influence was enhanced by the support of the Canadian delegation, on which the chair of the NGO task group sat as an NGO representative.[71]

CORPORATIONS AS ACTORS

Private business firms—especially multinational corporations—are important actors in global environmental issues because their interests are so directly affected by environmental regulation. Often they oppose national and international policies that they believe would impose significant new costs on them or otherwise reduce expected profits. Although some business leaders have become advocates for sustainable development in recent years, corporations have worked over the years to weaken several global environmental regimes, including ozone protection, climate change, whaling, and international toxic waste trade. When they face strong domestic regulations on an activity with a global environmental dimension, however, corporations are likely to support international agreement that would impose similar standards on competitors abroad. And they may prefer an international agreement if it has weaker regulations on their activities than those that they would expect to be imposed domestically.

Sometimes the interest of corporate business in general or a particular industrial sector in regard to an environmental regime is not clear or monolithic. In that case, the business sector or subsector that is most opposed to a new environmental regime tends to be more active in lobbying than those with less at stake. Although the Global Climate Coalition included a broad range of U.S. business sectors interested in the climate treaty negotiations in 1991–1992, those industries that were most strongly opposed to any meaningful legal commitment to controlling greenhouse-gas emissions (the coal industry, private electric utilities, and the auto industry) dominated the coalition's lobbying on the issue. Similarly, on the international hazardous waste trade issue, the chemical and waste-management industries both testified in favor of an international ban, but the position of the secondary metal industry, which strongly opposed such a ban, prevailed in the U.S. Chamber of Commerce.[72]

When some companies see a positive stake in a global environmental agreement, however, they can dilute the influence of those determined to weaken it. In the case of the biodiversity convention, the Industrial Biotechnology Association (IBA) opposed the convention in 1992, fearing that the provisions on intellectual property rights would legally condone existing violations of those rights.[73] But the issue was not a high priority for most of the industry, and two of its leading member corporations, Merck and Genentech, believed the convention would benefit them by encouraging developing countries to negotiate agreements with companies for access to genetic resources. After those companies joined environmentalists in calling for the United States to sign the convention in 1993, the IBA came out in favor of signing it.[74] Similarly, U.S. industries interested in promoting alternatives to fossil fuels began lobbying at meetings of the Intergovernmental Negotiating Committee of the climate convention in August 1994 and sharply reduced the influence of pro–fossil fuel industries, which had previously monopolized industry views on the issue.

Corporations have significant assets for influencing global environmental politics. They have good access to decisionmakers in most governments and international organizations and can deploy impressive technical expertise on the issues in which they are interested. They have national and international industrial associations that represent their interests in policy issues. In some circumstances, however, their influence is reduced by the perception that they represent narrow self-interest rather than global human interests.

Corporate Influence on Regime Formation

Corporations may influence global environmental regimes either indirectly by influencing regime formation or directly by undertaking business activities that weaken a regime or contribute to its effectiveness. To influence the formation of regimes, they may

□ shape the definition of the issue under negotiation in a way that is favorable to their interests;
□ persuade an individual government to adopt a particular position on a regime being negotiated by lobbying it in its capital;
□ lobby delegations to the negotiating conference on the regime.

The greatest success of corporations in defining an issue so as to shape the process of regime formation in their favor was the International Convention for the Prevention of Pollution of the Sea by Oil (1954). The seven major oil companies and global shipping interests (most of which were owned directly or indirectly by the oil companies) were the only actors with the technical expertise to make detailed proposals on the issue of maritime oil pollution. The technical papers submitted by the International Chamber of Shipping (ICS), composed of thirty national associations of shipowners, and the International Marine Forum, representing the interests of major oil companies, defined the terms of the discussion of the convention.[75] That ensured that the convention would be compatible with oil and shipping interests—and quite ineffective in preventing oil pollution of the oceans. That degree of success in defining an issue is unlikely to recur in the future because both governments and NGOs now have more expertise on issues being negotiated and NGOs are better organized and more aggressive.

In most global environmental issues, corporations have relied on their domestic political clout to ensure that governments do not adopt strong policies adversely affecting their interests. The domestic U.S. industry most strongly opposed to a ban on hazardous waste trade, the secondary metals industry, helped persuade U.S. officials to block such a ban in the negotiation of the Basel Convention. And on ozone depletion, Japan agreed to a phaseout of ozone-depleting chemicals only after some of its largest electronic firms said they would phase out their use by 2000.

In the case of the climate change regime, industry lobbying in some industrialized countries effectively blocked important policy measures needed to strengthen the regime negotiated in 1992. In the United States, the auto industry carried out a successful campaign against legislation setting stringent **Corporate Average Fuel Economy** (CAFE) standards, a key instrument for reducing U.S. emissions of carbon dioxide. In 1994, the National Association of Manufacturers and the U.S. Chamber of Commerce, in combination with the private electric power industry, used their clout in Congress to threaten the funding for the U.S. national climate action plan after the Clinton administration supported the negotiation of legal commitments reducing greenhouse-gas emissions beyond the year 2000.[76]

In Europe corporate lobbying on global environmental issues is directed primarily at government ministries traditionally aligned with industrial interests, such as ministries of economics, trade, and industry. In 1992–1993, industry associations in a number of European countries lobbied against the European Commission's carbon/energy tax proposal.[77] In at least one case, government ministries actively facilitated that campaign. The U.K. Department of Trade and Industry sent a letter to over 100 British trade associations inviting them to comment on the likely economic and administrative impacts of the Commission carbon/energy tax.[78] The net result of industry opposition was to make EC implementation of such a carbon/energy tax contingent on parallel action by the United States.

Industry associations have been actively involved in influencing the conferences negotiating on several global environmental regimes. In certain cases where the industry had particular technical expertise or relatively unchallenged influence over the issue, it was represented on one or more key countries' delegations. In the negotiations on Antarctic minerals in the mid-1980s, the American Petroleum Institute, the main umbrella organization for the U.S. oil industry, was represented on the U.S. delegation.[79] And the Japanese commissioner to the International Whaling Commission has generally been the president of the Japanese Whaling Association.[80]

Like NGOs, representatives of corporate interests lobby negotiations on environmental regimes primarily by providing information and analysis to delegations that are most sympathetic to their cause. In the case of the negotiations on the climate change negotiations, for example, coal interests were very active in advising the U.S., Russian, and Saudi delegations on how to weaken the regime.[81] And oil industry representatives were successful in lobbying for weak environmental controls in the Antarctic minerals regime being negotiated in the 1980s.

Corporations also may facilitate or delay, strengthen or weaken, global environmental regimes by direct actions that impact on the environment. These actions may be taken unilaterally or may be the result of agreements reached with their respective governments. Such actions may be crucial to the ability of a government to undertake a commitment to a regime-strengthening policy. The climate change and ozone-protection regimes are particularly sensitive to the willingness of corporations in key countries to take actions that would allow the international community to go beyond the existing agreement.

In the ozone-protection issue, the U.S. chemical industry delayed movement toward any regime for regulating ozone-depleting CFCs in the early 1980s, in part by simply reducing their own research efforts on substitutes for them.[82] More recently, CFC producers also have given impetus to an accelerated timetable for CFC phaseout by unilaterally pledging to phase out their own uses of CFCs ahead of the schedule already agreed to by the Montreal Protocol parties. In 1989, Nissan and Toyota pledged to eliminate CFCs from their cars and manufacturing processes as early as the mid-1990s. In 1992, Ford Motor Company pledged to eliminate 90 percent of CFC use from its manufacturing processes worldwide by the end of that year and to eliminate all CFCs from its air conditioners and manufacturing by the end of 1994.

In the case of climate change, the Japanese auto industry, which accounts for 20 percent of Japan's overall carbon emissions, adopted a goal of improving fuel efficiency by 8.5 percent above its 1990 level by the year 2000, thus encouraging a Japanese government commitment to the national goal of stabilization of carbon emissions at 1990 levels by 2000.[83] In the Netherlands a number of industrial sectors, including iron and steel, glass, cement, and textiles, signed long-term agreements with the Dutch government in 1992 to improve their energy efficiency by 20 percent from the 1989 level by the year 2000.[84]

Industry and Nonregime Issues

Corporations have their greatest political influence on a global environmental issue when there are no negotiations on a formal, binding international regime governing the issue. Under those circumstances, they are able to use their economic and political clout with individual governments and international organizations to protect their freedom to carry out economic activities damaging to the environment.

The issue of pesticide use in developing countries is an example of the power of major corporations to fend off pressures for a regime and to operate freely despite serious environmental consequences. Ten major agrochemical companies control 73 percent of the world pesticide market, and they have spurred the excessive use of pesticides in most developing countries through alliances with agriculture and trade officials who have subsidized pesticide imports, tied agricultural credit to pesticide use, and allowed the industry to provide misleading information to farmers. These companies have also enjoyed the strong support of governments of pesticide-exporting countries, some of which have provided subsidies for pesticide exports.[85] The pesticide industry has had considerable legitimacy in massively increasing sales of pesticides worldwide because of worldwide fears in the 1970s of a world food crisis and the widespread belief that chemical inputs are the key to greater production.

The agrochemical industry has enjoyed strong influence on the FAO's Plant Protection Service, which is responsible for the organization's pesticide activities. The industry's international trade association even had a joint program with the FAO to promote pesticide use worldwide until the 1970s.[86] This influence was instrumental in carrying out the industry's main strategy for avoiding binding international restrictions on its sales of pesticides in developing countries: a voluntary "code of conduct" on pesticide distribution and use, which was drafted by FAO between 1982 and 1985 in close consultation with the industry.

The logging of tropical rainforests for timber exports is another example of a global environmental issue on which multinational corporations have a major influence in the absence of any international regime. Major Japanese trading companies, such as Mitsubishi Corporation, have been heavily involved in logging operations in the Philippines, Indonesia, Malaysia, Papua New Guinea, Brazil, and Siberia. These companies have provided much of the financing for logging in those countries and then imported the raw logs—sometimes illegally harvested—or wood chips to Japan. They have also purchased timber from Myanmar, Thailand, Vietnam, Cambodia, and Laos. And they have had the cooperation of the Japanese government, which has subsidized the construction of roads to be used by the Japanese-financed logging in Malaysia and Papua New Guinea.[87] The governments of the tropical forest countries have been the main actors in fending off any move to establish an international regime for managing tropical forests, but multinational corporations have played a critical role in establishing and maintaining the international system of exploitation of those forests.

Although corporations have resisted strong international environmental agreements when they were not in their interest, in recent years a number of corporations have been positioning themselves as advocates of global sustainable development. Under greater public scrutiny of their environmental behavior and pressure from consumers for environmentally friendly products, these corporations have discovered that pollution prevention is good for profitability. The result is the emergence of a group of corporate leaders who support some of the main aspects of the new paradigm of sustainable development and take constructive positions on some key regime issues.

In the 1980s, a number of European and U.S. corporations participated in two world industrial conferences on environmental management, a joint endeavor of UNEP, the International Chamber of Commerce, and the U.S. Business Roundtable, intended to improve corporate environmental practices through voluntary initiatives. In 1991, at the request of UNCED secretary-general Maurice Strong, Swiss industrialist Stephan Schmidheiny enlisted a group of forty-eight chief executive officers of corporations from all over the world to set up the Business Council on Sustainable Development (BCSD) to support the objectives of the Earth

Summit. BCSD issued a declaration calling for the prices of goods to
flect environmental costs of production, use, recycling, and disposal and
for changes in consumption patterns.[88]

Although the BCSD was expected to disappear after Rio, most members decided to make it a permanent organization. It has since developed
into an international movement with regional branches in Latin America
and national BCSDs in Colombia, the Czech Republic, Indonesia,
Malaysia, Nigeria, and Thailand. BCSD has become actively involved in
the climate negotiations, creating a special task force to investigate and
develop conditions under which business investments could contribute
to reduced greenhouse-gas emissions under the climate convention.[89]

CONCLUSION

State actors have the primary roles in determining the outcomes of issues at stake in global environmental politics, but nonstate actors—IOs,
NGOs, and multinational corporations—influence the policies of individual state actors toward global environmental issues as well as the international negotiation process itself. Whether a state adopts the role of lead
state, supporting state, swing state, or veto state on a particular issue depends primarily on domestic political factors and on the relative costs
and benefits of the proposed regime. But international political-diplo-
matic consequences can also affect the choice of role.

International organizations, especially UNEP, WMO, and FAO, have
played important roles in regime formation by setting the international
agenda and by sponsoring and shaping negotiations on global environmental regimes and soft law norms. The Bretton Woods institutions and
certain U.N. agencies—particularly UNDP and FAO—influence state development strategies through financing and technical assistance. IOs also
seek to exert influence on state policy through research and advocacy of
specific norms at the global level.

NGOs influence the environmental regimes by defining issues, sway-
ing the policy of a key government, lobbying negotiating conferences,
drafting entire convention texts, and monitoring the implementation of
agreements. They have also sought to change the policies and structure of
major international institutions, such as the World Bank and the GATT,
with varying degrees of success. They have been more successful when
the institution in question is dependent on a key state for funding and
less successful when the institution is not so dependent or has no tradition of permitting NGO participation in its processes.

Corporations have used the same methods of influencing regimes as
NGOs, except for submitting draft texts and monitoring implementation.
They can sometimes employ special political assets, including particular

technical expertise, privileged access to certain government ministries, and political clout with legislative bodies to veto or weaken a regime. They can also directly affect the ability of the international community to meet regime goals by their own actions. They are able to maximize their political effectiveness in shaping the outcome of a global environmental issue when they can avert negotiations on a binding regime altogether.

THREE

□   □   □

The Development of Environmental Regimes: Nine Case Studies

The development of most global environmental regimes involves four stages: issue definition, fact finding, bargaining on regime creation, and regime strengthening. Within each environmental issue the sequencing of these stages and the length of time that each takes vary greatly. The stages are not always distinct; the definition stage may overlap the fact-finding stage, which may, in turn, overlap the bargaining stage.

Issue definition involves bringing the issue to the attention of the international community and identifying the scope and magnitude of the environmental threat, its primary causes, and the type of international action required to address the issue. An issue may be placed on the global environmental agenda by one or more state actors, by an international organization (usually at the suggestion of one or more members), or by a nongovernmental organization. The actors who introduce and define the issue often publicize new scientific evidence or theories, as they did in the case of ozone depletion, acid rain, and climate change. But issue definition may also involve identifying a radically different approach to international action on a problem, as it did in the cases of whaling, hazardous waste trade, African elephants, and Antarctic minerals.

The fact-finding process may be well developed or only minimal. In some cases, a mediating international organization has brought interested parties together in an attempt to establish a baseline of facts on which there is agreement. In cases where there is no such mediated process of fact finding and consensus building, the facts may be openly challenged by states that are opposed to international action. The fact-finding stage often shades into and becomes indistinguishable from the bargaining stage. Meetings ostensibly devoted to establishing the scope and serious-ness of the problem may also try to spell out policy options. During this stage, a lead state may begin to advance a proposal for international ac-tion and try to build a consensus behind it. International cleavages and coalitions begin to form.

The outcome of the bargaining process depends in part on the bargain-ing leverage and cohesion of the veto coalition. The members can prevent the creation of a strong international regime by refusing to participate in it or weaken it by insisting on a regime that has no teeth. However, one or more key members of the veto coalition usually make major concessions to make regime creation or regime strengthening possible. In certain cases, a regime may actually be created without the consent of key mem-bers of the veto coalition and thus remain a relatively ineffective regime, as in the case of acid rain.

The regime-building process does not end with the signing and ratifi-cation of a global environmental convention. Once established, regimes can be strengthened by further bargaining that reflects shifts in the under-standing of the environmental problem as well as in the domestic politics of some of the parties. Regime strengthening takes place in three ways:

- □ A protocol may be negotiated to establish concrete commitments, or targets and timetables, as in the case of the acid rain and ozone-pro-tection regimes.
- □ A convention or protocol may be amended by the conference of par-ties, as in the case of the ozone-protection regime.
- □ The conference of the parties to an existing convention may adopt a policy that mandates stronger action by the parties without amend-ing the convention, as in the cases of regimes on whaling and African elephants.

All three of these methods of strengthening an international regime take place within the regular meetings of the conference of the parties, which is provided for in all global environmental and natural resource conventions.

In this chapter, we analyze nine global environmental issues on which there have been multilateral negotiations during the past decade. Each is-sue will be analyzed in terms of the four processes of development of an issue and the role of veto coalitions in shaping the outcomes of bargain-ing. This sample of issues represents a wide range of environmental and political circumstances. It shows the similarities and differences in the political processes and provides a basis for addressing the question of why states agree to cooperate on global environmental issues despite divergent interests.

TRANSBOUNDARY AIR
POLLUTION (ACID RAIN)

Transboundary air pollution, or acid rain, is an issue on which a veto coalition has been divided and weakened over time by defections, permitting a strengthening of a regime that was initially extraordinarily ineffective. But the resulting regime has been undermined by the continued refusal of a few countries—especially the United States—to join. New scientific evidence was a major force for change in the position of key states, who switched from being part of the veto coalition to advocating a strong international regime for the reduction of acid rain. But the evidence has made no impact on the policies of the states remaining in the veto coalition.

Emissions of sulfur dioxide and nitrogen oxide became an international problem after industrialized countries raised the heights of their industrial chimneys by as much as six times in the 1960s in order to disperse pollutants into the atmosphere. Previously industries had polluted only the area immediately surrounding them, but now they exported their acid rain to other countries downwind of the sites.

The definition of transboundary air pollution as an issue in global environmental politics began in the late 1960s with Sweden as the lead actor. The first Swedish move was to introduce new scientific evidence that the acidification of Swedish lakes was related to sulfur dioxide emissions from outside Sweden. Sweden's efforts to put the issue of long-range transboundary air pollution on the international agenda were advanced by Sweden's offer to host the first U.N. environmental conference in 1972 in Stockholm.

There was still relatively little or no interest on the part of other European states. But Sweden and other Nordic states succeeded in getting the Organization for Economic Cooperation and Development (OECD) to agree to monitor transboundary air pollution in Europe in 1972, thus successfully completing the definition process. The OECD monitoring program from 1972 to 1977 was an international fact-finding program that established that pollution was being exported across boundaries and that the problem required international cooperation. In 1977, these monitoring programs were unified under a program sponsored by the Economic Commission for Europe (ECE), and thus included the communist states of Eastern Europe.

Within the ECE those states that had been the victims of this export of acid rain—notably Sweden, Finland, and Norway—took the initiative to negotiate for stringent and binding regulations on emissions of sulfur dioxide and nitrogen oxide.[1] But the industrialized states that were net exporters of acid rain formed a veto coalition, in large part because of their reliance on coal-fired power stations, which accounted for two-thirds of all sulfur dioxide emissions. Its members were the United States, the United Kingdom, the Federal Republic of Germany, Belgium, and Denmark, with the United Kingdom and the FRG in the lead role. The veto coalition rejected any agreement that included specific commitments to reduce emissions. Only after pressures from France, Norway, and Sweden did the FRG and U.K. accept vague obligations to endeavor "as far as possible" to reduce transboundary air pollution. The Convention on Transboundary Air Pollution, concluded in Geneva in 1979 with thirty-five signatories, was a toothless agreement that failed to effectively regulate emissions or transboundary fluxes of acid rain.[2] It did, however, set up an assembly of signatory parties to meet annually to review the implementation of the agreement, thus providing the institutional basis for a process of regime strengthening.

That process was impelled by new and more convincing scientific evidence of damage to European forests and historic buildings from acid rain. Some major exporters of acid rain—especially the FRG—began to change their stance in the early 1980s. At the first meeting of the assembly of signatory parties in 1983, Norway and Sweden proposed a program to reduce emissions of sulfur dioxide by 30 percent of 1980 levels by 1993 and were supported by three defectors from the veto coalition: the FRG, which had begun to experience forest damage, and France and Italy, which had less reason to hold out because they relied heavily on nuclear and hydroelectric power.[3] However, the United States and the United Kingdom continued to oppose formal pledges of emissions reductions.

In an unusual departure from diplomatic tradition, some states committed themselves formally to larger unilateral reductions, thus setting the standard by which other states would be judged. At a conference in Ottawa in March 1984, ten states pledged to reduce sulfur dioxide emissions by 30 percent and to substantially reduce other pollutants, especially nitrous oxide, thus forming the "Thirty-Percent Club." The club propelled agreement on the Protocol on the Reduction of Sulfur Emissions or Their Transboundary Fluxes by at Least 30 Percent (also known as the Helsinki Protocol), signed by twenty-one states in 1985. The protocol came into force in September 1987, but it lacked the adherence of three major exporters of acid rain: the United States, the United Kingdom, and Poland, which together represent more than 30 percent of total world emissions of sulfur dioxide.[4]

In negotiations on reducing nitrogen oxide emissions, three dramatically different positions were advanced by states and NGOs. Austria, the Netherlands, Sweden, Switzerland, and West Germany advocated a

An international group of scientists and activists tours North Carolina forests damaged by acid that comes from sources many miles away. Photo by James J. MacKenzie, World Resources Institute, July 1986.

30-percent reduction in emissions by 1994, but the United States demurred, arguing that it should be credited with previous abatement measures. (Environmental organizations, on the other hand, called for a 75-percent reduction over ten years.[5]) The Protocol Concerning the Control of Emissions of Nitrogen Oxides or Their Transboundary Fluxes (better known as the Sofia Protocol), signed by twenty-three European countries, the United States, and Canada in 1988, also reflected compromise between the lead states and the veto coalition. It required only a freeze of nitrogen oxide emissions or transboundary flows at 1987 levels while allowing most countries to postpone compliance until 1994 by providing credits for reductions in previous years—a concession to U.S. demands.

In summary, a small group of blocking states, led by the United Kingdom and the United States, either refused to join acid rain agreements or demanded that they be watered down. Although the international regime for acid rain, like others negotiated in the 1970s and 1980s, has lent itself to regime strengthening through a mechanism for regular review and action, it remains the weakest regime of any analyzed in this chapter, offering little or no protection to the victims of transboundary air pollution. The urgency of the issue was diminished somewhat by amendments to the U.S. Clean Air Act (1990) and the signing of the climate convention in 1992, since the commitments required in both cases will also have the effect of reducing acid precipitation in the long run.

OZONE DEPLETION

International negotiations to reverse the depletion of the ozone layer illustrate both the role of a veto coalition in weakening a global regime and the dissolution of that coalition because of a combination of scientific evidence and domestic political pressures in key states. The agreement ultimately produced by the bargaining process and continually strengthened since now stands as perhaps the strongest and most effective international environmental regime.

In 1975 UNEP took the first step in introducing the issue of ozone depletion to the international arena when it funded a study by the World Meteorological Organization on the theory advanced by two U.S. scientists that the depletion of the ozone layer was caused by chlorofluorocarbons (CFCs). But the political definition of the issue began in 1977 when the United States, Canada, Finland, Norway, and Sweden urged UNEP to consider the international regulation of ozone. A UNEP experts' conference in 1977 adopted the World Plan of Action on the Ozone Layer. The definition that emerged, however, was based on scientific uncertainty about the causes and seriousness of the problem. Although international action to regulate CFC use was suggested as a policy option, even the most enthusiastic proponents did not see it as an urgent problem.

The Coordinating Committee on the Ozone Layer, consisting of representatives of governmental agencies and NGOs, was established by UNEP to determine the extent of the problem. The fact-finding process was protracted because scientific estimates of the likely depletion fluctuated widely during the late 1970s and early 1980s. The methods of estimating future depletion of the ozone were still being refined, in fact, when UNEP moved to the stage of multilateral negotiation on a framework convention for protection of the ozone layer in 1981.[6] The Ad Hoc Working Group of Legal and Technical Experts for the Elaboration of a Global Framework Convention for the Protection of the Ozone Layer, which included representatives from twenty-four nations, began meeting in January 1982.

The bargaining process actually began, therefore, before there was a clear definition of the issue by proponents of international action. The United States, which alone accounted for 30 percent of worldwide production, was prepared to be the lead state in part because it had already been forced by domestic pressures to regulate CFCs, at least in aerosol cans, and wanted other states to follow suit. But it was essential to any ozone-protection regime that the other states that produced the CFCs be part of the agreement. The European Community, with four major producing states (Britain, France, Germany, and Italy) accounting for 45 percent of world CFC output and exporting a third of their production to developing countries by the mid-1980s, constituted a potential veto coalition. Germany was willing to support controls on CFCs, but the EC position was controlled by the other three producing countries, which wanted to preserve their industries' overseas markets and avoid the costs of adopting substitutes for CFCs.[7] Japan, which was a major user of CFCs, also became part of the coalition.[8]

The large developing countries—India, China, Indonesia, Brazil, and Mexico—also had some potential as a veto coalition. Their bargaining leverage depended on their potential capacity to produce CFCs and thus remain independent of industrialized-country exports. Although they produced less than 5 percent of the world's CFCs, their production was rising at 7 to 10 percent annually and, if not curtailed, could have reduced the impact of an ozone agreement by as much as 50 percent.[9] But these states did not take advantage of their veto power: No developing country played an active role in the early negotiations, and India remained outside the negotiations altogether until after the Montreal Protocol was signed in 1987.

The first proposal by the lead states (the United States, Canada, and the Nordic states) was for the simultaneous negotiation of a framework convention and of associated protocols, with binding obligations to reduce CFC use. The veto coalition steadfastly rejected any negotiation of regulatory protocols, arguing that the state of scientific knowledge was not sufficient to support such a protocol. The United States began in 1985 to define the issue as one of heightened urgency because of new evidence of the possibility of a collapse of the ozone layer at a critical point.[10] But the veto coalition held firm. The only agreement that could be forged, therefore, was a framework convention. The 1985 Vienna Convention for the Protection of the Ozone Layer was essentially an agreement to cooperate on monitoring, research, and data exchanges. It imposed no specific obligations on the signatories to reduce production of ozone-depleting compounds. Indeed, it did not even specify which compounds were the cause of ozone depletion. But because of a last-minute U.S. initiative, there was agreement to resume negotiations on a binding protocol on ozone protection.

Negotiations on such a protocol began in December 1986, with the lead states advocating a freeze followed by a gradual 95-percent reduction in production of CFCs and other ozone-depleting substances over ten to fourteen years. The industrialized-country veto coalition, supported now also by the Soviet Union, continued to advocate a production cap (meaning further growth) on the grounds that the evidence of danger from the ozone hole was not clear. The Toronto Group offered a 50-percent cut as a compromise, but as late as April 1987 the EC position was that it would not agree to more than a 20-percent reduction. Only at the Montreal conference in November 1987 did the EC Commission's representative agree to the 50-percent reduction. The evolution of the EC position from a production cap may have reflected several factors: disunity within the EC (with the FRG, Denmark, Belgium, and the Netherlands all urging strong regulation), the personal role played by UNEP executive director Tolba, relentless diplomatic pressures by the United States, and reluctance to be blamed for the failure of the conference.

The Montreal Protocol on Substances That Deplete the Ozone Layer was a compromise under which industrialized countries pledged to reduce CFC production by 50 percent of 1986 levels by 1999. Developing countries were permitted to increase their use of CFCs substantially for the first decade up to 0.66 pounds (0.3 kilograms) per capita annually.

The estimated net reduction in CFC use to be brought about by the agreement was less than half of the 85 percent generally regarded as necessary even to stabilize the level of ozone depletion. The protocol also permitted the continued production of some ozone-depleting chemicals and neglected to specify that alternatives to CFCs and halons must not be damaging to the ozone layer. It failed to include provisions for international monitoring of production and consumption of ozone-destroying chemicals and contained no real penalties for noncompliance.[11] Nor did it include a fund to defray the costs of substitutes for CFCs in the developing countries, a requirement urgently sought by the developing countries and successfully opposed by the United States, Japan, and the EC. For this reason, three of the most important members of the potential developing-country veto coalition (China, India, and Brazil) refused to sign the Montreal Protocol. But Mexico and Indonesia chose to sign the agreement, perhaps reflecting their greater vulnerability to trade sanctions against nonparticipants.

Within months of the Montreal accord, however, new scientific evidence gave the process of regime strengthening a strong impetus. British scientists discovered an "ozone hole," that is, springtime decreases of 40 percent of the ozone layer over Antarctica between 1977 and 1984. Then a 1988 report by 100 leading atmospheric scientists concluded that the Northern Hemisphere ozone layer had also been reduced up to 3 percent between 1969 and 1986. As a result, the EC decided in March 1989 to phase out all CFC production by the year 2000. At the first meeting of the parties in Helsinki in May 1989, the veto coalition began to shift its position dramatically: The EC members were among eighty nations—not including Japan or the Soviet Union—voting for a complete CFC phaseout by the year 2000 in a nonbinding declaration. In London in June 1990 at the second meeting to amend the protocol, a new coalition of thirteen industrialized states pushed for a 1997 deadline for final elimination of CFCs. The four leading CFC-producing states (the United States, Britain, France, and Italy), joined by the Soviet Union, favored a phaseout by 2000, thus constituting a new veto coalition against the proposed faster deadline.

The final London agreement on timetables for phasing out ozone-depleting chemicals not controlled under the original protocol may be viewed as a considerable victory for the lead states: Carbon tetrachloride was to be phased out by 2000, and methyl chloroform was to be eliminated five years later. Hydrochlorofluorocarbons (HCFCs), which were many times less damaging to the ozone layer than CFCs but were expected to increase rapidly in the future, remained uncontrolled.[12]

After more evidence of the seriousness of ozone-layer depletion in winter 1991–1992, the ninety parties agreed to further strengthen the regime at their annual meeting in Copenhagen in 1992. They accelerated the ban on all CFCs by four years and shortened timetables on other ozone-depleting chemicals. They also added HCFCs to the chemicals to be phased out: From a cap (3.1 percent of 1989 consumption of both CFCs and HCFCs weighted by ozone depleting potential), HCFCs are to be reduced gradually by 35 percent in 2004 to a complete ban by 2030, with all but .5 percent of HCFC use to be phased out by 2020.[13]

The European Commission proposed in 1993 that HCFC use be phased out by 2015, but the United States opposed it, arguing that it would reduce total damage to the ozone layer by less than .5 percent and that a significant proportion of the substitutes for HCFCs would be hydrofluorocarbons (HFCs), which are also potent greenhouse gases. In 1995 Sweden and other states proposed to phase out HCFCs by 2010 and to cut in half the cap from which the phaseout would be implemented. That would have reduced damage to the ozone layer much more than the earlier EC proposal, but the United States opposed the proposal, largely because it wanted to allow U.S. firms that had invested heavily in HCFC technologies as substitutes for CFCs to recoup their investments over 30 years or longer. The United States also pointed out that a rapid phase-out of methyl bromide would have have a much greater impact on the ozone layer than speeding up the HCFC phase-out

Even before the 1992 Montreal Protocol meeting, U.S. NGOs demanded a five-year phaseout of methyl bromide (the second most widely used insecticide in the world by volume) because it is a threat to human health and the ozone layer. Most of the production and use of methyl bromide is in the industrialized countries, but use is also growing in the developing world.[14] The 1993 Bangkok meeting of the parties agreed on the need to strengthen the treaty by phasing out methyl bromide.[15] The United States had already unilaterally frozen its production until 2001, when it will cease abruptly. Germany, Switzerland, and the Netherlands, which had virtually eliminated agricultural uses because of water contamination, and Italy and Denmark will phase out by 2001.[16] And in December 1993, the EU environmental ministers agreed to a 25-percent reduction by 1998.

The 1990 London meeting of the parties also created the Multilateral Fund for the Implementation of the Montreal Protocol. It is the first such fund established under an environmental agreement, and it remains controversial. The fund is administered by an executive committee made up of seven donor and seven recipient countries, carefully balanced geographically. Donor countries promised $240 million for 1991–1993 and another $510 million for 1994–1996 to help developing countries make a transition to alternatives to CFCs, but none had fully paid up as of August 1994.[17]

Funding of projects has also been delayed by contention over who would own technologies produced in developing countries with support from the fund. Some developing countries want the fund to support their research on substitute technologies that might compete with existing CFC alternatives already on the market. ICI and duPont, who own patents on new technologies, insist that most technology development assistance should be done through joint ventures in which the parent companies would still have controlling interests.

Another funding issue involves the question of what are the best substitutes for CFCs. NGOs have been critical that more than 60 percent of the proposed project funding would go to the replacement of CFCs with HCFCs and/or HFCs, which are likely to face tighter international controls in the future because they are potent contributors to global warming.[18] German refrigerator manufacturers are therefore pushing very different approaches, in this case hydrocarbon refrigerants (propane and isobutane) blown by cyclopentane. The multilateral banks and the ozone Multilateral Fund have yet to support those kinds of alternatives. As a result of these arguments, the fund has yet to finance an alternative chemical production facility in a developing country.

The ozone protection regime still faces major implementation challenges. Russia has already announced it cannot meet the Bangkok terms. And it is not yet clear whether the Multilateral Fund will become an effective means of promoting the phase-out of CFC production in the developing countries. Moreover, a significant illegal trade in CFCs emerged in 1994-1995 as the United States and Europe approached their respective cutoff dates for CFC manufacture, taking advantage of a new market created by the higher costs of replacement technologies.[19]

Nevertheless, the Montreal Protocol is the best example so far of a regime that has been continually strengthened in response to new scientific evidence and technological innovations. If these implementation problems can be overcome, it can actually reverse in future decades the damage to the ozone layer which has occurred since the 1960s.

WHALING

The fight to ban whaling worldwide illustrates the transformation of an international regime from one that permitted virtually unregulated exploitation of an endangered species into a global conservation regime, despite the continued resistance of a veto coalition led by a powerful blocking state—Japan. The process of decisionmaking on all commercial whaling, which took place entirely within the International Whaling Commission (IWC) on the basis of a majority vote, favored the forces supporting a ban. Even so, the power of the veto coalition, based on the ability to bolt the agreement at any time, has not yet been broken.[20]

Whaling is not an enterprise of significant economic dimensions worldwide. Nevertheless, it has generated great emotion, and opposing parties have often taken positions with little reference to science. For many environmentalists in the United States and Western Europe, whaling is a powerful symbol of humans' callous disregard for the environment. Whaling states, however, assert their right to pursue a traditional livelihood in a sustainable manner as a matter of national sovereignty.

A long history of overexploitation of whales, which had threatened many species with extinction, led to the establishment of the International Whaling Commission by the International Convention for the Regulation of Whaling in 1946. The convention prohibited killing certain species that were nearly extinct, set quotas and minimum sizes for whales commercially caught, and regulated the seasons for whaling.

But the IWC was a club of whaling nations. It met in secret each year to haggle over quotas that were set so high that the kill more than doubled from 1951 to 1962. In fact, more whales were being killed annually under the new regime than were being killed before the whaling regime went into effect. And the IWC had no power to enforce its regulations on the size of catch or even its bans on the killing of endangered species. Although the major whaling nations that were responsible for most of the catch were members of the IWC, many developing countries, including

China, South Korea, Brazil, Chile, Ecuador, and Peru, refused to join or to abide by its restrictions. They allowed "pirate" whalers, often financed by and selling to the Japanese, to operate freely.

The process of fact finding and consensus building played virtually no role in relations among the members of the IWC. There was no international organization to facilitate consensus building on the scientific facts on whaling. For many years scientific evidence was subordinated to the political and economic interests of the whaling nations; IWC's scientific committee routinely produced data and analysis supporting continued commercial exploitation. By the 1960s, the survival of the largest species, the blue whale, was in doubt, the finback stock was dwindling, and younger and smaller whales were being taken.

The plight of the whales seized the imagination of Americans who were beginning to learn more about the intelligence of whales and dolphins and led to popular demand in the United States for meaningful international protection. The United States, impelled by the Endangered Species Act (1969), declared eight whale species endangered in 1970 and then took the lead in defining the whaling issue internationally.[21] The United States led a regime transformation not by a process of fact finding and consensus building within the IWC but by creating a three-fourths majority needed under the treaty for a whaling ban.

At the 1972 Stockholm conference, the United States proposed an immediate moratorium on commercial whaling, which was adopted unanimously by fifty-two nations. But a whaling moratorium had to be passed by the IWC to have the force of law, and a similar proposal in the IWC was defeated 6 to 4, with 4 abstentions. The whaling states (Norway, Japan, the Soviet Union, Iceland, Chile, and Peru) constituted a veto coalition that was also a majority in the IWC.

The charter of the IWC, which did not limit membership to whaling states, provided a way to overcome the veto coalition by recruiting non-whaling states to the Whaling Commission. That is exactly what the United States, Sweden, and some other conservationist states did between 1979 and 1982. They recruited first the Seychelles and then seven other developing states, most of which viewed the whaling issue from their perspective that the oceans and their natural resources are the "common inheritance of mankind."[22]

The United States, as the lead state, also sought to weaken the veto coalition through the threat of economic sanctions. It used domestic legislation to ban imports of fish products and denial of fishing permits within the U.S. 200-mile zone to any country violating international whale-conservation programs. This put pressure on Chile and Peru, both heavily dependent on U.S. fishing permits and markets, to go along with a whaling moratorium.

In order to be adopted by the IWC, a moratorium required a three-fourths majority of the membership. By 1982, enough developing-country nonwhaling nations had entered the IWC to tilt the balance decisively. A five-year moratorium on all commercial whaling, to take effect in 1985, was passed 25 to 7, with 5 abstentions. The veto coalition, consisting of four states (Japan, Norway, Peru, and the USSR) that accounted for 75 percent of the kill and almost all the consumption of whale meat and other whale products, filed formal reservations to the moratorium but chose not to openly defy it when it went into effect.

Instead, Japan, Norway, and the Soviet Union all formally ended commercial whaling activity by the 1987–1988 whaling season. Then Japan, Iceland, and Norway unilaterally began carrying out what they called "scientific" whaling, which is permitted by the whaling convention. Most IWC members found no scientific merit in this whaling, conducted by commercial ships, which killed hundreds of minke whales annually. But the United States failed to ban imports of $1 billion in Japanese seafood annually because of the likelihood of Japanese retaliation on U.S. fish exports, choosing only the lesser sanction of denying the Japanese permission to fish in U.S. waters. And the United States, fearful of being denied use of its Air Force base in Reykjavik, reached two successive bilateral agreements with Iceland condoning its "scientific" whaling in 1987 and 1988. Only a boycott of Icelandic fish products by conservationists persuaded Iceland to pledge a halt in whaling, at least until 1991.[23] The Soviet Union, meanwhile, just continued whaling, bringing in the second largest catch in the world in the 1980s.[24] False reporting of the Soviet catch during those years may very well have skewed the decade's estimates of surviving stocks.

The "scientific" whaling policy was only a temporary stratagem pending a renewed effort to roll back the moratorium, as shown by the whaling states' request for a change in the status of the Northeast Atlantic minke whales from "protection stock" to "sustainable stock," thus opening the way for resumption of harvesting. At the 1990 IWC meeting, however, with the five-year moratorium ending, the United States led a majority of IWC members in blocking a proposal allowing limited commercial whaling in the Atlantic and extending the moratorium for another year instead. At the meeting, Iceland, Japan, and Norway resorted to the ultimate weapon of threatening to quit the IWC if the moratorium was not overturned at the following year's meeting.

Prior to the 1993 Kyoto IWC meeting, both Japan and Norway again prepared for another effort to end the whaling ban. Norway announced its intention to resume modest commercial whaling (160 minkes from the North Atlantic) in the 1993 season, reportedly because Prime Minister Gro Harlem Brundtland needed the Arctic whaling communities' votes in a tight upcoming election. Japan planned to request a resumption of commercial whaling of a limited number of Antarctic minkes and of 50 more by village fisherman off the Japanese coast. Meanwhile both governments spent large sums in public relations in nonwhaling countries in support of their arguments that minke whales were no longer endangered and that whaling villages, severely impoverished by the moratorium, were being denied the right to pursue a cultural tradition.[25] And Japan induced six Caribbean IWC members to support its position by providing funds for new fishing vessels and by paying their annual IWC membership fees.[26]

But the Kyoto meeting again extended the whaling moratorium for another year, rejecting Japan's requests. Norway resumed limited whaling in 1993 and came under increased pressure when the Clinton administration certified that Norway was eligible for U.S. trade sanctions and the U.S. House of Representatives called unanimously for the application of such sanctions. President Clinton delayed the application of sanctions, pending efforts to convince Norway to end its defiance of the moratorium.

More important, the whale-protection regime was further strengthened at the IWC meeting in Mexico in 1994 by the adoption of a long-term ban on all whaling below 40 degrees south latitude, creating a whale sanctuary that could protect up to 90 percent of the estimated 3.5 million great whales remaining. The big loser in the vote was Japan, which was taking 300 minkes from the Antarctic annually, ostensibly for "scientific" purposes.

While maintaining the moratorium on commercial whaling, the IWC has been discussing since the early 1990s the establishment of a new system of whale management that would permit a carefully limited catch of a whale species whose populations can be scientifically demonstrated to be large enough. Before such a system is adopted, the IWC will have to agree on much tougher enforcement measures than have been acceptable to whaling nations in the past.

The IWC will also have to be convinced that minke stocks in the northeast Atlantic are sufficiently abundant to permit such limited commercial whaling. Norway's 1989 estimate of 86,700 minke whales in the northeast Atlantic was accepted by the IWC's scientific committee as a possible basis for calculating eventual catch limits for the stock. But in 1995, it was revealed that there had been computer and mathematical errors in calculating the Norwegian estimate. The IWC scientific committee, meeting in May 1995, concluded that there was not yet a valid estimate of minke whale population in the northeast Atlantic and agreed to reach agreement on such an estimate during 1995.[27]

Meanwhile, both Japan and Norway appear determined to defy the whaling ban, and Iceland may join them in the future. Japan continues its lethal "scientific" whaling and may try to bring more small states in need of help for their fishing industries into the IWC to overturn the moratorium. Iceland, which quit the IWC in 1992, is under pressure at home to resume commercial whaling. But neither Norway nor Japan is likely to leave the IWC, regardless of decisions on population estimates and enforcement. And in the long run, sentiment and economics could undermine Norwegian and Japanese whaling. A strong majority of the Japanese public already opposes the killing of whales, and as the number of whale-watching vacationers increases each year, even Japanese and Norwegian whalers have taken tourists out to observe whales off their shores.[28]

Despite the defiance of the whaling states with regard to minke whales, there is a broad global consensus against hunting any whale species that could be endangered and on the need to take the precautionary approach in making such determinations. Even the whaling states do not disagree with that norm, and it will be the basis for any detailed set of rules for managing whale stocks that is adopted by the IWC in the future.

THE TRADE IN IVORY
FROM AFRICAN ELEPHANTS

The issue of saving the African elephant by preventing illegal trade in ivory from its tusks illustrates how the transformation of a veto state into a supporter of the regime can be brought about through diplomatic pressures. The context of that transformation suggests that such pressures, taking advantage of the potential embarrassment that could be created by a veto of the regime, were successful in part because the issue did not touch on interests considered to be crucial by the veto state.

The international trade in exotic wildlife is an enormous and lucrative business, worth an estimated $5 billion annually, of which nearly one-third is illegal. The worldwide market for live animals as well as for their parts and derivatives is an important cause of species loss, representing a systematic overexploitation of natural resources.[29]

The dramatic crash in African elephant populations in the 1980s—from 1.3 million in 1979 to 625,000 in 1989—was due partly to loss of habitat but mostly to killing for commercial sale of the ivory tusks.[30] In 1989, the market was worth an estimated $50–60 million annually. Tusks removed from dead elephants, usually killed by poachers, were shipped from African countries to be processed in the United Arab Emirates, Hong Kong, Macao, or China. Most of the worked-ivory products were sold in highly industrialized countries. Although the United States and Western

Europe have significant markets for ivory products, Japan dominates the world market, importing more than 80 percent of all African ivory products, making it the potential leader of a veto coalition.[31]

The umbrella regime for dealing with illegal traffic in wildlife products is the Convention on International Trade in Endangered Species, commonly known as CITES, completed in 1973. CITES combats commercial overexploitation of wild animals and plants by imposing trade sanctions against violators. It set up a secretariat, provided by UNEP, and a conference of the parties, which meets every two years to decide how to regulate trade in species in different degrees of danger. The treaty created three categories of species according to the threat to their existence, with various levels of controls over each: Those in Appendix I are threatened with extinction and are not to be traded except for scientific or cultural endeavors. Those listed in Appendix II are not yet endangered but are believed to merit monitoring and thus require export permits from the country of origin; those in Appendix III require export permits only if the country of origin has listed it in this appendix.

Nations that are the sources of wildlife trade generally support CITES because it helps them protect their valuable wildlife resources from poachers and illegal traders; importing countries often support it because it protects the interests of their legitimate dealers. In the negotiations on CITES the threat of a veto coalition forced the convention's strongest proponents to allow a party to the agreement to enter a reservation to the listing of a species as controlled or banned if the party claims an overriding economic interest in exploiting the species. Such a reservation makes that party in effect a nonparty with regard to that particular species.

As the largest consumer of illegal wildlife in the world, Japan was the leading blocking or veto state on many wild species. Japan made nine reservations to CITES when it ratified the convention and by 1985 added five more, and it refused to ban the import of a number of endangered species. Confronted with international criticism of its policies, however, Japan withdrew eight of its reservations between 1987 and 1994 and in 1987 passed a tough new law punishing traders in protected species.

The African elephant was listed under Appendix II of CITES beginning in 1977, and in 1985 a system of ivory export quotas in the countries with elephant herds was established by CITES to control the international traffic. But in 1988 the World Wildlife Fund and Conservation International (CI) redefined the issue, calling for a worldwide ban on trade in African elephant ivory. They sponsored a study of the African elephant by a group of elephant scientists, trade specialists, and economists in 1989 that made the case for placing the African elephant in Appendix I of CITES. The report concluded that the sustainable level of ivory production was 50 metric tons annually, whereas the world had been consuming 770 metric tons per year for a decade.[32]

The NGO report on the African elephant also represented the beginning of a relatively brief process of fact finding on the issue. But that process failed to achieve a consensus on the facts. There were counter-charges by some other elephant conservation specialists that the NGO report was based on inaccurate trade figures and had deliberately exaggerated the reduction in the elephant population.[33] Countries accepted or rejected the report depending on what policy they wished to support for other reasons.

The bargaining stage began when an odd international coalition including Kenya, Tanzania, Austria, the Gambia, Somalia, Hungary, and the United States initiated an effort to list the African elephant in Appendix I and ban trade in ivory products entirely. These efforts took place at the Seventh CITES Conference of the Parties in October 1989. Another unlikely coalition, uniting foes in southern Africa's struggle over apartheid (Botswana, Malawi, Mozambique, Zambia, South Africa, and Zimbabwe), opposed the listing. Underlying their resistance to the ban was the fact that although Africa's elephant population had declined by roughly one-half over the previous decade because of poaching and ivory trade, Botswana, South Africa, and Zimbabwe had succeeded in increasing their elephant herds by providing economic incentives to localities for conservation through the quota system.

After the conference defeated a compromise proposed by the CITES secretariat that would have distinguished between herds that needed the protection of an ivory trade ban and those that did not, a two-thirds majority put all African elephant herds in Appendix I but also created a special review process to consider the possible transfer of some of the sustainably managed herds before the next CITES meeting.[34] The southern African states lodged reservations against the ban and announced plans to sell their ivory through a cartel, with the proceeds to be used to finance conservation.[35]

It was Japan, however, not the African states, that determined the viability of the regime. A major consumer nation that had much to lose, Japan was expected to veto the ban. Nevertheless it decided not to enter a reservation. Under heavy pressure from NGOs, the United States, and the EC—and hoping to host the 1992 conference of parties—Japan changed its policy and thus made possible an effective regime to protect the elephants. Once the ban was in place, world prices for raw ivory plunged by 90 percent, radically reducing incentives for poaching and smuggling.[36]

To date, no country's elephants have been downlisted, but some illegal trade continues.[37] At issue again in the 1992 Kyoto meeting was the legitimacy of different strategies to rebuild the size of the elephant herds. Some southern African countries, for instance, have provided incentives to local communities to protect the remaining herds, and they insist that they should be allowed to resume limited hunting and trade. The IUCN, WWF, and the United States have some sympathy with a strategy that would seek to balance species protection with the needs of local African communities that could derive income from limited ivory sales, but most convention parties think it is too soon to assert that elephant populations have stabilized. They fear that resumption of ivory trade would once again stimulate illegal slaughter that the African governments would be unable to control. And the Species Survival Network, a largely U.S. and European coalition of about thirty animal rights and conservation groups, has so far persuaded the parties that conditions for downlisting have not been met.[38]

The southern African states were not a true veto coalition, however, because their position reflected an alternative wildlife management scheme that had worked in southern African countries to accomplish the same objective—saving the African elephant. The real issue was how Japan would deal with the issue in CITES. By demanding a reservation on African ivory, Japan would have frustrated international efforts to ban the trade.

INTERNATIONAL TOXIC
WASTE TRADE

Industrialized market economies generate more than 90 percent of the world's hazardous wastes, and as laws regulating hazardous waste disposal grow in those countries, individual firms have sought cheaper sites for their disposal. Most of the trade in hazardous wastes has been between industrialized countries. It is estimated that one-fifth of the total annual global trade in such wastes goes from industrialized countries to developing countries, most of which lack the capacity to monitor incoming shipments and dispose of them safely. These states, particularly the poorer states in Africa, Central America, and the Caribbean, have been tempted by offers of substantial revenues for accepting the wastes. In many cases the trade is illegal, the result of bribery of officials to allow the wastes to enter the country covertly.

The main exporters of hazardous wastes are Germany, Belgium, the Netherlands, Switzerland, and the United States, countries that all have stringent environmental regulations. Only a very small portion of the total waste trade is done in defiance of the receiving country's regulations, but even that constitutes, according to Greenpeace, a thousand egregious cases. The United States exports only one percent of its hazardous wastes, mostly to Canada and Mexico. Nevertheless, it was the United States that led the veto coalition in the 1980s, because of an ideological rejection of any limitation on its right to export.

A fact-finding process on the international trade in hazardous wastes began in 1984–1985, when a UNEP working group of legal and technical experts worked on a set of guidelines (called the Cairo Guidelines) on the management and disposal of hazardous wastes. The guidelines specified prior notification of the receiving state of any export, consent by the receiving state prior to export, and verification by the exporting state that the receiving state has requirements for disposal at least as stringent as those of the exporting state.

But this process did not satisfy key actors, notably the African states who were among the major recipients of illegal hazardous waste exports. The issue of banning international hazardous waste trade, as opposed to regulating it, was defined primarily by African states, who characterized the trade as a form of exploitation of poor and weak states by advanced countries and business firms. This definition of the problem drew support from some officials in the industrialized states: The Dutch minister of environment, for example, called it "waste colonialism."[39] In 1988 parliamentarians from the European Community joined with representatives from sixty-eight developing states from Africa, the Caribbean, and the Pacific calling themselves the ACP states, in demanding international arrangements banning international trade in wastes. The foreign ministers of the Nonaligned Movement also called for industrialized countries to prohibit all waste exports to developing countries.

The bargaining stage began in 1987 when UNEP organized a working group to negotiate a global convention on control of international trade in hazardous wastes. During the next year and a half major differences emerged between African and industrialized countries. The African states wanted a total ban on such waste exports, as well as export-state liability in the event of illegal traffic in wastes, because the developing countries had neither the administrative, technical, nor financial ability to enforce a ban on their own. The waste-exporting states wanted a convention that would permit the trade, providing importing countries were notified and agreed to accept it—what was called an "informed consent" regime.

At the final meeting in Basel, Switzerland, in March 1989, the veto coalition, led by the United States, took advantage of the fact that the waste-exporting states could have continued to find poor countries willing to accept wastes. The veto coalition gave the waste-importing states a choice: Accept an informed consent regime or get none at all. The Organization of African Unity proposed amendments to prevent the export of wastes to countries that lack the same level of facilities and technology as the exporting nations and to require inspection of disposal sites by U.N. inspectors, but the industrialized countries rejected the amendments.[40]

The Basel Convention on Control of Transboundary Movements of Hazardous Wastes and Their Disposal allowed hazardous wastes to be exported to countries whose facilities for storage are less advanced than those of the exporting country as long as the importing state had detailed information on the waste shipment and gave prior written consent. Agreements between signatory states and nonsignatory states were permitted by the convention, although they were supposed to conform to the terms of the convention. Critics charged that the convention did not go any further than existing regulations in industrialized countries, which had failed to curb legal or illegal waste traffic. Moreover, the convention's enforcement provisions were weakened by lack of precision on key definitions, such as "environmentally sound" and "hazardous wastes," and by lack of liability provisions.[41]

As in other global environmental issues, the signing of the Basel Convention began a new phase of maneuvering and bargaining for a stronger regime, but it did not take place in the Basel Convention conference of parties alone. Within months the veto coalition was splitting under pressure from developing countries. In April 1989, thirty states (not including the United States) and the EC pledged publicly to dispose of wastes at home and to ban the export of hazardous wastes to countries that lack the legal and technological capacity to handle them.[42] Later in 1989, after extended negotiations, the European Community also reached agreement with the sixty-eight former European colonial ACP states to ban waste shipments to all sixty-eight members, after ACP negotiators rejected a proposed EC exception for countries with "adequate technical capacity."[43] This concession by the EC appears to have reflected particular conditions affecting member states: a French decision to give priority to cultural and economic ties with France's former colonies, heavy pressure on the U.K. from its former colonies, and a weak commitment by the FRG to the veto coalition because of its lack of interest in exporting to developing countries.

In January 1991, twelve African states, under the auspices of the Organization of African Unity, signed the Bamako Convention, banning the import into their countries of hazardous wastes from any country. They thus underlined the African determination to end the international hazardous waste trade. These multilateral and unilateral bans on hazardous waste trade created, in effect, a stronger waste trade regime outside the Basel Convention, although it excluded Latin American and Asian states from its scope.

The Basel Convention came into effect in May 1992 without ratification by any of the major exporting states that had been the victorious veto coalition in the negotiations. None of them was ready to push for the convention's implementation, and it remained a very weak regime.[44]

But in less than two years, the rapidly growing demand for a complete ban on hazardous waste trade would transform the Basel Convention from a weak regime into a strong one. By early 1994 over 100 countries had banned the import of hazardous wastes, although not all of them had the administrative capacity to do so unilaterally.[45] Some of the credit must go to Greenpeace, which published an exposé volume of 1,000 cases of illegal toxic waste exports.[46] The Clinton administration decided in 1994 to reverse U.S. policy toward hazardous waste trade. In preparation for the March 1994 Geneva meeting of the Basel Convention parties, which the United States would attend only as an observer, the administration announced its intention to call for a ban on all hazardous waste exports to developing countries, and a ban on such exports to any country within five years—exempting only scrap metal, glass, textiles, and paper, which are widely traded for recycling.[47]

But at the Geneva meeting, a broader coalition of states pressed for a complete ban on hazardous-waste exports from OECD countries to non-OECD countries, including those exported for recycling.[48] It was argued that shipments of recyclables were often not recycled by just dumped in a developing country and that the OECD countries would never be forced to reduce their own excessive waste as long as they could ship it out. The G-77 was the lead state coalition calling for such a complete ban to go into effect immediately. Denmark was only a step behind, calling for such a ban to begin in 1995. The United Kingdom, Australia, Germany, the Netherlands, Japan, Canada, and the United States wanted to exempt recyclables. China and the former socialist states of Central and Eastern Europe came out in favor of the G-77 proposal.

Despite intensive lobbying by exporting countries, particularly for allowing bilateral agreements on hazardous-waste exports for recycling, the G-77 would negotiate only on the timetable for its implementation. Confronted with non-OECD unity, the veto coalition began to divide, as the Netherlands shifted to the G-77 position. Italy offered a new proposal for a total ban that was ultimately endorsed unanimously by the Secretariat of the European Council of Ministers.

The remaining veto states could get no more than a delay in the implementation of a total export ban. The 64 nations that were party to the convention and 38 other states that had not yet ratified adopted by consensus a total immediate ban on hazardous-waste exports from OECD countries for final disposal to non-OECD countries and an end to *all* hazardous-waste exports, including recyclables, by December 31, 1997.[49] The United States, Germany, and the European Commission did not accept the verdict of the COP as final, arguing that the ban did not constitute an amendment of the Convention and was not binding international law. But a reversal of the COP decision is unlikely, given the political unity of non-OECD countries on the issue.

The strong regime on international hazardous-waste trade that emerged from the 1994 COP represented a complete reversal of the original Basel convention regime. In an astonishingly short time, an international environmental issue that had deeply divided North and South moved decisively to conclusion. The evolution of the Basel Convention shows how veto power can dissipate when economic relations are suddenly altered. Once the hazardous-waste trade issue became a matter of political symbolism uniting developing countries behind the demand for a complete ban, it eliminated the leverage of waste-export states that had weakened the waste-trade regime in 1989.

THE ANTARCTIC ENVIRONMENT

The regime for Antarctica negotiated in the 1980s was fundamentally redefined in the process: What started as negotiations to regulate mineral exploitation concluded in a regime to protect the environment. The usual roles of state actors are reversed in this case: The veto coalition was composed of states who wished to ban economic activities that could imperil the environment. Antarctica also illustrates how important the "rules of the game" are for global environmental politics: The Antarctic Treaty system requires an unusually high degree of consensus to make binding decisions. The difficulties of creating a new regime within that framework were ultimately advantageous to those campaigning for environmental protection in the region.

Antarctica, which constitutes about 10 percent of the earth's land and water areas, is the only continent that has not been exploited for economic purposes. But it is believed to contain considerable mineral wealth, including reserves of uranium, gold, silver, and other precious metals under the Antarctic Peninsula and oil and natural gas offshore.[50] Given the extreme conditions in Antarctica, which increase the likelihood of accidents and decrease the ecosystem's ability to recover from disruption, ecologists fear that mineral exploitation would pose serious threats to the environment.

Antarctica is governed by the Antarctic Treaty of 1959, which bans military activities and radioactive wastes in the continent and sets it aside as a research preserve. The original twelve signatories to the Antarctic Treaty (Argentina, Australia, Belgium, Chile, France, Japan, New Zealand, Norway, South Africa, the United Kingdom, the United States, and the Soviet Union) include seven that have made territorial claims in Antarctica and five others that insist on viewing the continent as the common property of humankind.

Antarctica is under the collective management of thirty-eight states, called the Antarctic Treaty Consultative Parties (ATCPs), including the twelve original signatories and twenty-six other states who have since signed the treaty and have been accepted by the original signatories as having done substantial scientific research activity there. Other states,

Protesters at the McMurdo U.S. base point up the danger of exploiting Antarctic mineral deposits. Photo by Midgley.

even if signatories to the Antarctic Treaty, may attend the meetings of the ATCPs only as observers. Thus the ATCPs are a relatively exclusive club, consisting of countries with the resources for scientific research.[51]

The Antarctic Treaty was supplemented by three agreements to protect the environment: Agreed Measures on the Conservation of Antarctic Fauna and Flora of the continent in 1964, the Convention for the Conservation of Antarctic Seals in 1972, and the Convention on the Conservation of Antarctic Marine Living Resources (CCAMLR) in 1980. But compliance with all these agreements is voluntary; the treaties failed to establish an environmental review body or regulatory authority, thus leaving individual member states to interpret agreements and resolutions on environmental protection. The CCAMLR requires a consensus of parties on conservation measures and therefore limits environmental protection to what is acceptable to the most shortsighted party.

In 1972 the Second World Conference on National Parks, cosponsored by the IUCN, noted the "great scientific and aesthetic value of the unaltered natural ecosystems of the Antarctic" and called for the negotiation of a "world park" regime that would ban all mineral exploration in the continent. The proposal was formally supported by New Zealand in 1975 but never raised in meetings of the ATCPs.

Meanwhile most of the ATCPs, driven by sudden price increases in the international oil market, agreed that an international regime was needed to govern eventual exploration for Antarctic oil and gas resources. The United States, in particular, believed that Antarctica might become a vital source of supply in the future and was one of the few ATCPs to oppose a moratorium on exploration until a minerals regime was negotiated. No fact-finding process was carried out by the ATCPs before the bargaining process began. By 1977, the ATCPs were already discussing the principles of such a regime.[52]

Negotiations began in 1981 and continued for the next seven years.[53] A division developed between the most enthusiastic pro-mining states (the United States, West Germany, Japan, Britain, and France) and states geographically closer to Antarctica (Australia, Argentina, and Chile), which wanted stronger conservation provisions.[54] This coalition won some concessions from the most pro-mining states, but it agreed to a regime that could have permitted minerals exploitation in Antarctica.

The Convention on the Regulation of Antarctic Mineral Resources Activities (CRAMRA, 1988) would have blocked any exploration for minerals in the absence of a consensus of all members that the activity would not violate specific environmental standards, thus reversing the rule in the CCAMLR that economic activities can proceed unless there is a consensus on measures to restrict them.[55] Nevertheless, environmentalists doubted that the ATCP states could be counted on to put environmental protection ahead of economic development once the race for mineral wealth began and feared that the regulatory committees provided for in the treaty would be subject to political horse-trading at the expense of the environment.[56]

Before the new convention could go into effect, the political process took a sudden dramatic turn, as a veto coalition quickly took shape behind Australia. In May 1989 Australia, influenced by the environmentalist vote in the previous election, announced that it would not sign the convention but would work for a comprehensive environmental protection convention, including provision for an Antarctic World Park, first proposed by IUCN. To take effect, the minerals treaty required the ratification of sixteen of the twenty ATCPs who were signatories as well as all seven of those with territorial claims. That meant that Australia could single-handedly veto the minerals regime.

Australia's pronouncement simultaneously redefined the issue once again and began a new phase of bargaining. In August, France—another claimant state—jointly proposed with Australia that Antarctica be designated as a nature preserve, asserting that mining was not compatible with environmental protection there. Belgium, Italy, Austria, Greece, India, and the European Parliament then joined the call for making Antarctica a permanent wilderness preserve. Finally, New Zealand, formerly a strong supporter of the minerals regime process but under strong pressure from environmentalists, abandoned the minerals treaty in early 1990 and indicated that it would work with France and Australia to protect Antarctica from mining. With the tide now running against the minerals regime, the U.N. General Assembly voted overwhelmingly in 1989 in favor of an Antarctic World Park.

The United States at first strongly resisted Australia's initiative, but it was soon subject to its own domestic pressures. After the U.S. Congress passed two pieces of legislation prohibiting mining activities in Antarctica indefinitely and backing the world park proposal, the United States countered with a proposal for a legally binding moratorium, though still not a permanent ban, on minerals exploration in Antarctica. At the 1990 ATCP meeting the parties agreed to pursue the negotiation of a new "comprehensive legal instrument" on the environmental protection of Antarctica, which would prohibit any exploration for mineral resources in the region.

At a special meeting of the treaty parties in December 1990, the concept of a long-term legal moratorium was discussed, but there was no agreement on how long it should last or what would follow its termination. The United States, the United Kingdom, and Japan led a new veto coalition that resisted an indefinite ban. But at the second session of the meeting in April 1991, Japan broke ranks and joined the advocates of such a ban. A compromise proposal was tabled for a fifty-year ban on mineral-related activity in Antarctica that could be lifted only with the support of all twenty-six of the present ATCPs, thus continuing to give each of them a veto.

At another meeting in Madrid two months later, the proposal was supported by every ATCP except the United States. After two weeks of intensive lobbying by other states, the United States agreed to a new compromise that would permit a repeal of the mineral ban by three-fourths of the twenty-six ATCPs,[57] and the Environmental Protocol to the Antarctic Treaty was signed. In early 1995, the treaty had not yet received the ratifications to come into force, though the United States had agreed to ratify and was waiting only on enabling legislation for implementing specific parts of the convention.

The agreement on a fifty-year mining ban represented another stunning reversal of a regime negotiated earlier. The collapse of the proposed minerals regime was in large part due to the salience of environmental issues in parliamentary elections in several countries and the aggressive and persistent lobbying of NGOs, especially the Antarctic and Southern Oceans Coalition. It was also facilitated by the Antarctic Treaty regime it-

FIGURE 3.1 Cumulative emissions of carbon dioxide from fossil fuels for twenty-five countries with the highest emissions, 1950–1989

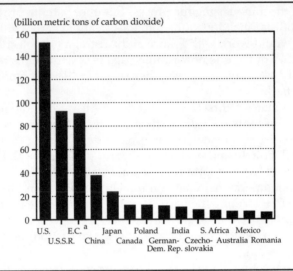

(billion metric tons of carbon dioxide)

[a] The European Community (EC) comprises 12 countries: Belgium, Denmark, France, Germany, Greece, Ireland, Italy, Luxembourg, the Netherlands, Portugal, Spain, and the United Kingdom.

Source: World Resources Institute, *World Resources, 1992–93* (New York: Oxford University Press, 1992), p. 206.

self, in which a few parties have special veto powers, thus making it possible for Australia to lead an unlikely veto coalition in defeating the major powers' efforts on behalf of the regime. And it was made easier by the fact that no country was in fact dependent on or planning to invest in mineral exploitation in Antarctica.

GLOBAL WARMING

Global climate change, or greenhouse warming, is the prototype of the global commons issue. All nations are affected by the earth's climate system, and broad international cooperation is required to mitigate the threat of global warming. Although the impacts of greenhouse warming are expected to vary from one region to another, suggesting to some the possibility of winners and losers, that notion is based on the erroneous assumption that greenhouse warming will stop at a predictable point. In fact, in the absence of a global agreement to reduce greenhouse gases, no state can anticipate any stabilization in the climate, and its capacity for adaptation could well be overwhelmed by continued warming.[58]

FIGURE 3.2 Per capita emissions of carbon dioxide in North and South, 1950–1987

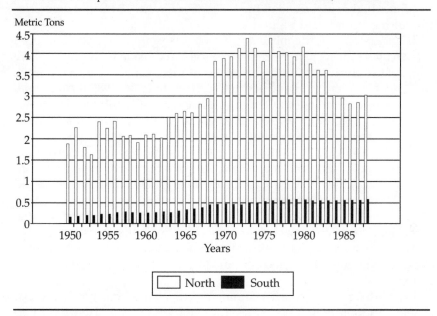

Source: Ishac Diwan and Nemat Shafik, "Investment, Technology and Global Environment: Towards International Agreement in a World of Disparities," in Patrick Low, ed., *International Trade and the Environment* (Washington, D.C.: World Bank, 1992), p. 271.

Building a regime to mitigate global climate change is technically and economically feasible. But it is complicated by the multiple sources of emissions that contribute to global warming, by scientific uncertainties, especially the chemistry of the atmosphere, and by dependence on global climate modeling, which is far from an exact science.[59] Even more important, however, is the fact that energy is central to every nation's economy, and the policy changes required to reduce greenhouse-gas emissions raise politically difficult policy questions of who should bear the immediate costs. Even to stabilize the global concentrations of carbon dioxide (which would not reduce the warming to which earlier emissions have already committed the earth) would require reducing current emissions by roughly one-half. That would necessitate major gains in conservation and switching from coal and oil to natural gas and renewable sources, which would affect powerful economic and political interests in many countries.

Most greenhouse-gas emissions have come from the burning of fossil fuels in the highly industrialized countries. A comparison of cumulative emissions of carbon dioxide from fossil fuels show that U.S. and Soviet Union emissions far exceeded those of any other country. (See Figure 3.1.) On a per capita basis, emissions of energy-based carbon dioxide from the

North have been ten times higher than those from the South and were five times higher at the end of the 1980s. (See Figure 3.2.) Rapid deforestation of the tropics and natural sources of methane, neither of which is well understood, also contribute to global warming.[60] It has long been known by scientists that the buildup of carbon dioxide in the atmosphere could cause climate warming by means of the greenhouse effect. But the process of defining the issue began to accelerate in the 1985–1986 period. The World Meteorological Organization and UNEP took the first major step with a 1985 conference in Villach, Austria, that produced a new scientific consensus that greenhouse warming was a serious possibility.[61] And in 1986 WMO, the National Aeronautics and Space Administration (NASA), and several other agencies issued a three-volume report concluding that climate change was already taking place at a relatively rapid rate. The unusually hot summer of 1988 accelerated media and congressional attention and even thrust the climate issue into the presidential campaign. The testimony of prominent U.S. scientists suggesting that the climate was already changing irreversibly, primarily because of carbon dioxide emissions, further contributed to the definition of the climate change issue.[62]

In an attempt to establish a common factual basis for negotiations that would focus on policy options, WMO and UNEP organized the Intergovernmental Panel on Climate Change (IPCC). It had working groups on scientific knowledge, on the social and economic impacts of global warming, and on response strategies. Each had a core membership of ten to twelve states, including one or two of the major developing countries (China, India, Brazil, and Indonesia). The final report of the working groups—approved by the participating states after long, grueling negotiations in August 1990—reaffirmed that global warming is a serious threat.

Bargaining on regime creation began when some states, pressured or supported by their environmental NGOs, pushed for a strong global regime built around specific targets and timetables for greenhouse-gas emissions reductions. A conference in Toronto, sponsored by the Canadian government in June 1988 and attended by government officials, scientists, and representatives of industry and environmental NGOs from forty-six countries, was the first to call for a comprehensive global convention and protocols, a reduction in carbon dioxide emissions by about 20 percent of 1988 levels by the year 2005, and establishment of a world atmosphere fund financed partly by a tax on fossil fuel combustion. Regime development was given a boost when the G-7 meeting in Paris in 1989 endorsed the idea of a convention.

Throughout negotiations on a regime to mitigate global warming, targets and timetables were the central issue. At the Noordwijk conference in the Netherlands in 1989, the United States, the Soviet Union, China, and Japan, which together accounted for more than half the world's carbon dioxide emissions from fossil fuels, acted for the first time as a blocking coalition on global warming. The United States and Japan argued that further study of the goal of reducing carbon emissions was needed, and the Soviet Union rejected action on straightforward economic grounds.[63]

In the eighteen months that followed, the coalition of lead states (Norway, Sweden, Finland, and the Netherlands) squared off with the United States, as leader of the veto coalition, on whether the negotiations should produce a protocol with specific obligations on emissions. The lead states called for negotiation of a framework convention to be paralleled by negotiation of a protocol limiting emissions to be completed no later than a year after the convention. The United States insisted on a framework convention with no parallel negotiations on protocols, arguing that regulating carbon releases would require major changes in lifestyle and industrial structure. But in October 1990, Japan broke ranks with the United States on the issue by committing itself to stabilizing its greenhouse-gas emissions at 1990 levels by the year 2000. That left the United States and the Soviet Union alone among industrialized countries rejecting a target and timetable for controlling emissions in a climate regime.[64]

The negotiation of a climate convention began officially in February 1991, conducted by the Intergovernmental Negotiating Committee (INC) for a Framework Climate Convention, created by the U.N. General Assembly. The EC assumed a lead role in the negotiations by virtue of its commitment to returning its joint carbon dioxide emissions to 1990 levels by the year 2000. Germany, Denmark, Austria, Australia, the Netherlands, and New Zealand had committed to reducing their emissions by 2000 or 2005. The United States alone among industrialized countries resisted the inclusion of any binding commitments to targets and timetables.

Had binding commitments for controlling greenhouse emissions been included in the text, the developing countries' agreement would have been crucial to the regime. Although their share of such emissions, including carbon dioxide releases from deforestation, was estimated at around 45 percent of the worldwide total, they were expected to account for two-thirds of total emissions by 2025. The biggest rapidly industrializing countries (China, India, and Brazil), which already accounted for 21 percent of global emissions from all sources in 1989 (about the same as the United States), were a potential veto coalition.[65]

What was to have been the final round of negotiations in February 1992 ended without resolution of the issue of a stabilization target and timetable.[66] With the deadline of the Earth Summit only weeks away, the negotiators agreed to one more session in April. German, British, Dutch, and other EC member states sent officials to Washington before the session in an unsuccessful effort to persuade the United States to go along with a commitment to stabilization of emissions at 1990 levels by the year

2000. But during the April session, President George Bush personally called German prime minister Helmut Kohl to ask him to drop his government's demand for the stabilization commitment in return for Bush's participation in the Earth Summit. Bush announced his decision to attend the Rio conference only after the final text of the climate change convention was adopted without reference to binding commitments to controlling greenhouse gases.[67]

The Framework Convention on Climate Change was signed by 154 countries in Rio in June 1992. It declares as its goal the restoration of greenhouse-gas emissions in 2000 to "earlier levels"—a phrase interpreted by the EC to mean 1990 levels—but does not commit any government to hold emissions to a specific level by a certain date. Nor does it address a climate change goal after the year 2000. Of a lengthy list of commitments in the agreement, providing national reports is probably the only one that is enforceable. But the text does provide for regular review of the "adequacy" of the commitments.

The Framework Convention on Climate Change came into force in March 1994 after ratification by the minimum necessary fifty states.[68] The climate regime that resulted from the exercise of veto power by the United States was generally regarded as a weak one. The process of strengthening the regime had begun when the EC issued a statement upon signing the convention calling for an early start on negotiation of a protocol with binding targets and timetables. A detailed discussion of the struggle to implement and strengthen the climate regime is provided in Chapter 5.

BIODIVERSITY LOSS

Biodiversity loss has been recognized by the scientific community as one of the most serious environmental threats facing humankind, but negotiation of a regime for conserving biodiversity has suffered from serious differences over the definition of the problem and from resistance to strong legal obligations by a veto coalition of states holding most of the world's biodiversity. Combined with a weak commitment on the part of the United States and other industrialized states, these problems have contributed to a relatively weak regime.

By the early 1980s a scientific consensus had begun to emerge that the rate of species extinction had increased alarmingly. And the IUCN General Assembly requested the director-general of IUCN to set in motion a process aimed at producing a preliminary draft of a global agreement on conserving the world's genetic resources.[69] The United States took the lead in putting the issue of biodiversity loss on the international agenda in 1987, getting the UNEP Governing Council to create an ad hoc working group of experts to study an "umbrella convention" to rationalize activities in biodiversity conservation.[70] But it quickly became apparent to the experts that an umbrella convention would be an unworkable, and probably sterile, approach to the problem.

When the UNEP ad hoc working group began meeting in 1990, the issue of a biodiversity convention became entangled in a North-South struggle over plant genetic resources and **intellectual property rights** (IPR), the rights of businesses, individuals, and states to legal protection of their discoveries and inventions. Up to that time, plant genetic resources had been regarded in international law as part of the "common heritage of mankind" and thus freely available to companies who wished to use them to create new commercial seeds. But developing-country states had long been dissatisfied with the fact that the hybrid seeds based on the genetic resources obtained from their countries were protected by intellectual property rights and thus were available to them only at much higher costs. In 1983, developing countries had tried to press for change in that system through the nonbinding FAO Undertaking on Plant Genetic Resources. That agreement applied the concept of the "common heritage of mankind" not only to the original genetic resources but also to the hybrid seeds created by the seed companies, which would have deprived the companies of intellectual property rights. But that maneuver ran into determined opposition from states in which seed companies were located (Canada, France, West Germany, Japan, the United Kingdom, and the United States), which refused to sign the Undertaking and boycotted the FAO's Commission on Plant Genetic Resources until it reassured them that the intellectual property rights of seed companies would be respected.

Having failed to change the IPR system through the FAO, some developing countries rejected in the UNEP working group the previously accepted notion that their genetic resources were part of the common heritage of mankind. They insisted instead that those resources belong to the states in which they are located, and that access to genetic resources should be on the basis of "mutual agreement between countries." They also asserted that provision for noncommercial access to biotechnologies based on plant genetic resources found in the South had to be a central element in any biodiversity convention. The industrialized countries, with the exception of the Nordics, initially opposed the inclusion of biotechnology in the convention, defining the scope of the regime to include only conservation of biodiversity in the wild and mechanisms to finance such efforts.[71]

The official negotiations on a biodiversity convention were completed in just five sessions over a relatively brief span of nine months from July 1991 to May 1992, with more than 100 states participating in the final session in Nairobi. The bargaining, polarized largely along North-South lines, was shaped largely by four factors: the veto power of developing countries over biodiversity conservation provisions, the veto power of industrialized countries over technology transfer and financing, the aggressive role played by UNEP executive director Mostafa Tolba, and the implicit deadline imposed by the Earth Summit in Rio in June 1992. The resulting regime relies more on economic incentives than on legal obligations for biodiversity conservation, and it left key states in both North and South unsatisfied with provisions on technology transfer and financing.

The convention puts access to genetic resources under the authority of the state in which they are found and calls for access to be granted on "mutually agreed terms." Thus companies interested in prospecting for genetic resources in a particular country have to negotiate with entities designated by the government of that country over the terms of that access, including royalties from any biotechnologies based on genetic resources transferred as the result of the agreement. Such deals are supposed to provide a new economic incentive for developing countries to conserve biological resources.

The scope of the conservation provisions was narrowed by the unwillingness of key actors to entertain the possibility of quantitative targets for percentage of land set aside for biodiversity conservation. That idea was raised informally by Germany early in the negotiations, but a veto coalition led by countries holding a large proportion of the world's biodiversity (Mexico, Brazil, and Indonesia) vociferously opposed such tough conservation provisions. And most European countries argued that such targets would embarrass those countries that had already cut down most of their forests.[72] They were never formally proposed in the negotiations.

Although the United States, sometimes supported by India, weakened the conservation provisions, the final text does obligate the parties to develop national strategies for conservation and sustainable use of biological diversity, to integrate conservation and sustainable use of biological diversity into relevant economic development policies and programs, to inventory and monitor biodiversity resources and processes that affect them adversely, and to preserve indigenous conservation practices.

The most contentious issues—transfer of technology and financing—could not be resolved at the final negotiating session to the satisfaction of all the key parties. On technology transfer, India, on behalf of the Group of 77, had tried and failed to get language obligating the industrialized countries to compel biotechnology companies to turn over patented technologies to developing countries. The United States succeeded in getting a sentence clearly guaranteeing that any technology transfer under the agreement would be on terms that protected intellectual property rights. But India insisted that the same sentence had to be applied consistent with an ambiguous compromise paragraph calling on parties to ensure that intellectual property rights are "supportive of and do not run counter to" the convention's objectives. The United States objected that the ambiguous paragraph could be read as hostile to intellectual property rights.

The provisions on the convention's financial mechanism were equally divisive. The donor countries and most Latin American countries supported the Global Environment Facility (GEF), created by the donor countries and managed primarily by the World Bank, as the funding mechanism for the convention. But Asian and African states, led by India and Malaysia, were angry about the provision of the climate convention making the GEF the interim financial mechanism. They demanded the creation of a freestanding biodiversity fund having nothing to do with the World Bank, which they felt was controlled by the donor countries.[73]

UNEP secretary-general Tolba, confronted with the possibility of a failure to reach agreement in time for the Rio conference, took over the negotiations personally. In an extraordinary intervention that was protested by both the United States and France, Tolba in effect suspended the rules, replaced the designated chair of the conference, and wrote his own text, which he submitted to the delegations as a fait accompli to be accepted or rejected shortly before the diplomatic conference that would formally adopt the convention.[74]

The text designated the GEF as the interim funding mechanism, with conditions relating to transparency and democracy, until the first conference of the parties but also had the GEF functioning under the authority of the conference of the parties (COP)—something the donor countries had rejected. It appeared to leave open the possibility that the COP could determine what levels of financial resources would be contributed by donor countries. Both Malaysia and the United States declared that the compromise on finance was unacceptable and expressed dissatisfaction with the provisions on technology transfer as well.

Other industrialized countries also had concerns, particularly on the financial mechanism, but felt that it was the best agreement that could be reached in time for the treaty to be opened for signature at the Earth Summit only ten days later. They chose to issue their own interpretations of the text on financing and to sign the convention in Rio. One hundred and fifty-three countries signed the convention in Rio, but the United States refused to do so, citing the provisions on financing and intellectual property rights.

The United States reversed its position after the Clinton administration came into office in 1993 and signed the convention in June 1993.[75] The convention entered into force on December 29, 1993, after thirty countries—six industrialized countries and twenty-four developing countries—had ratified the convention. The United States failed to ratify the convention, however, and participated in the first COP of the convention only as an observer.

Eucalyptus saplings planted to prevent soil erosion. Lompoul, Senegal, 1984. Photo by J. Isaac, UN/DPI.

DESERTIFICATION

The desertification convention is one of only two international regimes that was established at the initiative of the developing countries despite the resistance of industrialized countries. The desertification, which affects many regions of the world, had been the subject of international cooperation for two decades, since the first major drought in sub-Saharan Africa, but it was put on the global environmental agenda in 1992 only because of the persistence of African countries and because it became linked with other issues in UNCED. As the first treaty after UNCED, it was looked upon by some as a test of whether governments had the political will to follow up on Agenda 21 commitments.

The stage of issue definition in the case of desertification was plagued by complexity, vagueness, and disagreement on whether it was indeed a "global" problem. Desertification was defined by UNEP and by most specialists as sustained land degradation in arid, semiarid, and dry subhumid areas resulting mainly from adverse human impact.[76] But the term "desertification" evokes images of deserts advancing and destroying productive land, whereas scientists have found no evidence to support claims that the Sahara is expanding at an alarming rate. Foes of a convention exploited that fact: At one point in the UNCED negotiations, the United States dismissed the term "desertification" and suggested substituting "land degradation."[77] Some donor countries objected to the designation "global" because that might imply that treaty implementation efforts would be eligible for funding from the Global Environment Facility.[78]

African countries encountered other problems in defining the issue of desertification. First, desertification does not involve resources or life-support systems of global interest, as do other environmental issues on which regimes have been negotiated. It affects countries not suffering from desertification only because it threatens the economies and societies of a large number of countries. Second, a bewildering array of natural and social factors appears to affect land degradation in drylands, including overpopulation, climatic cycles, social and economic structures, poor pastoral or agricultural practices, bad policies on the part of governments and donors, and North-South economic relations. So it was difficult to articulate simply and clearly either the nature of the problem or the international actions needed to address it.

Indeed, for many African countries, there is a strong link between poverty alleviation and desertification control. The African countries' definition of the problem emphasized the need for additional funding for as yet unidentified activities. These countries hoped that a desertification convention would help them gain access to additional funding through the Global Environment Facility, which had rejected desertification as one of the global environmental problems it could finance.[79]

Finally, the African countries' attempt to define the desertification issue was hampered by the fact that the earlier Plan of Action to Combat Desertification (PACD), launched in the late 1970s, was generally acknowledged to have been a failure. A UNEP evaluation of the plan had blamed the failure on both African governments and the donor community for not giving the issue priority. UNEP had also found that only $1 billion of the $9 billion provided by donor agencies from 1978 to 1983 was spent on direct field projects.[80]

So when the issue of a desertification convention was first raised in UNCED, only France, with its special ties with Africa, expressed support for the idea. Most industrialized countries and the World Bank argued that the primary problems were with the structure and macroeconomic policies of African governments (such as excessive taxes on agriculture and failing to grant enforceable property rights) and that policy reforms, better planning, and more popular participation would achieve better results than a new international program or formal agreement.[81] Moreover, the G-77 failed to endorse the African call for a desertification convention in the communiqué of the 1992 Kuala Lumpur ministerial meeting, dominated by host government Malaysia.

Despite these problems in the definition of the issue of desertification, it was put on the global agenda because of African persistence and because the United States unexpectedly supported the African position. At the Earth Summit in Rio, the United States, after opposing a desertification convention throughout the UNCED negotiations, shifted to backing such a convention in the hope of getting African support on forests and on the remaining issues in the Rio Declaration.[82] Other industrialized countries then followed suit, but the EC initially resisted the U.S. proposal. Finally the EC relented, and the call for a desertification convention became part of Agenda 21.[83]

Negotiations by the Intergovernmental Negotiating Committee on the International Convention to Combat Desertification began in May 1993 and were completed in a brief fifteen months. The formal fact-finding process, carried out in an "information sharing segment" at the first session of the INC, focused primarily on socioeconomic strategies for slowing and reversing desertification and on reports from individual countries rather than on scientific understanding of the problem. That process produced general agreement on the importance of such strategies as integrating arid and semiarid areas into national economies, popular participation in antidesertification efforts, and land tenure reform.[84] As a result, the convention would be the first to call for affected countries to provide for effective participation by grassroots organizations, NGOs, and local populations, both men and women, in the preparation of national action programs.[85]

The bargaining revolved not around commitments to environmental conservation actions but around financial, trade, institutional, and symbolic issues. The African countries were the lead states. The Organization of African Unity (OAU) had detailed draft sections for every section of the convention, some of which were accepted as the basis for negotiation.

Whether debt and trade issues should be included within the scope of the convention was a central issue, affecting the obligations, action programs, and regional annexes as well as sections on scope, objectives, and principles. The OAU and other developing countries asserted that external debt burdens and commodity prices, among other international economic policy issues, affect their ability to combat desertification. The industrialized countries argued that those North-South economic issues could be negotiated only in other international forums. They did agree to general obligations to "give due attention" to the trade and debt problems of affected countries in order to create an "enabling international economic environment" for those countries.

Differences over financial resources and the financial mechanism nearly caused the negotiations to collapse. Some members of the G-77 and China demanded commitments to "new and additional" financial resources and creation of a special fund for desertification as the centerpiece of the convention. The industrialized countries were united in rejecting any provision for new and additional financing, agreeing only to ensure "adequate" financial resources for antidesertification programs. The developed countries felt they bore no responsibility for the problem of desertification worldwide, unlike the issues of ozone depletion and climate change, and were therefore unwilling to incur any obligation to increase their financial assistance to affected countries.[86] They insisted that the overhead associated with a special fund would reduce the resources needed in the field and that existing resources could be used more effectively. They also vetoed the use of GEF funds unless the project contributed either to prevention of climate change or to biodiversity conservation.

The deadlock on a funding mechanism was broken only after the United States proposed a "global mechanism" under the authority of the conference of the parties, to be housed within an existing organization, which would improve monitoring and assessment of existing aid flows and increase coordination among donors. Developing countries remained dissatisfied because such a mechanism would not increase development assistance to African and other countries suffering desertification. But they ultimately accepted it as the only compromise acceptable to the donor countries.[87]

TABLE 3.1 Veto States and Regime Creation or Strengthening

Issue	Key Veto States	Basis of Veto Power	Veto State Concession
Acid rain	Germany	Percent of emissions; exports	Joining the "30-Percent Club"
Ozone depletion I	EC Commission	Percent of CFC production	Agreeing to 50-percent cut
Ozone depletion II	EC Commission	Percent of CFC production	Agreeing to phaseout
African elephant ivory	Japan	Percent of imports	No reservation to CITES uplist
Whale protection	Japan and Norway	Percent of catch	No unilateral resumption of whaling (1986–93)
Hazardous waste trade	United States, EU, Japan	Percent of exports	Agreeing to ban exports
Climate	United States	Percent of CO_2 emissions	Agreeing to stabilization goal
Antarctic	United States, U.K., Japan	Potential for mineral exploitation	Agreeing to world park
Biodiversity	United States	Percentage of financing of GEF	Signing the agreement
Desertification	EC, United States	Percentage of ODA	Agreeing to negotiate regime

The problem of how to reflect the priority to be given to Africa, called for in the UNGA resolution on the convention, while meeting demands from other regions for equitable treatment, arose in negotiating regional annexes to the convention. The original intention of African and industrialized countries' delegations was to negotiate a regional implementation annex only for Africa by the deadline of July 1994, but other developing-country delegations demanded that implementation annexes for their own regions be negotiated simultaneously with the one for Africa. In the end, each regional grouping got its own annex, but the priority for Africa was ensured by a special resolution that encouraged donor countries to provide financial support of national action programs in Africa without waiting for the convention to ⌐ into force.

The International Convention to Combat Desertification was opened for signature in October 1994 and was to enter into force ninety days after the fiftieth ratification. By early 1995, it had been signed by ninety-seven countries and was expected to go into effect sometime in 1997.

CONCLUSION

These case studies of environmental regime formation and strengthening show that the successful negotiation of global environmental regimes almost always depends on inducing one or more key states in a veto coalition to go along with a central element in the proposed regime. The veto states usually either change their own understanding of the problem because of new scientific evidence or change in political leadership or are moved by some combination of domestic pressures and the fear of negative reactions by governments and public opinion in other states. As Table 3.1 shows, in each of these cases, one or more veto states either agreed to the central obligation proposed by the lead-state coalition or accepted the regime in general despite earlier rejection.

New scientific evidence has helped move veto states on some issues (acid rain and ozone depletion) but has been secondary or irrelevant in other issues (whaling, hazardous waste trade, Antarctic minerals, and African elephants). International considerations were primary in several cases: Japan's concern with economic and diplomatic ties with other major trading nations and its international image helped tilt its stand on the ivory ban. French and British desires to maintain close relations with former colonies were a factor conditioning their views on the hazardous waste trade issue. The threat of trade sanctions constrained Japan and (until 1993) Norway from openly defying the ban on whaling.

In other cases (Antarctica and climate), domestic political developments played a key role in facilitating agreement. On Antarctica the United States softened its opposition to a mining ban when Congress supported such a ban, and Australia and France shifted from supporters of a mining regime to supporters of the world park concept because of clear signals from the public. The United States dropped its veto role on targets and timetables in the climate change regime because a more sympathetic administration came into office.

Regime formation also requires leadership by one or more states committed to defining the issue and proposing a detailed policy approach as the basis for the regime. Sometimes that lead role is played by states that are motivated by particular vulnerability (Sweden, Finland, and Norway on acid rain; the African countries on hazardous waste trade and desertification) and sometimes by a state that has an advantageous legal or other status (Australia in the regime for Antarctica).

But as these case studies show, the United States has greater diplomatic influence on other state actors and IOs than any other state. When the United States has taken the lead, as it did on the Montreal Protocol on ozone depletion, whaling, or the African elephant, the result has been a much stronger regime than would otherwise have been established. But when it has been a veto state, as in the sulfur dioxide protocol to the acid rain convention, the hazardous waste trade convention, and the climate convention, the result is a significantly weaker regime. Only rarely, as in the case of the Antarctic negotiations, did a U.S. veto role not seriously undermine the regime, and that was because of the peculiar rules of the Antarctic Treaty, which permitted Australia and France to nullify U.S. influence.

It is evident from these case studies that no state actor plays a lead or veto role on all global environmental issues. The United States has played both roles, as have Germany and France as well as the EC as a whole. Norway was a lead state on acid rain, climate change, and ozone depletion and with the lead states on all but whaling and has had a prime minister (Gro Harlem Brundtland) who headed the commission that produced the pivotal report on sustainable development, *Our Common Future*. Yet Norway found itself in the unaccustomed role of veto state on whaling because of the importance of that industry to a key political constituency in Norwegian politics.

As these cases of environmental regimes established or strengthened during the 1985–1994 period indicate, the international community has been able to reach an impressively large number of agreements to reduce environmental threats. Many of these agreements were believed impossible to achieve only a few months before they were successfully completed. Moreover, they have been negotiated more rapidly than were previous treaties dealing with environment and natural resources, indicating a process of international learning about how to reach agreement on complex and contentious environmental issues. The Law of the Sea convention took nine years to negotiate, and the Antarctic minerals treaty took seven (without being completed), but the biodiversity convention took only nine months to negotiate, and desertification and climate conventions were completed in fifteen and sixteen months, respectively.

Global environmental regimes also have evolved from agreements that originally had limited membership (whaling, Antarctic, acid rain) to conventions that have achieved nearly universal adherence. The climate treaty had 154 signatories and the biodiversity convention 167. Finally, some of the new regimes (climate, biodiversity, hazardous waste trade, and desertification) have the potential for affecting fundamental economic development strategies, production technologies, and even domestic political processes.

FOUR

□ □ □

Global Economics, Development, and Environmental Politics

The arena of global environment has become increasingly intertwined with the politics of international economic relations and policies in recent years. Trade and environment, the financing of sustainable development, and consumption patterns were not on the international political agenda at all a decade ago. But several developments converged to change all that: the growing influence of environmental consciousness on trade policies, the emergence of environmental regimes requiring major social and economic transitions in all societies, and the convening of history's first global negotiations encompassing both environmental and economic policies—the United Nations Conference on Environment and Development (UNCED).

As linkages with economic relations and development have multiplied, the boundaries of global environmental politics have broadened. In this chapter we analyze a number of political issues and processes involving both environmental problems and economics and development: the wide-ranging negotiations in the UNCED, tensions within the General Agreement on Tariffs and Trade (GATT) over trade and the environment, and the establishment and subsequent restructuring of the Global Environment Facility for financing global environmental agreements.

These issues and processes are not just about North-South differences. Conflicts of interest and differing perspectives among industrialized countries have surfaced in the UNCED negotiations, in debates over trade rules relating to the environment, in the renegotiation of the International Tropical Timber Agreement (ITTA), and in the restructuring of the facility for financing global environmental conventions.

But North-South relations have been an important political dynamic in each of the cases covered in this chapter. In the UNCED negotiations, North and South clashed on a wide range of economic and political issues related to sustainable development. In the negotiations on trade and environment, North and South squared off over the issue of environmentally related trade restrictions against developing-country products. And in negotiations on the Global Environment Facility, North and South had to reconcile divergent models of governance of multilateral institutions.

In each of these political processes, some of the outcomes reflect the force of inertia and the difficulty of changing institutions. But the same negotiations can also be viewed as part of a longer-term process of evolution toward environmentally sound norms governing trade, finance, management of global commons, and even domestic development patterns. Like negotiations for formal environmental regime formation and strengthening, these negotiations on economic policies and institutions are being impelled by social and political forces for change that are gaining momentum, including increased scientific data on environmental degradation, growing popular consciousness of the environment, and networks of nongovernmental organizations dedicated to making societies environmentally sustainable.

NORTH-SOUTH INEQUALITIES AND THE ENVIRONMENT

Inequitable economic relations between North and South have been a crucial element of the political context of global environmental politics. The developing states' perceptions of the global economic structure as fundamentally inequitable often shape their policy responses to global environmental issues and their strategies for negotiating on those issues. Moreover, unfavorable trends in North-South economic relations since the mid-1970s have not only sharpened the inequalities between North and South but weakened the bargaining position of the South in issues involving North-South economic relations.

A surge in commodity prices and the Organization of Petroleum Exporting Countries' (OPEC) successful manipulation of oil supplies in the early 1970s encouraged the developing countries to attempt to restructure the whole global economic system at the U.N. General Assembly in 1974. The South called for a bold but largely unrealistic plan, the **New International Economic Order** (NIEO), which would include a new system of international commodity agreements, a unilateral reduction of barriers to imports from developing states in industrialized countries, enhancement of developing countries' capabilities in science and technology, increased Northern financing of technology transfer, and changes in patent laws to lower the cost of such transfers.[1]

From the late 1970s onward, however, the NIEO faded from the global political agenda as economic trends turned against the South, and the North consequently felt it could disregard such Southern demands for change. Falling commodity prices devastated the economies of those countries that were heavily dependent on commodity exports. Between 1980 and 1991, the weighted index for thirty-three primary commodities exported by developing countries, not including energy, declined by 46 percent.[2] And heavy debt burdens, taken on at a time when commodity prices were high and Northern banks were freely lending dollars from Arab oil revenues, siphoned off much of the foreign exchange of many developing countries. At the beginning of the 1990s, no less than forty severely indebted countries were spending the equivalent of 30 percent or more of their export income on debt repayments—well beyond what capital markets normally regard as the threshold of financial crisis.[3]

During the 1990s trade barriers erected by industrialized countries against imports of manufactured and processed goods from the developing countries continued to increase even as most developing countries (under pressure from international financial institutions) were lowering their own barriers to imports.[4] Industrialized-country tariffs on textiles and clothing and other products of particular importance to developing countries' exports tended to be the highest tariff rates in industrialized countries, which often increase tariff rates on goods in proportion to the degree of processing involved. New kinds of **nontariff barriers** to trade, such as antidumping and countervailing duty actions, export-restraint agreements such as the Multi-Fibre Arrangement, and direct subsidies have been used to protect industries in the industrialized countries against imports from developing countries. As a result of such trade barriers, developing countries were losing an estimated 3 percent of their collective income by the end of the 1980s.[5]

The negotiations on liberalization of world trade, known as the Uruguay Round, were started in 1985 under the auspices of the GATT and helped reduce some of those barriers, but the overall impact appears to have been slight. The GATT Uruguay Round agreement adopted in April 1994 was expected to benefit the rapidly industrializing countries of East Asia and Latin America, though not nearly as much as they had expected. And the cost to the sub-Saharan African countries, which are the weakest competitors in the world trade system, could be as much as $2.6 billion annually by the beginning of the next century. As a result of these global trade and financial pressures, real annual growth of per capita incomes was negative for Africa, the Middle East, and Latin America dur-

POPULATION CONTROL IN MEXICO

Jeff Danziger in *The Christian Science Monitor* ©1990 TCSPS.

ing the 1980s, and it continued to be negative for developing countries as a whole in 1990 and 1991.[6] Despite the rapid growth in a number of East Asian economies in the 1980s, the income gap between the industrialized world and the developing world continued to grow. Whereas the richest 20 percent of the world controlled 70 percent of global gross domestic product (GDP) in 1960, the richest 20 percent controlled 82.7 percent of global GDP by 1989.[7]

Existing patterns of North-South economic relations have contributed to the degradation and depletion of natural resources. Sudden increased demand in the North for certain commodities has increased their price and stimulated increased exploitation of the resource. When Japan began major imports of tropical timber in the 1960s and 1970s, for example, it raised tropical timber prices and impelled the Philippines and Indonesia to step up their exports of raw logs and processed timber products.[8]

But the pressure on natural resources also increases when falling commodity prices are combined with debt burdens and protectionism. Countries that are indebted and heavily dependent on commodity exports often have adjusted to falling prices by increasing the volume of commodity exports, thus depleting agricultural land, forests, and other natural resources. For example, several of the Sahelian countries increased their cotton production by 20 percent in the 1980s even as world cotton prices fell by 30 percent. The expansion of cotton production forced grain farmers off their land, encouraged heavy use of pesticides, and exacerbated the problem of soil depletion.[9]

Northern protectionism also forces developing countries to exploit their natural resources more heavily. Subsidies to agricultural exporters in the United States and other OECD countries deprive developing-country producers of markets and depress world prices for those goods, exacerbating trade imbalances and developing-country indebtedness. European beef exporters undercut African producers by massive subsidies, for example, and thus dominate African markets.[10] Often poor countries adjust to this loss by expanding acreage for export crops or livestock. Depressed food prices discourage marginal farmers in food-exporting developing countries from making the investments in soil conservation and water management necessary for sustainable agricultural development. Meanwhile, subsidized prices for exportable agricultural commodities provide powerful incentives for the agricultural sector in developed countries to use more fertilizers, pesticides, and water, polluting groundwater supplies and depleting the underground aquifers.[11]

NORTHERN AND SOUTHERN PERSPECTIVES ON THE GLOBAL ENVIRONMENT

The developing countries' views on global environmental issues have been shaped to a considerable extent by their preoccupation with economic growth, their fears of high costs for environmental protection, and their general distrust of the policies of industrialized states. Developing countries have generally regarded the negotiation of global regimes on ozone depletion, climate change, biodiversity loss, and conservation of endangered species as a Northern agenda. Their own environmental priorities have been urban air and water pollution, the erosion and salinization of agricultural land, and toxic chemical contamination; but for most developing countries, economic growth, employment, and overcoming poverty have been the dominant concerns.

Although some officials of developing countries, particularly in environmental ministries, recognized the seriousness of local and global environmental degradation for their own economic future, many of them regarded environmental regimes for ozone and climate and the proposed world forest convention as a means by which industrialized countries would maintain their control over resources and technology or even gain control over resources now located in the South. One developing-country delegate to the second meeting of the parties to the Montreal Protocol in 1990 declared that for "some countries," the protocol was a "pretext to place new obstacles in the way of efforts by developing countries to develop their economies."[12] And some officials of developing countries viewed the efforts of industrialized countries to bring them into a global climate-change convention as a ploy to constrain economic development in the South so that the developed countries could dominate the world's remaining oil resources.[13]

Developing countries, many of which were already subject to macroeconomic policy conditions on loans from multilateral banks, reacted strongly to any suggestion that industrialized countries would also impose environmental conditions on economic assistance or restrict their exports on environmental grounds. The Conference of the Nonaligned Movement (NAM) held in September 1989 expressed concern about "a growing tendency toward external impositions and increased conditionalities on the part of some developed countries in dealing with environmental issues."[14]

Despite growing disparities among the developing countries between rapidly industrializing countries and debt-ridden countries that experienced little or no growth in the 1980s, developing countries share a common view of the relationship between global environmental issues and North-South economic relations. They insist that the industrialized countries, because of their historical dominance in the production and consumption of CFCs and combustion of fossil fuels, are responsible for the thinning of the ozone layer and greenhouse warming. More generally, they identify wasteful Northern patterns of excessive consumption as a key cause of global environmental degradation. According to one study, developed countries have 28 times more cars and use 13 times more paper products per capita than developing countries (see Table 4.1). Each person in the United States uses 45 barrels of oil annually, compared with 1 barrel of oil for each Indian citizen.[15]

Based on such comparisons, developing-country officials as well as NGOs began to demand in the early 1990s that industrialized countries reduce their share of what they call "environmental space"—the use of the earth's limited natural resources and environmental services—and permit developing countries to use more of that environmental space in order to raise their living standards.

Developing countries also believe that the North should bear the financial burden of measures to reverse the ecological damage. In the negotiations for each global environmental regime, as well as in the UNCED negotiations, demands from the South for "new and additional" funding (i.e., funding over and above existing levels of international development assistance) for developing countries' implementation of the agreement have been a central issue.

Another consistent theme in developing-country views of global environmental issues is the inequality in governing structures of international organizations such as the World Bank, which allows a minority of donor

TABLE 4.1 Consumption Patterns for Selected Commodities: Distribution Among Developed and Developing Countries

Category	Products	World Total (MMT)[a]	Share (%) Dvlpd.	Share (%) Dvlpg.	Per Capita (Kg. or MSq.)[b] Dvlpd.	Per Capita (Kg. or MSq.)[b] Dvlpg.
Food	Cereals[c]	1801	48	52	717	247
	Milk[d]	533	72	28	320	39
	Meat[e]	114	64	36	61	11
Forest	Round wood[f]	2410	46	55	388	339
	Sawn wood[g]	338	78	22	213	19
	Paper, etc.[h]	224	81	19	148	11
Industrial	Fertilizers[i]	141	60	40	70	15
	Cement	1036	52	48	451	130
	Cotton & Wood fabrics[j]	30	47	53	15.6	5.8
Metals	Copper	10	86	14	7	0.4
	Iron & Steel	699	80	20	469	36
	Aluminum	22	86	14	16	1
Chemicals	Inorganic Chemicals	226	87	13	163	8
	Organic Chemicals	391	85	15	274	16
Transport Vehicles	Cars	370	92	8	0.283	0.012
	Commercial Vehicles	105	85	15	0.075	0.0006

[a] Millions of metric tons. Cotton and wood fiber total consumption figures in billion square meters and per capita consumption figures in kg. or square meters.

[b] Per capita data are calculated.

[c] Cereals data 1987.

[d] Milk data include cow milk, buffalo milk, and sheep milk (1987).

[e] Meat data include beef, veal, pork, mutton, and lamb (1987).

[f] Round wood includes fuel wood + charcoal and industrial round wood (1988).

[g] Sawn wood includes wood extracted from sawlogs and veneer logs (1988).

[h] Paperboards include newsprint, printing and writing papers and other paper plus paperboard (1988).

[i] Fertilizer consumption data include nitrogen, phosphate, and potash fertilizers.

[j] Cotton fabrics plus woolen fabrics; synthetics, which will alter these figures substantially, are excluded. USSR and China excluded due to nonavailability of data.

Source: Consumption Patterns: The Driving Force of Environmental Stress, a report prepared for the United Nations Conference on Environment and Development. (Bombay: Indira Gandhi Institute of Development Research, October 1991), p. 8.

countries to outvote the rest of the world. Developing countries have demanded that institutions making decisions on how to spend funds on the global environment should have a "democratic" structure, i.e., one in which each country is equally represented. Thus developing countries did some of their toughest bargaining in negotiations relating to the environment when they resisted the donor countries' proposed governance structure for the Global Environment Facility.

The South also has demanded that transfer of environmental technologies on concessional terms be part of the agreements on the major conventions and on UNCED's Agenda 21. In the Montreal Protocol negotiations, for instance, developing states demanded a guarantee from the industrialized countries that corporations would provide patents and technical knowledge on substitutes for CFCs to them. In 1990 India tried unsuccessfully to get language into the amended protocol that would make the obligations of developing states to phase out CFCs subject to the private transfer of technology.

A few European states and numerous Northern NGOs have supported the South's view on environmental space and its demands for resource transfers. And most industrialized countries accepted the South's argument in the UNCED negotiations that Northern consumption patterns were responsible for much global environmental degradation. The willingness of Northern countries to permit developing countries to have a relatively long grace period before having to comply with the ozone and climate conventions reflects the general acceptance that poor countries had relatively little responsibility for those problems. But the North generally emphasizes the responsibility of all countries to contribute to solving global environmental problems, which implies a need for developing countries to avoid duplicating the unsustainable historical development patterns of the industrialized world. And most wealthy countries have been extremely reluctant to give up their control over institutions that involve financial resources or their freedom to determine how much money they will commit to a given global environmental convention.

The ultimate reckoning over North-South equity and responsibility still lies in the future. Developing countries have been willing to sign and ratify global environmental regimes even though they did not secure the financial and technology arrangements they had demanded. But their willingness to take the actions needed to make climate and biodiversity conventions effective will depend in part on whether nations can work out new forms of North-South cooperation reflecting greater commitment from some of the key industrialized countries.

RAESIDE/*Times-Colonist*, Victoria, Canada. Reprinted with permission.

THE EARTH SUMMIT NEGOTIATIONS ON
SUSTAINABLE DEVELOPMENT

The United Nations Conference on Environment and Development was a monumental effort by the international community to reach consensus on principles and a long-term workplan for global sustainable development. The conference in Rio de Janeiro in June 1992, which came to be known as the Earth Summit, was the first truly global summit meeting, drawing the participation of 110 heads of state. Conceptually, its explicit focus on integrating environmental and development policies represented a major step forward from the Stockholm conference of twenty years earlier.

The major output of UNCED was a nonbinding agreement called Agenda 21 (referring to the twenty-first century), which is a global plan of action for more sustainable societies worldwide. Negotiations on Agenda 21 were the broadest and most complex international talks ever held. The 294-page comprehensive Agenda 21 encompassed every sectoral environmental issue as well as international policies affecting both environment and development, and the full range of domestic social and economic policies, all adding up to 38 chapters and 115 separate topics. The confer-

UNCED, Rio, 1992. NGO representatives join hundreds of thousands who signed the Earth Pledge leading up to the Earth Summit. Photo by Charles V. Barber, World Resources Institute.

ence also produced two nonbinding sets of principles—one on environment and development in general, the other, in lieu of a forest treaty, on the sustainable management of the world's forests. The climate and biodiversity conventions, which were negotiated independently of the UNCED process on parallel tracks, were opened for signature at the Earth Summit and were often mentioned as UNCED-related agreements.

Objectives and Strategies of North and South

UNCED was the first opportunity in more than a decade for developing countries to engage the industrialized countries in bargaining that could encompass the North-South economic issues of greatest concern to the South. The heads of some developing-country governments believed that Northern countries' worries about threats to the global environment gave the South new bargaining leverage regarding North-South economic issues.[16] Some influential experts in the South were also urging a broad cross-sectoral bargaining strategy that would ask for firm commitments from the North to debt relief, better terms of trade, market access, and increased official development assistance (ODA) in return for the South's cooperation on the biodiversity and climate conventions and other UNCED agreements.[17]

But no such comprehensive bargaining strategy emerged from the developing-country caucus in the four PrepComs. The developing countries had not forgotten that their efforts in the 1970s to play hardball politics to get the NIEO had met a decisive defeat.[18] Whereas a few developing countries were ready to take a more confrontational stance toward the North, the least developed countries, saddled with debts and heavily dependent on the North for loans and development assistance, felt far more vulnerable economically in the 1990s than they had in the 1970s. They were wary about antagonizing powerful industrialized countries in the UNCED.[19] Moreover, developing countries also wanted to advance some global environmental proposals through Agenda 21, such as bans on hazardous waste trade and ocean dumping of low-level nuclear wastes, so they recognized that they had a stake in the success of the negotiations as well.

So the G-77 countries limited their negotiating objectives to obtaining whatever additional ODA they could in conjunction with Agenda 21, defending their right to exploit their own resources and inserting political points favorable to Southern interests wherever they could in texts on sectoral issues (forests, energy, hazardous wastes), cross-sectoral issues (finance and technology transfer), and the two sets of principles. In particular, their negotiators pushed for the following four principles:[20]

☐ New and additional development assistance should be provided through a mechanism with equal representation for developing countries in decisionmaking.
☐ The North must reduce its consumption of natural resources and environmental services in order to give the South adequate "environmental space" for its development.
☐ No restrictions should be imposed on imports by industrialized countries because of environmental problems beyond the territory of the importing country.
☐ The North must transfer relevant environmental technologies to the South on preferential and concessional terms.

The G-77 identified forests as the main point of leverage because the United States in particular had made it clear that it was eager to have a convention on the world's forests. But that point of leverage was never used because exploiting it would have required the South to make concessions to Northern concerns on forests in return for Northern concessions on other issues. And for a few key timber-exporting countries, such as Malaysia and Indonesia, avoiding any restrictions on their freedom to exploit forest resources was top priority.

Among the industrialized countries, two contrasting approaches to a negotiation strategy were discernible in the UNCED process. The Bush administration's strategy for UNCED negotiations, based on the assumption that UNCED represented a potential threat to U.S. interests, was aimed at averting any initiatives that would limit U.S. freedom of economic action worldwide.[21] The United States was prepared to veto any initiatives that could be viewed as redistributing economic power at the global level, that would create new international institutions, or that would require additional budgetary resources, technology transfers, or changes in domestic U.S. policies.

The Netherlands and the Nordic countries advocated responding to at least some of the economic grievances of the South in the UNCED process. They were prepared to support the principle that industrialized countries should change their consumption patterns in order to "make space" for development in the South. They also supported at least some of the key demands of the developing countries on financial resources, including a separate fund that would have mandatory contributions from donor countries and a higher global target for worldwide developmental assistance.[22]

Only one country—the United States—had the economic and political power and the expertise to play the lead role in such a complex and wide-ranging set of North-South negotiations, had it chosen to do so. European states were active in UNCED preparations, but because of differences among its members, the EC was incapable of acting in a unified manner on most issues. Japan was constrained by a perceived need not to offend the United States.[23] Most EC countries and Japan had no clear overall strategy for negotiations and often supported specific U.S. positions, especially with regard to developing-country demands for reform of existing economic policies and institutions.

The United States could have increased the chances of far-reaching agreements on a number of sustainable development issues, such as energy, consumption patterns, finance, and trade, had it decided to play a lead role in North-South bargaining. But instead the United States played more the role of veto power on those issues. The result was that other OECD countries often were not pushed to move beyond least-common-denominator positions, and developing countries were not offered any real bargains.

The Negotiating Process

Stretching over nearly two and a half years, the negotiating process leading up to the Earth Summit included two planning meetings, four lengthy PrepComs, and one final negotiating session at the Rio conference itself, which was originally to have been essentially ceremonial in nature.

Jim Morin. *The Miami Herald*. Reprinted with permission.

Because the delegations were slow to begin negotiations on substantive issues at PrepComs I and II in 1990 and 1991, the conference secretariat, under the direction of Secretary-General Maurice Strong, was directed to prepare negotiating texts for Agenda 21 for consideration by the delegations at PrepCom III (August-September 1991). Many of the proposals prepared by the secretariat were both innovative and ambitious and reflected considerable input from NGOs. Some delegations, including the United States and the United Kingdom, did not like many of these proposals. The U.S. delegation did not trust the secretariat to be "objective," believing that UNCED secretary-general Maurice Strong had his own agenda.[24] Many of the secretariat proposals were put in square brackets, indicating objection by one or more governments, and ultimately eliminated from the text, but many of them did survive. Tensions between the secretariat and the delegations peaked before the final PrepCom, after only four issues actually reached the negotiation stage at PrepCom III. Eighty to ninety percent of the negotiations remained to be completed in the final, month-long PrepCom IV in New York City from March 3 to April 4, 1992. The task facing negotiators in New York was so daunting that the secretariat urged key delegations to negotiate only the "high points" of Agenda 21 and leave the rest to the secretariat.[25]

The delegations rejected that alternative but could agree on only about 85 percent of the text sent to the Rio conference. The first seven days of the eleven-day Earth Summit in Rio thus became, in effect, "PrepCom V." To deal with unfinished issues, PrepCom chair Tommy Koh established eight "contact groups" whose work was to be approved by the plenary meeting. When the main committee ran out of time on June 11, some points on three issues—forests, finance, and atmosphere—remained unresolved. They had to be turned over to ministers to resolve in a few hours of intense negotiation behind closed doors.[26]

New Norms for Development and the Environment in Agenda 21. Negotiations on Agenda 21 registered the state of international consensus on the full range of issues affecting the long-run sustainability of human society, including domestic social and economic policies, international economic relations, and cooperation on global commons issues. On domestic policies, the developing countries accepted surprisingly strong language relating to popular participation in sustainable development. In chapters on poverty, sustainable agriculture, desertification, and land degradation, provisions were adopted that call for decisionmaking on natural resources management to be decentralized to the community level, giving rural populations and indigenous peoples land titles or other land rights and expanding services such as credit and agricultural extension for rural communities. The chapter on major groups calls on governments to adopt national strategies for eliminating the obstacles to women's full participation in sustainable development by the year 2000.[27]

Among the more important norms agreed to in the document, despite the reluctance of both developing countries and some industrialized countries, are provisions calling for the removal or reduction of subsidies that are inconsistent with sustainable development (such as the sale of U.S. timber from public lands at prices below the full costs of production) and the improvement of price signals through environmental charges or taxes. Implementation of those norms would be a major step toward more sustainable development worldwide.[28]

Proposals by the secretariat for new initiatives on developing-country indebtedness and North-South trade were frustrated by Northern vetoes. The United States rejected a secretariat proposal for further cooperation to reduce debt owed to commercial banks by some developing countries, expansion of official bilateral debt reduction, and relief of debt owed to multilateral financial institutions.[29] Similarly, language in the negotiating text that hinted at the desirability of new commodity price arrangements was deleted at the insistence of the United States and other OECD countries.[30]

A number of proposals to create a new global environmental regime or strengthen an existing one were the subject of negotiations. One such proposal was for a new legally binding ban on all transboundary movement of hazardous wastes that would supersede the Basel Convention, which had not yet been ratified by enough countries to go into force. The G-77 countries were united behind the proposal, and the EC was willing to support some amendment of the Basel Convention, but the United States insisted on support for the Basel Convention without further amendment. The final compromise leaned toward the U.S. position, calling for ratification of both the Basel and Bamako Conventions.[31]

Developing countries and their allies prevailed, however, on the issues of a new regime for dumping of low-level radioactive wastes and on strengthening the voluntary norms for regulating the global pesticide trade. Most developing countries, joined by Iceland and some of the Nordics, called for new international controls on radioactive waste dumping. The United States, the United Kingdom, France, Finland, and Argentina argued that the issue should be handled by the International Atomic Energy Agency (IAEA).[32] But the United States, the EC, and Japan, which initially rejected a compromise proposal that would have encouraged the London Dumping Convention to expedite its studies of the issue of replacing the voluntary moratorium on ocean dumping of nuclear wastes with a ban, finally gave in and accepted that language.[33]

On the regulation of trade in pesticides, the G-77 wanted the voluntary "prior informed consent" procedure (i.e., that exporting countries inform governments of importing countries about dangerous pesticides they intend to export to those countries and obtain their explicit consent before the shipment) into a legally binding international agreement. The United States initially opposed that proposal on the dubious ground that it would require a change in U.S. laws, but after prolonged negotiations with the EPA, the U.S. delegation went along with it.[34]

The issues of depletion of the world's fish stocks and land-based sources of marine pollution were too complex and contentious to permit substantive consensus on new norms in UNCED. Nevertheless, delegations were able to agree to future international negotiations under U.N. auspices aimed at strengthening existing norms, including the possibility of legally binding rules.

After persistent lobbying by African delegations, UNCED agreed to the convening of an international conference on a binding desertification agreement by 1994. Most OECD countries were very skeptical about the idea of negotiating a convention on the issue of desertification, and the issue would not have been put on the global political agenda in the absence of the extraordinary political circumstances of the Earth Summit. And the small island developing states (SIDs), brought together in the early 1990s by the common threat of sea-level rise from global warming, won recognition of their unique environmental and development problems. Agenda 21 called for a global conference on the sustainable development of small island developing states, which was held in 1993 and 1994 and produced a detailed plan of action and commitments of financial and technical assistance from several donor countries and international organizations.[35]

Consumption Patterns and Population. At UNCED the issue of inequitable consumption patterns as a cause of global environmental degradation was elevated to a new status in international politics at the insistence of the developing countries. The issue was woven through several chapters of Agenda 21 as well as the principles document, making it a major theme of the entire conference.

Industrialized countries were asked to accept responsibility to change their "unsustainable lifestyles." The United States initially tried to change the secretariat's draft text on consumption so that poverty and industrialized-country consumption were given equal weight as causes of environmental stress, but the G-77 balked. When the issue was taken up again in Rio, the United States ultimately conceded, accepting essentially the same text for those paragraphs that it had rejected earlier. Moreover, industrialized countries agreed to "take the lead in achieving sustainable consumption patterns" and to a review of progress in this regard as a "high priority."[36]

Energy-consumption issues produced varied patterns of alignment and cleavage. The United States insisted on the elimination of a secretariat proposal for nationally determined targets for reducing per capita energy consumption in industrialized countries, despite the fact that the EC had been willing to agree to such language.[37] When proposals for reducing fossil fuel use did not distinguish between North and South, however, key developing countries joined the veto coalition. The G-77, following the lead of India, Pakistan, and Nigeria, all of which subsidize fossil fuel use, joined the United States and oil-producing countries in opposing proposals for energy taxes that would encourage improved efficiency in energy consumption, for measures to prevent discrimination against renewable energy sources in domestic energy markets, and for stronger energy-efficiency standards for specific technologies.[38]

Population was not included in the original scope of the conference as established by the U.N. General Assembly. It was added to the agenda only after the industrialized countries agreed with the proposal of the developing countries that it be paired with consumption in the same chapter. But neither the North nor the South tried to strike a bargain that would establish targets for limiting both population and consumption.

*"And may we continue to be worthy of consuming a
disproportionate share of this planet's resources."*

Drawing by Lorenz; © 1992 The New Yorker Magazine, Inc.

Negotiations on key paragraphs on population at PrepCom IV revolved around the use of the term "family planning," which the Vatican
and some pronatalist countries were determined to keep out of the text.[39]
All interested parties, including population and women's organizations,
finally agreed to substitute "responsible planning of family size" for
"family planning" and called for governments to give men and women
the "same right to decide freely and responsibly on the number and spac-
ing of their children." However, a series of qualifiers such as "as appropriate" were added to satisfy the pronatalist interests.[40]

Financial Resources. The negotiations on financial resources for implementation of Agenda 21 and global environmental agreements began
with the G-77 presenting an ambitious set of negotiating objectives at
PrepCom IV (March-April 1992):

☐ a special Green Fund for Agenda 21 with "new and additional"
   funding and an equal voice for all parties in governance;

☐ a separate fund for each global environmental convention instead of all funds being disbursed through the Global Environment Facility (GEF);

☐ a real increase in funding for the World Bank's lending window for the poorest countries;

☐ an increase in current levels of ODA to 0.7 percent of donor countries' GNP by 1995 and to 1 percent of their GNP by the end of the century.

But donor countries insisted that the GEF must be the only funding mechanism on global environmental issues and offered no new ODA commitments.[41] The G-77 then compromised on or abandoned all of its demands except its opposition to the GEF as the only mechanism for global environmental funding. And when the EC was inflexible on that issue, the G-77 decided to terminate the financial negotiations until the Rio conference, hoping to enhance its bargaining leverage on the issue of ODA targets and timetables.[42]

In Rio, the G-77 accepted the GEF and focused instead on a commitment by all OECD countries, including the United States, to achieving the target of 0.7 percent of GNP going to ODA by the year 2000. It also asked for a "substantial initial financial commitment" to Agenda 21 by the OECD countries and a pledging conference at the next UNGA session. Those demands left plenty of room for a last-minute compromise on increased financial commitments. But in the end all the G-77 got was a reaffirmation that those countries who supported the ODA target would implement it. The United States maintained its decades-long rejection of any target for future ODA levels in relation to GNP; the EC was divided on the issue.[43]

The failure of the G-77 to win any significant concession on financial resources reflected both the veto power of the OECD countries on the issue and the unequal bargaining power of the North and South at the end of the negotiations. Some OECD delegations, including the United States, had been worried at PrepCom IV that failure to come up with an acceptable financial chapter to Agenda 21 could cause the UNCED to "crash"—i.e., collapse without agreements.[44] But by the opening of the Earth Summit itself, it was clear that the G-77 did not intend to walk out of the conference over financial resources, and the United States and other donor countries relaxed. When asked in Rio whether the G-77 would accept a text that lacked even a provision for a pledging conference, a U.S. official responded, "They won't have any choice."[45]

Forest Principles. The United States, supported by most of the OECD countries, proposed at PrepCom II the negotiation of a global forest convention outside the UNCED framework. At the July 1990 summit of the G-7 countries in Houston, the United States had proposed a framework

"And see this ring right here, Jimmy? . . . That's another time when the old fellow miraculously survived some big forest fire."

The Far Side. © 1989 FarWorks, Inc. Dist. by Universal Press Syndicate. Reprinted with permission. All rights reserved.

convention—one that would have required no binding commitments to forest conservation. Mistakenly thinking such an agreement would be easy to achieve, the Bush administration viewed such a forest convention as its main initiative at the UNCED. But at PrepCom II the G-77 rejected the negotiation of a binding agreement before Rio and agreed only to negotiation of a nonbinding "Authoritative Statement of Principles on the World's Forests."[46] At PrepCom III only the United States continued to call for a forest convention to be signed in Rio.[47]

Negotiations on the forest principles quickly became polarized between the "global responsibility" approach of the United States and Canada and the "sovereign discretion" approach of Malaysia and India.[48] The United States and Canada tried to link the principle of the sovereignty of countries over their own forest resources with the principles of national responsibility and global concern for forests. Canada's proposals would have established that forests are of interest to the international community, that international standards should be implemented in forest management, and that targets and time frames should be included in national forestry plans.

But Malaysia and India saw these formulations as an effort to establish the legal principle that forests are "global commons" or part of the "common heritage of mankind," thus giving industrialized countries some right to interfere in the management of the tropical forest countries' resources.[49] Malaysia, as the world's largest exporter of tropical logs, had a particularly intense interest in the issue. It was determined to become a "fully developed country" by the year 2020 using export earnings from timber and other export crops grown on land converted from forests.[50]

Malaysia and India forced Canada to weaken its key principles on international interest and guidelines. The G-77 also objected to a reference encouraging trade in "sustainably managed" forest products and to U.S. efforts to get some language keeping open the possibility of a forest convention. But the United States, which had already objected to targets and timetables in the climate negotiations, broke ranks with Canada and opposed targets and timetables in national forest plans.[51]

The final version of the forest principles document only hints at the fact that forests are a global environmental issue and drops both the idea of international guidelines for forest management and any reference to trade in "sustainably managed" forest products. The agreement was widely regarded by OECD countries as worse than no declaration at all because it appeared to legitimize unsustainable forest management policies.[52]

The Rio Declaration. The negotiations on the text of the Rio Declaration of Principles also pitted the North's vision of universal responsibility for the global environment against the South's insistence on sovereignty and a more equitable allocation of rights to use "environmental space." At PrepCom IV the G-77 submitted a draft of the document, which included the following among its principles:[53]

☐ common but differentiated responsibility for the global environment,
☐ apportionment of equal shares of environmental space,
☐ no use of environmental considerations to justify trade restrictions unless based on multilateral agreement,
☐ the right of all nations to development, and

□ the sovereign right of all states to utilize their own natural resources pursuant to their own environmental policies and their development and economic priorities.

Although the G-77 agreed to drop the principle on environmental space and some others that were most objectionable to the OECD countries, stalemate persisted through PrepCom IV over the remaining principles.[54] After nearly a month of negotiations, PrepCom chair Tommy Koh of Singapore had to draft his own text, which he submitted to the plenary in the early morning of April 4 as "The Rio Declaration."

Koh's draft bowed to G-77 concerns on the "right of development," the sovereign right to exploit resources, the eradication of poverty, and "common but differentiated responsibility." But it also deleted one principle that identified industrialized countries' consumption patterns as the "main cause" of environmental degradation and another that called for new and additional resources and technology transfer on preferential and concessional terms.[55]

Even so, the United States indicated at the final plenary of PrepCom IV that it could not accept several of the principles in Koh's draft, including the principle of "common but differentiated responsibilities."[56] Other delegations also indicated that they were not happy with certain principles. Koh nevertheless prevailed on the PrepCom to agree to send his text to the Rio conference without any brackets by promising that there would be further negotiations on the text in Rio.[57] Koh, who had no intention of reopening the declaration for renegotiation in Rio, was exercising his ability as chair to discourage dissent on a negotiating text.

Before the Rio conference, the United States came under intense pressure not to reopen the text on the ground that it represented such a delicate balance that the entire endeavor would be imperiled.[58] In Rio, the U.S. delegation, isolated on the issue, tried unsuccessfully to get changes in several places in Agenda 21 in return for acceptance of Koh's Rio Declaration text.[59] The United States then submitted four reservations on the Earth Charter along with six others on Agenda 21 and the forest principles, joining Saudi Arabia, the only other country insisting on such "interpretative statements" at the conference.

The Rio Declaration reflects to a much greater degree than the Stockholm Declaration twenty years earlier the political agenda of the developing countries. The strong role played by Chairman Koh helped to overcome some of the objections to G-77 principles by the United States and other OECD countries and thus tilted the balance more toward the developing-country perspective than would otherwise have been the case.

UNCED as Snapshot and Dynamic Process. Did UNCED demonstrate that both North and South will block progress toward global sustainable development or that the global system is continuing to evolve toward norms of sustainable global human development? The answer depends on the optic used to view the outcomes.[60] The negotiations did illustrate the tendency of multilateral negotiations to give the most obdurate states veto power over promising initiatives and more moderate positions. The United States and other industrialized countries failed to commit significant new resources to support sustainable development and blocked secretariat proposals for change in industrialized countries' consumption patterns and in North-South economic relations. Developing countries in turn blocked the establishment of international norms for forest management and joined the United States in preventing agreement on accelerating the transition to sustainable energy systems.

A longer-term perspective on the UNCED negotiations, however, would emphasize that they did establish new norms in a number of areas, such as popular participation in resource management, sustainable consumption patterns in industrialized countries, prices that reflect environmental costs, and reduction of subsidies for resource consumption that are inconsistent with sustainable development. Even though these norms are not legally binding and may not be implemented in most countries in the short run, their formal adoption by consensus at a global summit meeting makes it more likely that they will be put into practice in the future.

Agenda 21 also set in motion new processes both within and among nations toward progress on sustainability. It called for new international negotiations on formal regimes on desertification, overfishing, the international pesticide trade, and land-based sources of marine pollution and on a plan of action on small island states. Those negotiations have either been completed or are still in process. Although Agenda 21 did not contain strong language on population, an effective women's caucus was forged in the process that became a major influence on the 1994 Cairo conference on population, which was widely regarded as a triumph for the population agenda.

Finally, Agenda 21 was the impetus in many countries, including, for example, the Netherlands, Australia, Belgium, Canada, India, Thailand, and the United States, for creation of new national commissions—often involving broad representation of various social sectors—to discuss and recommend actions to achieve sustainable development.

If one assumes an international system in which patterns of relations are static or cyclical in character, therefore, UNCED negotiations provide ample evidence for the hypothesis that the world faces deadlock on efforts to achieve sustainable development. But if the system is assumed to be still in evolution, the UNCED experience also marks an important new stage in the longer-term development of the national and international norms and institutions needed to meet the challenge of environmentally sustainable development.

TRADE AND THE ENVIRONMENT

The relationship between trade and the environment emerged in international politics only in the 1990s.[61] It became a high-profile international political issue in 1992 during the height of negotiations on the North American Free Trade Agreement (NAFTA), which was seen as a symbol for economic integration between countries at different stages of economic development. The spark was the U.S. ban on tuna from Mexico and Venezuela on the ground that their fleets did not meet U.S. standards for minimizing dolphin kills in tuna fishing. The U.S. trade ban was the subject of a controversial decision by a GATT dispute-resolution panel that symbolized the clash between free trade and the GATT—now renamed the World Trade Organization (WTO)—on one hand, and environmental objectives, on the other.

Conflicts between environmental trade restrictions and the desire for free access to markets have divided some OECD countries from some developing countries but have also pitted some industrialized countries against others. Moreover, they have pitted environmental ministries against trade ministries within the same government. In virtually every country the trade and finance ministries are more powerful than the more recently established environmental ministries, but the environmental ministries in the OECD countries are generally much stronger than their counterparts in the developing countries.

The actual number of trade controversies involving restrictions over environmental issues have been relatively few, and only three cases had been actually brought before GATT dispute panels by 1995—all of them stemming from complaints against U.S. trade measures. But because the international system is at the beginning of a process of defining norms regarding trade and the environment, each controversy has prompted strong positions and stirred emotional responses on both sides.

Trade-Environment Links

The links between trade and the environment have generated at least four distinct types of international political issues:[62]

□ Multilateral trade rules have tremendous impacts on the environment by affecting the volume of production activity and the incentives trade provides for either sustainable or unsustainable production and use.

☐ Multilateral trade rules may be used to override domestic environmental standards in order to ensure market access for particular products.
☐ Unilateral trade restrictions can be used as means to protect the environment beyond the jurisdiction of the country applying those restrictions; the GATT can be used to challenge some of those restrictions.
☐ Lower environmental standards or nonenforcement of standards in some countries causes some industries in higher-standard countries to call for unilateral trade measures to increase tariffs on lower-cost imports and thus level the playing field.

The second and third issues have generated most of the international controversy to date. Many environmental laws authorize restrictions on trade for a variety of policy objectives related to the environment, both domestic and international. Such laws have been called "environmental trade measures" (ETMs) and include import prohibitions, product standards, standards governing production of natural resource exports, and mandatory ecological labeling schemes.[63] But exporters that are disadvantaged by such environmental measures sometimes charge that they are intended to protect domestic producers from foreign competition, and in a few cases, the governments of the exporting countries have brought such complaints to GATT's dispute-resolution panels.

The United States has taken the lead in defending the right to use ETMs for environmental objectives, and it is no accident that it has been the target of all three cases brought before GATT/WTO dispute panels. As the largest single market in world trade, the United States has a unique capability to exert pressure on the environmental and trade policies of other countries, and it has been pressured by environmental NGOs to do so, at least in marine conservation issues. The United States used trade restrictions in conjunction with its leadership role to end commercial whaling and to protect dolphins from excessive killing by tuna fishermen and marine mammals generally from the use of destructive drift nets. The U.S. threat to ban Korean fish products from the U.S. market and to prohibit Korean fishing operations in U.S. waters persuaded South Korea to give up whaling as well as drift-net operations in the Pacific Ocean.[64] And the United States banned wildlife-related exports from Taiwan in 1994 after finding that that country had violated CITES by failing to control trade in rhino horn and tiger bone.

Japan and the members of the European Union have shown little interest thus far in using trade for international environmental purposes. Unlike the United States, the EU has not had pressure from NGOs to use trade aggressively for external environmental purposes, and it lacks the legal authority to do so.[65] Only in the Netherlands and Austria have public pressures resulted in ETMs for international environmental goals. The European Court has handled a number of disputes over ETMs for domestic environmental purposes, however, and in most cases has reaffirmed the legitimacy of individual countries' ETMs.

Developing countries are concerned about the use of ETMs by industrialized countries, even for domestic environmental purposes, because they view them as potential barriers to their exports. Rapidly industrializing countries fear that the United States in particular will use ETMs to protect its domestic industries, just as it used antidumping legislation for that objective in the past. In negotiations on the UNCED Rio Declaration and in the Uruguay Round, developing countries have clashed with the United States over ETMs related to extrajurisdictional issues. In the UNCED, India and South Korea proposed that unilateral actions to deal with environmental problems outside the jurisdiction of the importing country "should be avoided," a proposal that became Principle 12 in the draft Rio Declaration. The U.S. delegation objected but bowed to the consensus on the declaration in Rio, although it submitted an interpretative statement on Principle 12 that "in certain situations," such ETMs might be "effective and appropriate means" of addressing environmental concerns beyond the jurisdiction of the importing country and specifically referred to forest management as an example.[66]

India again tried to get a ban on unilateral ETMs into the statement on the work program on trade and environment of the new WTO, but the compromise adopted referred back to Principle 12 of the Rio Declaration. U.S. officials then argued that the reference to Principle 12 incorporates the U.S. interpretive statement on the principle as well.[67]

NGOs have played the key role in issue definition and agenda setting on trade and environment. Environmental NGOs have pressed governments to make environmental protection an objective of trade policies and trade agreements. U.S. environmental NGOs demanded provisions in the North American Free Trade Agreement that would address the environmental impacts of that agreement, including environmental assessments and commitments to environmental cleanup. They failed to get any environmental provisions in the agreement itself but did get an environmental "side agreement" that created the first U.S.-Canadian-Mexican environmental commission.

It was also because of NGO pressures that the issues of protecting domestic standards against challenge under free-trade rules and using trade measures for environmental issues that are beyond domestic jurisdiction have been in the political spotlight. The Bush administration was forced by NGO lawsuits to implement the trade ban on Mexican and Venezuelan tuna to protect dolphins.

Environmental NGOs also have argued that basic trade rules and institutions have been systematically biased against the environment. The GATT was created in the 1940s when the environment was not an issue domestically or internationally. Trade rules and mechanisms that are used to handle disputes between trading partners have long been geared primarily to removing barriers to free trade. Moreover, the deliberations of GATT dispute panels are carried out in secret with no opportunity for nongovernmental testimony or briefs.

NGOs demanded changes in GATT rules to guarantee a country's right to set environmental domestic standards as high as it wished, to allow NGO participation and greater openness in the GATT's deliberations, and to reform the dispute-resolution process to ensure that environmental experts are included in cases involving the environment. NGO efforts to get environmental provisions in the Uruguay Round agreement came late in the process and produced only a last-minute commitment in 1994 to set up the Committee on Trade and Environment. Many NGOs opposed the GATT Uruguay Round agreement in 1994, based on the absence of any environmental provisions. In 1994 the fear that the WTO, operating in secret, could threaten U.S. laws became a major theme of domestic political opposition to the Uruguay Round agreement in the United States.

Trade officials of most countries as well as the GATT secretariat have great faith that increased trade liberalization will lead to economic growth, which will in turn lead to greater investment in environmental protection. They argue that trade-restricting measures usually only stunt economic growth and are generally ineffective in accomplishing environmental objectives. They also fear that domestic economic interests will use the environment as a cover for protectionist aims.

Free-trade advocates have been particularly vociferous in opposing ETMs aimed at influencing environmental issues beyond the boundaries of the importing country. The secretariat of the GATT published a paper in 1992 denying that the GATT Articles interfere with a country's right to protect its own environment but asserting that they did not permit a country to influence other countries' policies by threatening their market access.[68]

Disputes over Environmental Trade Measures

The GATT Articles, the document that codifies the basic principles of the world trade system, determine how trade measures can be used to protect the environment. Those rules allow countries to discriminate against an imported good only on the basis of the product's characteristics, not on the basis of the process by which it was produced. Article XX allows exceptions to this principle if "necessary to protect human, animal or plant life or health," but until recently those exceptions were not seen as applying to trade-restricting measures to protect exhaustible resources beyond the jurisdiction of the importing country.

GATT dispute-resolution panels have the authority to determine whether a particular trade measure is compatible with the GATT Articles based on a complaint by a state alleging that its market access has been unfairly restricted by the measure. Those panels consist of trade specialists from three or five contracting parties with no stake in the issue who have been agreed to by both parties to the dispute. Dispute-panel rulings are normally submitted to the WTO Council (which includes all parties to the agreement) for approval. Under the old GATT dispute-resolution rules, a ruling could be vetoed by a single member of the GATT Council. However, the Uruguay Round agreement adopted in 1994, which created the WTO, provides for automatic acceptance of a dispute-panel ruling by the WTO Council within sixty days unless there is a consensus within the council to reject it. If a country fails to bring its law into conformity with the decision, its trade partners could take retaliatory trade measures against it, although it is doubtful that smaller countries will risk taking such measures against the United States.

The GATT/WTO dispute-resolution panels have been a focal point of political contention over the legitimacy of specific ETMs. Of the three dispute-panel decisions on ETMs that have been handed down as of the beginning of 1995, two represented defeats for a major U.S. international environmental policy; the third represented at least a partial victory for a key domestic U.S. environmental regulation.

The first such dispute-panel report, the 1991 panel decision on the U.S.-Mexican tuna-dolphin dispute, was a major factor in shaping the politics of trade and environment issues in subsequent years. As a result of it, developing countries became more determined to create international rules against what they regarded as unfair trade pressures. Meanwhile the GATT panel decision prompted many environmental NGOs in the United States to press even harder for changes in the GATT, including provision for ETMs covering issues beyond the jurisdiction of the importing country.[69]

Mexico had filed a complaint with the GATT charging that the U.S. embargo against Mexican yellowfin tuna—imposed under an amendment to the 1972 Marine Mammal Protection Act (MMPA) because of the Mexican fleet's killing dolphins at twice the rate of the U.S. fleet in catching tuna—was a protectionist measure on behalf of the U.S. tuna industry. Mexico and Venezuela asked why they should forgo export earnings and a low-cost source of protein for their own people to reduce the incidental impact on a marine mammal that was not an endangered species.[70]

The GATT panel found that the U.S. ban was a violation of the GATT because it was concerned only with the process of tuna fishing rather than with the product. It also ruled that GATT Article XX, which allows trade restrictions for human health or the conservation of animal or plant life, cannot justify an exception to that rule because the article does not apply beyond U.S. jurisdiction. The GATT panel's ruling on the tuna-dolphins issue reflects the tendency of most trade specialists to view any restrictions on trade for environmental purposes as setting a dangerous precedent that could destroy the entire world trade system. It may also have been influenced by the fact that eight governments or agencies spoke against the U.S. tuna ban before the panel and that not a single party spoke for it.[71]

Because of Mexico's strong interest in completing the negotiations on NAFTA, the United States was able to work out an agreement with Mexico that prevented the GATT panel decision from being presented to the GATT Council. So the European Union brought a second complaint on the U.S. tuna ban to a GATT dispute panel in 1994. The EU charged that its exports of tuna were adversely affected by the MMPA's "secondary embargo" against imports of tuna from intermediary nations that fail to certify that they do not buy tuna from nations embargoed under the law.

The GATT panel found the U.S. ban incompatible with the GATT Articles, but it accepted two key contentions of environmental critics of the GATT. It rejected the EU's arguments that dolphins are not an exhaustible natural resource and that Article XX applies only to the protection of resources located within the territory of the country applying the trade measure in question. But it held that such measures could be used only to conserve those resources directly and not to change the policy of another state—a distinction that is difficult, if not impossible, for policymakers to apply in practice—and thus found the U.S. MMPA incompatible with the GATT Articles.[72] When the GATT Council met following the panel decision, the EU, Japan, and Southeast Asian and Latin American countries demanded that the United States implement the ruling, but the council made no final decision. Meanwhile, Mexican and Venezuelan tuna fleets have dramatically reduced dolphin mortality in their operations and continue to petition the United States to end its ban on their tuna.[73]

The third GATT panel case over an ETM, also brought by the European Union in 1994, was over two domestic U.S. environmental regulations— the 1978 "gas guzzler" tax and the CAFE (Corporate Average Fuel Economy) standards.[74] The "gas guzzler" tax levied taxes on auto models whose fuel efficiency falls below 22.5 miles per gallon, with the size of the tax depending on how far the model's rate was from the minimum. The EU argued that treatment of its cars under the measure was discriminatory, since the tax fell disproportionately on cars of European origin, and that it was not effective in conserving fuel because only a small proportion of cars in the U.S. market were subject to the tax. But the GATT panel found that the gas-guzzler tax did not unfairly protect U.S. auto manufacturers and that although the measure may not be as effective in fuel conservation as a fuel tax, it has had the desired effect.

On the related issue of U.S. CAFE standards, the GATT panel ruled slightly differently. The CAFE legislation, passed in 1975, was aimed at doubling the average fuel efficiency of the automobiles sold in the U.S. market within ten years. It requires that automakers' domestic fleets average at least 27.5 miles per gallon of gasoline and that the total fleet of foreign-made automobiles sold in the U.S. market must meet the same average. Failure to meet the fleet average results in a fine of $5 for every tenth of a mile per gallon below that average multiplied by the number of automobiles in the manufacturer's fleet. U.S. manufacturers can average their large fuel-consuming vehicles with smaller, more fuel-efficient models; European manufacturers, who sell almost entirely larger luxury automobiles in the U.S. market, cannot. The EU argued that the law worked to the disadvantage of limited-line car producers concentrating on the top of the car market and that individual foreign cars are treated differently from domestic cars. The United States insisted that the CAFE legislation is based on objective criteria and was not aimed at affording protection to domestic production.

The panel found that CAFE was intended to promote fuel efficiency. But the requirement that foreign fleets must be accounted for separately, based on ownership and control relationships rather than characteristics of the products themselves, was found to give foreign cars less favorable conditions of competition than domestically produced cars. The panel also found that the requirement was not aimed at conserving fuel. It concluded that the separate foreign fleet accounting could not be justified under the exceptions in Article XX(g) and recommended that the United States be requested to amend the CAFE regulation to eliminate that requirement.[75]

Other ETMs announced by Austria and the Netherlands affecting tropical timber products led to controversies with exporting countries but were dropped before they reached a GATT dispute panel. In 1990, the Austrian parliament passed a law establishing a mandatory labeling scheme for all tropical timber, a voluntary program of labeling sustainably managed tropical timber, and a new 70-percent customs duty on all tropical timber imports, with the import tariffs to be used to fund tropical rainforest protection projects in the exporting countries (along with new and additional Austrian funding).

But Malaysia and Indonesia attacked the Austrian law at the GATT Council meeting in November 1992. They argued that it constituted a unilateral action dealing with environmental challenges outside Austrian jurisdiction, that it was inherently discriminatory because it applied only to tropical timber rather than to all kinds of timber, including temperate and boreal timber, and that the real motive behind it was to protect the Austrian timber export industry, which accounts for 8 percent of Austrian export earnings. In support of the Malaysian-Indonesian position, all ASEAN states agreed to boycott Austrian products. Austria, fearing both an unfavorable GATT dispute-panel decision and a boycott that Austrian companies claimed could cost them more than half a billion dollars, dropped both the import tariff and the mandatory labeling scheme. Austria later submitted a paper to a GATT working party criticizing unilateral trade restrictions aimed at changing the environmental policies of another country.[76]

In 1993, the Dutch government adopted a unilateral import ban on timber that was not sustainably produced, to go into effect in 1995. The Dutch initiative was adopted despite the reported conclusion of the Ministry of Economic Affairs that the proposed ban would violate Article XI of GATT, which essentially bans quantitative limits on imports. The Netherlands apparently hoped that a new multilateral agreement on tropical timber that was under negotiation in 1993–1994 would provide a way around this problem by establishing binding international commitments on the tropical forest countries for sustainable management of their forests. But after the negotiations produced no such legal commitments, the Netherlands concluded that it could not institute the ban in the immediate future.[77] It is worth noting that there might have been a different outcome to either the Austrian or Dutch efforts had they been undertaken by a larger trading state like Germany or had the backing of the European Union.

Environmental Standards and Competitiveness

As industries have become more sensitive to nontariff factors in the comparative costs of goods in world trade and environmentalists have discovered the concept of unpaid environmental costs, the issue of trade-restricting measures to eliminate alleged competitive disadvantage conferred by lower environmental standards has emerged. Exports of goods that are produced under low environmental standards have been likened both to a subsidy and to "dumping," i.e., the export of products at prices below the cost of production. The practice has been called ecological dumping, or "ecodumping,"[78] and is related to the broader concept of "social dumping"—the idea that low standards for environmental protection, worker health and safety, or even artificially depressed wages are unfair trading practices. Some environmentalists and U.S. legislators have proposed leveling the playing field for international trade in a particular product by imposing increased tariffs in relation to the unpaid environmental costs of production, although no government has yet adopted or advocated such a measure. The option of "green countervailing duties" would be inconsistent with current GATT rules, which allow trade measures against explicit subsidies but not against implicit subsidies. Developing countries charge that such duties would be nontariff barriers—barriers such as quotas that discourage imports—and would violate their right to determine domestic environmental standards appropriate to their level of development.[79] Moreover, empirical evidence does not support the proposal's underlying assumption that higher environmental standards have created competitive disadvantages for most industrial sectors.[80]

But environmental groups and officials in a number of OECD countries have called for changes in GATT rules that would allow such discrimination. Several variants of "green countervailing duties" have been proposed in the U.S. Congress since 1990. These proposals have been motivated primarily by the interests of import-sensitive industries. The U.S. trade representative also indicated interest in 1994 in an agreement aimed at leveling the playing field with regard to environmental costs.[81] In 1994, forty environmental organizations, mostly from the North, urged that the WTO include on the agenda of a new trade and environment committee the practice of ecodumping and the possibility of tariff discrimination on the basis of production methods.[82]

In several European countries, notably Belgium and France, the concept of "social dumping" has long been widely accepted as a cause of production shifting to countries with low social standards and has now simply been extended to environmental standards. The European Parliament, as well as France and Belgium, has called on the GATT to address ecological dumping. The "Green Group" in the European Parliament has accused the pulp and paper industry of the Canadian province of British Columbia of gaining unfair trade advantage over the EC paper industry by overlogging its old-growth forests.[83]

But the developing countries, fearing that the issue of social dumping will be used to disguise protectionist measures, have made it clear they will resist putting it on the agenda of the WTO. The fate of a U.S. proposal (supported by France, Belgium, Spain, and Luxembourg) to include labor standards as an issue to be included on the agenda of the new preparatory committee for the transition from the GATT to the WTO shows how difficult it will be to get GATT to deal with the ecodumping issue. Despite the U.S. disclaiming any social-dumping approach to the linkage between labor standards and the environment, the developing countries refused to consider any reference to labor rights in the declaration. They feared that some OECD countries would push for rules that would permit them to accuse poor countries of social dumping and to curb their exports.[84]

Trade and Forest Management: The Politics of the International Tropical Timber Organization

The politics of the International Tropical Timber Agreement demonstrates that an organization devoted primarily to expanding trade is unlikely to make serious commitments to sustainable development. When it was first signed in 1984, the ITTA, as the only agreement governing international trade in tropical timber, seemed to many environmentalists to be the best available instrument for improving the way commercial logging is carried out. But the original agreement failed to ameliorate the rate of destruction of forests in timber-exporting countries such as Malaysia and Indonesia. And the new ITTA, completed in 1994, actually represents a retrogression from responsibility for sustainable forest management.

The ITTA's failure to curb the mining of forests for export is related to the structure of the International Tropical Timber Organization (ITTO) and the motivation of its members. The ITTO, which includes twenty-two producing states and twenty-six consuming states accounting for 95 percent of the international trade in tropical timber, is dominated by timber-trading interests on both sides of the producer-consumer divide. The organization has a unique voting scheme that allocates votes among producer states equally on the basis of their export volume and their remaining forests. This system ostensibly aimed at providing a modest incentive for forest conservation, but it has not worked that way.

Japan is the most powerful consuming country in the organization, representing about 40 percent of the 1,000 consuming-country votes in the ITTO Council and financing most of the organization's administrative costs. Japan's main interest has been to maintain its access to tropical timber at relatively low cost. Most European states are interested in maintaining a flow of tropical hardwood to their furniture industries. And the United States, which is both the world's largest importer of finished hardwood products and the world's largest exporter of softwood products, has generally eschewed a leadership role within the organization. The main interest of producer countries has been to obtain funding for more modern logging equipment and to increase their share of processing of tropical timber in order to increase their export earnings.

Although NGOs lobbied for several years to get the ITTO to adopt codes of conduct and an action plan for shifting to sustainably managed forests by phasing out conventional logging and substituting less destructive logging methods, the ITTA has had little effect on logging practices. Nonbinding guidelines for sustainable management of timber to be applied by the year 2000 were adopted in 1990, but they did not include specific standards for sustainable management or provisions for regular reporting or review of performance.[85]

When the ITTA was renegotiated from 1992 to 1994, moreover, both producer and consumer states conspired, in effect, to ensure that no one would be held accountable even for these broad guidelines in the new agreement.[86] Producer countries, led by Brazil and Malaysia, agreed to include the year 2000 target in the new agreement only if it applied to all types of forests and if "new and additional resources" were provided to producer countries for that purpose.[87] Although they raised legitimate international equity issues, it is clear that producer countries were using the "all timbers" demand to further weaken the objective of sustainable forest management by the year 2000 or keep it out of the text entirely. They knew that some EC countries were not prepared to accept the broadening of the scope of the agreement to temperate and boreal timber, or to commit themselves to new and additional funds.

The resulting agreement, reached in January 1994, let both producer and consumer countries off the hook regarding any formal commitment to sustainable management.[88] "Objective 2000" is referred to only in the preamble of the agreement, and consumer countries issued a separate statement with respect to their own forests that committed them only to continuing the forestry management techniques they are already practicing. The agreement's objectives hint at a broadening of scope to include nontropical timbers but allow the consumer countries to insist that the scope of the agreement is still tropical timber.[89] Moreover, the agreement rules out in advance any unilateral trade sanctions against countries failing to meet the avowed 2000 objective of sustainable management.

It is unlikely that the ITTA, the one trade agreement with an environmental mandate, can evolve into an instrument for sustainable management of forests. Unlike the whaling convention, which allowed antiwhaling states to join the treaty organization and ultimately overwhelm pro-whaling states with their accumulated votes, the structure of the agreement ensures that major tropical timber producers and importers will continue to dominate it. The impetus for international agreement on sustainable forest management will have to come from elsewhere. Other possibilities for advancing that objective are examined in Chapter 5.

The Future of Trade and Environment Issues

The WTO Committee on Trade and Environment (CTE) will be the main political forum for dealing with the nexus between trade and environment in the coming years. But given the suspicions of most developing-country members about the linkage between trade and environment, it remains unclear whether the CTE will be accorded the status of a standing, or permanent, committee of the WTO.

One of the contentious issues to be played out in the CTE is the transparency of the WTO in regard to the public. The United States, under pressure from NGOs and public opinion, proposed in 1994 that NGOs be permitted to observe the CTE's proceedings and is likely to continue to push within the CTE for opening it up to environmental NGOs and for making the dispute-resolution process more transparent. But the United States now seems isolated on the transparency issue. Delegations from developing countries and other industrialized countries agreed in principle on the need to increase the transparency of the organization but reject the environmental NGO movement worldwide, which they perceive as dominated by U.S. NGOs, as participants in the WTO's decisionmaking.[90] They also oppose breaching the confidentiality of the dispute-resolution process. The prospects for change will depend on whether NGOs and public opinion in other countries successfully elevate the issue of transparency and whether rising public opposition in the United States to the secrecy of the WTO is seen by other countries as a serious threat to the organization.

The CTE will also be dealing with the trade implications of ecolabeling schemes that are proliferating, particularly in the European Union.[91] Such schemes, some sponsored by governments and some by private business or NGOs, use labels indicating that products are environmentally friendly based on overall analysis of the entire life cycle of the product from production to disposal. Their purpose is to raise consumer awareness and ultimately make manufacturing designs more sensitive to environmental impacts.

Developing countries have expressed justifiable concerns that such ecolabeling schemes will be skewed in favor of domestic producers, which have already influenced the selection of product categories to be covered or excluded, as well as the criteria for obtaining the desired label. Ecolabeling schemes may favor a domestic industry by virtually mandating a particular technology or production process, ignoring the fact that another technology or process may be equally or more environmentally sound. In the case of a proposed private German labeling scheme for textiles, for example, natural dyes that are used more in developing countries are excluded by the criteria for environmentally friendly chemicals. And developing countries are not the only ones questioning some ecolabeling schemes: The United States has supported the lobbying of its pulp industry in making representations to the EU about an ecolabeling system that focuses on the use of chlorine in manufacturing paper, fearing it would create a severe disadvantage for the United States in the European market.[92]

The demands for equity in determining ecolabeling schemes and the potential for conflicting standards in different schemes are likely to increase interest in multilateral negotiations on minimum environmental standards, which would allow countries to maintain higher standards. The WTO is generally recognized as having no mandate or expertise to negotiate environmental standards, prompting some environmentalists and trade specialists to call for negotiation of minimum standards under the auspices of UNEP or a new multilateral "World Environment Organization."[93]

Multilateral agreement on minimum standards for production processes in various industrial sectors would reduce conflicts over ecolabeling schemes. And similar agreements on minimum international standards for managing forests, marine mammals, and fishery resources would ease international conflicts over extrajurisdictional ETMs. The most rapidly developing countries are likely to agree to such minimum standards only if the threat of unilateral trade measures or ecolabeling systems is perceived as worse than the risks of international standards. The history of negotiating international norms on whaling, dolphin-safe tuna fishing, and drift-netting suggests that such agreements may be achieved, but only after tough bargaining in which the threat of unilateral trade measures is maintained, at least by the United States.

THE POLITICS OF FINANCING GLOBAL ENVIRONMENTAL REGIMES: THE GLOBAL ENVIRONMENT FACILITY

The new generation of global environmental regimes, especially those for climate and biodiversity, will require transitions to environmentally sound technologies and new natural resource management strategies. Such transitions require difficult political decisions that are likely to meet resistance from powerful interests, as well as investments to ease the transitions. The latter makes the question of external financing for developing-country implementation a key issue in every one of these agreements. And as financial assistance assumed greater importance in environmental regimes, control over the use of that assistance emerged as a new issue in global environmental politics.

A three-year international struggle over the Global Environment Facility reflected the political tensions among the state actors involved in environmental regime formation. Established in 1991 as a three-year pilot project to support several global environmental objectives (controlling climate change and protecting the ozone layer, biodiversity, and international waters), the GEF was a contentious issue from the beginning. Donor countries identified the GEF as the only channel through which they would commit new and additional resources for global regimes, but developing countries rejected it. And despite the fact that its funding is extremely modest in relation to the environmental challenges it addresses (just $1.2 billion for the three-year pilot phase and $2 billion for the first three years of the postpilot phase), the GEF represented the first major North-South battle over the governance of a global environmental institution.

The GEF was begun as essentially an arm of the World Bank, with UNEP and UNDP providing technical and scientific advice. Influenced primarily by their finance ministries, France and West Germany, which took the lead in proposing the GEF, and most of the donor countries wished primarily to avoid a separate fund for each global environmental convention and to keep control of other funds out of the hands of developing-country majorities and of UNEP executive director Tolba, whom they distrusted. So the donor countries insisted on putting control over project planning and financing decisions in the World Bank, in which they had most of the votes on the governing board. The United States, however, did not support the GEF initially, mainly because of its skepticism about the need for a climate change treaty that would require additional financing.[94]

The G-77 firmly opposed the GEF as the sole funding mechanism for environmental agreements on the grounds that it had been set up by a few industrialized countries without consultation with the developing countries themselves, and that it would be run by the World Bank, which was controlled by industrialized countries. They charged that it would focus only on environmental issues of interest to the North, rather than on those of concern to the South.[95] And developing countries could participate only by contributing $2 million to the GEF—a sum that discouraged most of them from participating.

In the UNCED PrepComs, the G-77 proposed a separate fund that would be governed on the basis of one country, one vote as an alternative to the GEF. But developing countries were by no means united on the GEF issue: Countries such as India and Malaysia, which were not as concerned about getting financing from the GEF, took a position of all-out opposition; poorer countries such as Ecuador and sub-Saharan African countries saw it as a source of potential funding for projects.[96]

Most NGOs in both North and South, meanwhile, found the central role of the Bank in the administration of the GEF unacceptable. They were especially incensed at the fact that most GEF projects were actually attached to larger World Bank projects, suggesting that the Bank was simply doing more of the same through the GEF. U.S.-based NGOs also criticized the GEF's lack of openness and accountability and its failure to consult with grassroots groups in the recipient countries and permit NGOs to attend the meetings of GEF participants as observers.

Whether the GEF would be accepted by developing countries as the funding mechanism for global environmental conventions ultimately depended on reaching agreement on a governing structure. Donor countries wanted a governing structure based on the World Bank model, with weighted voting according to financial contribution and decisions made by a qualified majority. Developing countries demanded a governing structure based on full equality for all participants, as in the U.N. General Assembly, with decisions made by a simple majority.

In May 1992 the climate and biodiversity conventions both accepted the GEF as the "interim" funding mechanism in return for the promise that the GEF would have "equitable and balanced representation" (climate convention) and be "democratic" (biodiversity convention), suggesting that the donor countries had given up their insistence on the World Bank model for governance of the GEF.

It took nearly two more years, however, to work out the details of a system of governance that would satisfy both donor and developing countries. In the end, the developing countries won significant concessions from the donor countries: The two groups of countries agreed to a voting system requiring both a 60-percent majority of the members of the governing body (one state, one vote) and a 60-percent majority of states making the contributions for a decision. They also agreed that in addition to a GEF "council" in which a smaller number of countries would represent the entire membership of the GEF, there would also be a participants' assembly with universal membership that would meet less frequently.[97]

Negotiators tentatively agreed that the GEF Council would have 30 seats, but the developing countries insisted on having as many seats as the donor countries and former socialist states combined. France objected at first to a lesser number of seats on the council for donor countries and walked out of the negotiations. But the donor countries finally agreed, in March 1994, that the council would have 16 developing-country members, 14 developed-country members, and 2 members from Central and Eastern Europe and the former Soviet Union.

Under the original GEF proposal, project approval would have been left entirely to the World Bank. The issues of the GEF Council's authority vis-à-vis the implementing agencies and the independence of the GEF secretariat from the World Bank were added to the negotiating agenda only because U.S. environmental NGOs persuaded the Clinton administration to change the U.S. position. The G-77 welcomed the new U.S. position on these issues; European donor countries were initially resistant.

The growing worldwide furor over the Bank's involvement in India's Sardar Sardovar project to dam the Narmada River and the report of an independent review panel evaluating the first two years of the GEF's pilot phase helped change the European position. Criticism of the Sardar Sardovar project by environmental and human rights groups and unfavorable media reports about its environmental damage and large-scale

ruption reached a new peak in 1993. And the review panel, es-
by the GEF secretariat under pressure from NGOs, charged that
had shifted projects from its regular portfolio to the GEF and
had exaggerated the level of consultation with governments, NGOs, and
affected communities.[98] European governments, which had been the
World Bank's strongest supporters, finally went along with U.S. proposals to give the CEO of the GEF—who could not be on the World Bank
staff—final approval of all projects, to permit four GEF Council members
to request that an individual project be put on the agenda for a council
meeting, and to allow 40 percent of the council members to veto a project
thus placed on the agenda.

The agreement to restructure the GEF illustrates the importance of the
United States shifting from a negative role on financing to a lead role. U.S.
success in that role was facilitated by the fact that the GEF was still new
and unformed as an institution, as well as by developments that made
other donor countries more flexible on the issue of functional independence from the World Bank. Second, the GEF negotiations suggest that,
despite the fact that industrialized countries controlled the financial resources at stake, the developing countries could prevail on governance issues when they were united among themselves and when they were allied with Northern NGOs and the industrialized countries were divided.
Finally, the experience demonstrates again the agenda-setting role of
NGOs in getting issues of independence from the Bank into the negotiations, which was necessary to bring about crucial changes from the original World Bank model.

CONCLUSION

Issues that involve the nexus of economic relations, patterns of development, and the environment have become central elements of the field
of global environmental politics. Certain features of North-South trade relations and heavy developing-country indebtedness are linked with
faster rates of natural resource depletion. Inequities in North-South economic relations and consumption patterns have shaped developing-
country attitudes toward negotiations on environmental issues. Three
major developing-country themes in global environmental politics are the
need for industrialized countries to reduce their occupation of "environmental space," to take primary political and financial responsibility for
reversing environmental degradation, and to give developing countries
equal representation in the mechanisms dispensing financial resources
for implementing environmental regimes and sustainable development.

UNCED produced a set of nonbinding agreements (Agenda 21, the Rio
Declaration, and the Statement of Forest Principles) that could be consid-

ered as an umbrella regime for sustainable development worldwide. Those agreements were weakened by the United States and other key state actors' vetoes of many proposals, but Agenda 21 in particular established new norms in many areas and galvanized action on a number of issues on which there was not yet an international regime. And the UNCED process further strengthened the role of NGOs in global environmental politics.

Linkages between trade and environment include the impact of trade liberalization on environmental degradation, the possible overriding of domestic environmental regulations by free-trade rules, the use of trade restrictions to promote environmental protection beyond a state's borders, and the alleged impact of lower environmental standards on trade competitiveness. The international community has begun to establish rules on environmentally related trade restrictions through the GATT's dispute-resolution process. But the outcomes of disputes over environmental trade measures are shaped in some cases by the relative market power of the parties involved rather than by rulings by the GATT's dispute panels.

The International Tropical Timber Organization was founded as an effort to reconcile its trade objectives with sustainable development of forests, but its domination by timber-trading interests negated its environmental objectives. Ecolabeling schemes, intended as an alternative to trade restrictions, are seen by many countries as discriminatory and a threat to market access. One way to reduce or eliminate disputes over environmental trade measures and ecolabeling systems is probably to reach multilateral agreements on minimum environmental standards.

The Global Environment Facility, the primary source of external financing for the implementation of environmental regimes, was the subject of prolonged North-South contention over governance. The issues were whether governance would be based on the weighted voting or one-nation–one-vote models and whether the GEF would be an arm of the World Bank. Developing countries won an equal voice in decisionmaking, and participating states agreed to make the GEF's secretariat functionally independent of the Bank.

FIVE

□ □ □

The Future: An Agenda for Global Environmental Politics

The past decade has seen an unprecedented explosion of international negotiations and cooperation on the global environment. With the climate and biodiversity conventions and the Law of the Sea convention all going into effect in 1993 and 1994, the international community now has the basis for a new international environmental legal order. All of these conventions will continue to evolve in the coming years as new protocols are negotiated and political and technical problems of implementation confront the parties. But a number of new issues involving environmental regimes are already on the international political agenda for the next few years. Among the issues on which negotiations on new regimes are either already under way or are possible are the depletion of the world's fishery resources, land-based sources of marine pollution, worldwide sale of pesticides, the security and sustainable use of freshwater resources, and deforestation. Most of these negotiations were called for by Agenda 21 at the Earth Summit.

Today governments are involved every month in new rounds of international negotiations preparing for regimes that are soon to go into effect, reviewing and strengthening existing regimes, or negotiating on new regimes. One specialist on international environmental law argues that the international community is suffering from "treaty congestion," with more treaties than it is yet able to implement effectively.[1]

In the next few years, therefore, the central challenges in global environmental politics will be to strengthen the regimes that have been negotiated through new protocols and amendments and to devise ways to im-

147

plement them more effectively. New proposals are likely to be discussed for improving the monitoring and enforcement of global environmental conventions as well as for financing them. And beyond legally binding agreements, new international initiatives will be discussed for assisting, encouraging, and financially supporting sustainable development worldwide, some based on Agenda 21 and others going beyond that document.

STRENGTHENING EXISTING REGIMES

Targets and Timetables for the Climate Convention

The convention on climate change entered into force in 1994 as a framework convention that lacked legally binding obligations to reduce carbon dioxide emissions to a specific level. But a few states, led by Germany and strongly supported by a well-organized international network of NGOs, are determined to press the other parties to the convention to strengthen the climate regime significantly. The two main challenges facing the conference of the parties (COP) in the coming years will be to establish obligations both for the immediate goal of stabilization of emissions and the longer-term goal of stabilizing actual concentrations of greenhouse gases in the atmosphere.

The major industrialized countries are publicly committed to the objective of stabilizing carbon dioxide emissions at 1990 levels by the year 2000. But achievement of that goal is far from ensured. Germany reported in 1994 that its emissions had already dropped almost 16 percent since 1987, primarily through restructuring East Germany's energy-inefficient economy.[2] The former Soviet state's energy use was flat because of serious economic depression. But both Japan and the EU as a whole were projecting in 1994 that their emissions of carbon dioxide in the year 2000 would be substantially higher than their 1990 levels unless they took new economic measures to reduce them.[3] And despite the Clinton administration's commitment to meeting the stabilization goal, NGO analysts predicted the cuts that would be achieved by the mostly voluntary U.S. plan would fall about 5-percent short of the stabilization goal.[4]

Even as they struggle to meet the emissions stabilization goal, major parties to the convention must also come to grips with the long-term challenge of reducing worldwide carbon dioxide emissions by as much as 60 percent or more just to stabilize current atmospheric concentrations of CO_2. Even before the convention entered into force, the signatories, meeting as the Intergovernmental Negotiating Committee in February 1994, came to an informal consensus that further measures were needed to reduce emissions beyond 2000. The European Union, again taking the lead role, proposed informally the negotiation of a protocol for targets and timetables beyond 2000, in which the larger developing countries would be included. Already, Canada, Denmark, Germany, and the Netherlands have announced unilateral commitments to reduce their own emissions 20 percent below 1990 levels by 2005. Germany assumed the lead-state role on the issue, submitting a formal proposal for a protocol that would commit OECD countries to stabilization of emissions at 1990 levels by the year 2000 and require timetables for those countries to reduce emissions of carbon dioxide by 20 percent below 1990 levels.

The first COP of the climate convention in March–April 1995 agreed to negotiate by the end of 1997 quantitative limits on greenhouse gas emissions beyond the year 2000 but could not agree on whether those limits would be reductions or which countries would have to negotiate the commitments. The JUSCANZ group (Japan, United States, Canada, Australia, and New Zealand) constituted a new veto coalition, opposing any negotiation of emissions reductions, and most developing countries rejected any quantitative commitments on their part. To reduce emissions beyond the year 2000, the industrialized countries will have to adopt new economic measures that would help bring about fundamental changes in energy use—especially carbon taxes, which impose fees on energy sources in direct proportion to the amount of carbon per unit of energy produced. Phased in at sufficient levels over a period of years, carbon taxes would ensure that some structural changes in transport and energy-use systems take place and that the transition to alternative energy sources is accelerated.

EU energy and environment ministers agreed in 1993 to a $10 tax per barrel of crude oil by 2000, but EU finance ministers insisted that it be linked to parallel taxes in the United States and Japan. Similarly, Japan agreed to enact a carbon tax, but only on the condition that the United States adopts a similar measure. Some EU member states, including Germany and Denmark, have been prepared to have the EU implement such a tax without regard to a U.S. commitment. Others, including the Netherlands and Luxembourg, are concerned that their industries will be put at a competitive disadvantage without such conditionality. The poorer EU members, such as Ireland and Spain, want the level of each country's carbon tax to reflect different levels of economic development, and the United Kingdom has opposed an EU-wide carbon tax on principle.[5]

The United States remains the main obstacle to carbon taxes in the industrialized world. All of the major potential measures for stabilizing and then reducing U.S. CO_2 emissions—increased car fuel efficiency, gas or carbon taxes, upgrading industrial generating and residential energy efficiency—either have met powerful resistance in Congress or have been viewed by the Clinton administration as politically unacceptable to voters.[6]

Even if all industrialized countries agree to substantial post-2000 emissions-reduction targets, the climate convention can be effective only if developing countries also agree to formal commitments to control their emissions. The developing world's carbon emissions grew by 82 percent from 1970 to 1992; during the same period, OECD countries' carbon emissions increased only 28 percent. As a result, developing countries' share of total world emissions surpassed that of OECD countries around 1983 and has remained over 50 percent ever since, with China as the largest developing-country contributor.[7] If the major rapidly industrializing countries were to stay on their present greenhouse-gas emissions growth paths over the next few decades, it would more than wipe out a 20-percent reduction on the part of OECD countries. To induce developing countries to accept limitations on their emissions, however, the industrialized countries will have to show that they are serious about cutting their own emissions.

The developing countries have long argued that the industrialized countries created the global warming problem and that there should be a differentiated set of commitments for developing countries in the climate regime, as there is under the Montreal Protocol. They will want any formula for reducing greenhouse-gas emissions below business-as-usual projections to be based on cumulative releases over several decades and to take into account the huge differences in per capita emissions between North and South. Developing countries may also try to limit any commitments to emissions from fossil fuel burning, excluding emissions of methane and carbon emissions from tropical deforestation. Adopting these bases for calculating commitments would shift far more of the burden to the industrialized countries. However, the industrialized countries can be expected to insist on current or recent-year gross emissions as the basis for calculating allowable emissions in the future, which would mean a greater burden for developing countries.

A major problem that will require special attention by the parties to the climate convention is the projected growth in China's greenhouse-gas emissions. Given the combination of rapid economic growth, population growth, and increased reliance on coal, it is possible that China's annual carbon emissions alone could reach 2.25 billion tons by 2050 and that they could account for 40 percent of worldwide emissions.[8] China, as well as India, Thailand, and Indonesia, are expected to experience the largest increase in coal use in the world by the year 2000, in part because of shifts in fuel mixes toward even greater reliance on cheap indigenous coal.[9] For these coal-intensive countries, rapidly leapfrogging fossil fuels and introducing inexpensive solar energy technologies may be the only way to avoid an explosion of carbon emissions in future decades. Such technologies could be commercialized much more rapidly if fossil fuel energy is priced more realistically.

One of the bases for an agreement on controlling greenhouse gases is the fact that developing countries are generally so inefficient in their use of energy. That inefficiency implies both economic and environmental benefits to be gained from reducing their carbon emissions by promoting energy efficiency. A number of country studies have shown that just by making low-cost policy shifts that would not require external financing—such as eliminating energy subsidies—many rapidly developing countries could cut energy-related carbon emissions by up to 50 percent or more.[10] With additional financing for new energy-efficient technologies, even greater reductions could be achieved.

The major rapidly industrializing countries are unlikely to agree to curbs on their greenhouse-gas emissions without far-reaching commitments by industrialized countries to financial and technology transfers. Such financial commitments will have to go far beyond the modest amounts already pledged to the GEF to provide financing—primarily through the World Bank and other multilateral financial institutions—of new energy-efficient technologies for lighting, transport, industry, and other uses and to help develop renewable energy systems.

Another issue to be resolved is how the provision in the climate convention for **joint implementation** (JI) should be implemented. That provision allows countries or private firms to invest in emissions-reduction measures in other countries where the marginal costs are lower and ultimately to receive some form of international credit. JI could provide the main source of transfers of capital and technologies from industrialized to developing countries in the coming decades.

Whether joint implementation can be used by an industrialized country to achieve credits toward stabilizing its emissions by the year 2000 had not yet been settled by 1995. China and the G-77 have opposed regarding JI projects as a substitute for existing national commitments to stabilization of emissions by the industrialized countries. Some developing countries view JI as a cheap way for industrialized countries to avoid radical changes in their own consumption patterns by helping developing countries make the relatively easy first-stage changes and leaving them with the more expensive subsequent steps. Moreover, without a target for developing countries' emissions, it would be difficult to assess whether individual projects would provide resources that would not otherwise be funded. JI is likely to be officially sanctioned by the conference of the parties, therefore, only after both industrialized and developing countries have committed to emissions-reduction targets and timetables beyond the year 2000.

Making the Biodiversity Convention Effective

The prospects for forging new arrangements to make the biodiversity convention effective in the next few years are dimmed by the international political context as well as by the characteristics of the regime itself. Although a few countries, including Sweden, Australia, New Zealand, and Germany, have been active in trying to get the parties to come to grips with key problems, there is no strong coalition of lead states that is strongly committed to the success of the treaty. The future role of the United States, which had moved from veto state to supporting state, is highly uncertain given its failure to ratify the convention in 1994 and the strong opposition of the Republican-controlled Senate.

Another problem with the biodiversity convention is that, unlike the Montreal Protocol or even the climate convention, it does not have any quantitative target or timetable for international action. The absence of any target for conservation makes it more difficult for the COP to determine its priorities for implementing and strengthening the convention. That difficulty was illustrated by the first meeting of the COP in the Bahamas in November 1994, where participants showed little willingness to tackle some of the central problems of the convention. Among the issues on which the COP of the biodiversity convention will decide over the next few years, national reporting and the negotiation of protocols on conservation in the agriculture and forestry sectors will have the greatest impact on the effectiveness of the treaty. But based on the initial COP, those are not likely to get the most attention.

In the absence of quantitative commitments to conservation, national reports on implementation of the convention are the only mechanism available to hold the parties accountable for making progress in implementing their own national strategies. Since the periodicity and contents of these reports are not specified in the convention, it will be up to the COP to decide the issue. The first meeting of the COP made no decision on the question, so it will be on the agenda for the second COP in November 1995. Some countries, such as Brazil and India, which have in the past opposed stringent reporting requirements in various international environmental forums, are likely to argue for leaving the periodicity and/or organization of reports up to national authorities. The countries most strongly committed to the convention will probably push for mandating regularity and uniformity in format.

The COP is unlikely to agree, however, to any process that would subject the reports to any official process of review. That will be a job for NGOs, who will be able to assess the accuracy of the reports as well as the substance of the policies, just as the Climate Action Network did with regard to the climate action plans of the industrialized countries.

The COP will also decide in the coming years what protocols to negotiate. Its first protocol is almost certain to be one on biosafety, which the Scandinavian countries, the G-77, and China have all called for, citing a number of potential threats to biological diversity from the transfer, handling, or use of living modified organisms (LMOs). The United States has been alone in asserting that a biosafety protocol is unwarranted, whereas the United Kingdom and the Netherlands, supported by the EU, proposed voluntary biosafety guidelines outside the convention without ruling out eventual negotiation of a protocol. The first meeting of the COP established an open-ended ad hoc group to discuss the issue and report to the second meeting of the COP.

Far more important to the success of the convention would be the negotiation of a protocol on agricultural biodiversity. Although the convention implicitly includes agricultural biodiversity within its scope, it contains no operational provisions relating to it. The problem to be addressed is the genetic erosion of food crops worldwide because of the replacement of thousands of traditional varieties with a few high-yielding ones. The renegotiation of FAO's International Undertaking of 1983 in the FAO Commission on Plant Genetic Resources has been proposed as one way of producing such a protocol. Such negotiations would probably pose a conflict between the rights of farmers and local communities to the benefits of products derived from local genetic resources and those of seed companies.

A protocol on forests would also go to heart of the convention, since most of the world's biodiversity is located in the world's tropical forests. The idea of a forest protocol has been pushed by environmental NGOs who see the biodiversity convention as the most advantageous forum for discussing multilateral agreements on forests. Many would like to reintroduce the idea of legal commitments to increasing the protected areas of forests. IUCN's Environmental Law Center is developing ideas on a forest protocol, and several industrialized countries, including Germany and Canada, are sympathetic. But India and Malaysia are opposed to negotiating on forests within the biodiversity convention. Most G-77 countries are likely to follow their lead, dooming the proposal for the foreseeable future.

The issue of whether the GEF will be the convention's funding mechanism was debated but not resolved at the first meeting of the COP. The parties could agree only to designate the GEF the "interim funding mechanism" until the second COP meets to choose a permanent funding mechanism. The G-77 countries continued to oppose the designation of the GEF as the institutional structure to operate the funding mechanism despite the fact that they had negotiated a comprehensive agreement on reorganizing the GEF earlier in the year. Given that there is no practical alternative to the GEF as that structure, the G-77 appears to view the position of rejecting the GEF as a bargaining chip to be used to win concessions on other issues.

Determining the strategy and priorities for funding projects to implement the convention was one of the key tasks before the first meeting of the COP and a key test of whether the COP was capable of formulating a coherent funding policy. It also invoked political sensitivities. A major issue is how much of the available funds should be allocated—according to scientifically based priorities—to projects in "threatened hotspots" (the small group of tropical rainforest regions that harbor up to 40 percent of all terrestrial biodiversity and are at greatest risk in terms of species extinction) and how much to projects in "megadiversity countries" (the dozen or so countries that have up to 70 percent of the earth's biodiversity, including Indonesia, Mexico, India, and Brazil). Alternatively, how much should be allocated to helping all the countries inventory their biodiversity resources and build their capacity to formulate and implement biodiversity conservation plans?[11]

These issues could divide the G-77 between megadiversity countries and smaller countries. It is not surprising, therefore, that the COP resisted the idea of prioritization in discussions on funding guidance. In the end the COP adopted a list of fourteen criteria that would have covered virtually any project that might be proposed. The effect of such vague guidance is to give the GEF the real responsibility for determining program priorities, despite G-77 rhetoric insisting that GEF operate under the COP's authority.

THE NEXT GENERATION OF GLOBAL
ENVIRONMENTAL REGIMES

Conserving Global Fish Stocks

One of the global environmental problems demanding urgent international cooperation is the worldwide decline of fish stocks from overfishing. The world fish catch grew fivefold between 1950 and 1989, then started to decline, but the more valuable species, such as mackerel and herring, were in decline well before that. The FAO now reports that all seventeen major ocean fisheries have either reached or exceeded their natural limits and that nine of them are in serious decline.[12] The primary reason for the decline is too many fishing boats with too much modern fishing technology, such as bigger nets, electronic fish-detection equipment, and mechanized hauling gear. Much of the overcapitalization of fishing, moreover, is from government subsidies: The FAO reports that $54 billion of the $92 billion in operating costs of the world's fishing fleets were met by government subsidies in 1989.[13]

Ninety percent of the fish catch worldwide is taken within the 200-mile (320-kilometer) **exclusive economic zones** (EEZs) under national jurisdiction, but fish migrate from one EEZ to another and between the EEZs and the high seas. Problems of migrating and straddling stocks and high-seas fisheries are now left to regional agreements. The U.N. Convention on the Law of the Sea (UNCLOS) establishes only very general rights and obligations of states regarding conservation and use of these migratory resources.

The U.N. Conference on Straddling and Highly Migratory Fish Stocks, called for in Agenda 21, was driven in large part by Canada's dispute with the EU over fish stocks that straddled the Canadian EEZ and the high seas. The conference began in March 1993 under the auspices of the U.N. General Assembly to consider ways of improving international cooperation on the problem. The conference held three sessions in 1993–1994 and met twice in 1995 to complete the negotiation of a regime, with the final session in July-August 1995.

The sharpest conflict in these negotiations is between the seventy coastal fishing states and the ten nations that have technologically advanced fleets ranging thousands of miles and processing enormous quantities of fish as they are caught. The long-range fishing states, including the European Union, Japan, South Korea, Taiwan, Poland, China, and the United States, are accused by coastal states of abusing their right to fish international waters; long-range fishing states in turn point out that mismanagement of EEZs by coastal fishing states is responsible for the most serious overfishing problems.[14]

Led by the EU, Korea, and Japan (which has the largest fishing fleet in the world and the largest fish catch), the long-range fishing states called for nonbinding guidelines rather than a legally binding instrument. They have long argued that regulation of fishing practices should be left to regional or subregional organizations. The coastal states, led by the "like-minded" caucus (Argentina, Canada, Chile, Iceland, New Zealand, Norway, and Peru) advocated a legally binding agreement for high-seas fishing. Canada, Chile, and Russia implied that they would seize ships on the high seas if nations failed to agree on such binding rules.[15] At the same time, most coastal states resisted international rules that would limit their freedom to manage their 200-mile zones. Some called for leaving responsibility for regulation in the EEZs to subregional and regional organizations and agreements.

The United States, which has both long-range and coastal fishing fleets, was in a pivotal position to broker an agreement. Initially, it opposed a binding convention on straddling and migratory stocks in the belief that stronger conservation rules would be adopted if the agreement were nonbinding. But in mid-1994, it joined the like-minded caucus in supporting a binding agreement. The negotiating text produced by the conference chair did take the form of a legally binding agreement, covering both high seas and EEZs.[16] But it imposed relatively few obligations on coastal states, mainly because Canada, which led the like-minded caucus, had resisted international regulations on coastal state management as a breach of its sovereignty.

The United States pushed Canada to accept tougher obligations on coastal states, hoping to get long-range fishing states to accept a binding agreement that would limit high-seas fishing in return. Canada did agree in 1994 to stronger language on coastal zone management, reducing the imbalance between the obligations assumed under the agreement by long-range fishing states and coastal states.

That shifted the focus of negotiations back to the distant-water fishing fleets and the issue of high-seas overfishing. In March 1995, tension between Canada and the EU escalated over Spanish and Portuguese fishing outside Canadian waters of the same stocks denied to Canadian fishermen. Three incidents in which Canadian ships aggressively pursued, seized, or cut the nets of Spanish trawlers illustrated the difficulty of enforcing fisheries agreements on the high seas. The Canadian actions polarized the conference but increased the incentive for both sides to reach agreement on new rules.

The March 1995 round of negotiations left the coastal states and long-range fishing states far apart on the issue of the right of coastal states to board ships on the high seas that they suspect of having violated the agreement. The Chairman's draft leaned toward the position of coastal states, allowing wider latitude for such high seas boarding than the EU, Japan, Korea, and China were prepared to accept. Boarding on the high seas and other related enforcement issues were still capable of blocking final agreement as the last scheduled round of talks approached.

The most effective approach to conserving straddling and migratory stocks would have been to establish strict limits on entry into the fishing industry and set a numerical limit on the total catch and a percentage of the total catch per entrant. But that approach would have required putting many fisherman out of business and thus would involve political costs for governments. Instead the draft relies on general principles of conservation of fish stocks, such as requirements to apply the "precautionary principles," to take measures to "ensure long-term sustainability and promote optimum utilization" of the stocks, and to "eliminate overfishing and excess capacity."

The draft agreement obligates parties to take into account scientifically based limits on exploitation of specific fish stocks but does not spell out those limits. Nor does it establish binding standards for sustainable management of fish stocks or for such problems as overcapitalization of fishing fleets, excessive fleet size, vessel reflagging, or inappropriate fishing gear. Instead the text calls on relevant coastal states and long-distance-fishing states to reach agreements on these issues that apply both within the EEZs and beyond them. Even if a legally binding agreement does emerge from the process, it will be at best only a framework convention— the first step toward a meaningful regime for reversing the problem of overfishing.

Security and Sustainable Use of Shared Freshwater Resources

Another issue demanding international agreement in the near future is ensuring adequate freshwater for nations that must share common water resources. That will require agreements on sustainable water use as well as equitable sharing of international rivers. As noted in Chapter 1, total water use worldwide has increased nearly fourfold over fifty years, but per capita availability of water in developing countries has continually declined. In both highly industrialized and developing countries, freshwater is a finite resource that has too often been treated as though it were infinite and free.

Scarcity of freshwater resources may be linked with international conflict when two or more countries rely on the water of the same river. Forty percent of the world's people depend on water that originates in another country.[17] The waters of the Zambezi River, which runs through eight countries; the Tigris-Euphrates, which is shared by Turkey, Syria, and Iraq; and the Aral basin, where five republics of the former Soviet Union are competing for a diminishing, badly damaged resource, have long been the cause of international tensions and sometimes violent conflict. The Nile waters, which flow through nine countries, are used mainly by the two downstream nations, Sudan and Egypt, whose economies are overwhelmingly dependent on them. Ethiopia, the source of most of the Nile waters, has not been in a position to develop the river, but neither has it been willing to negotiate a binding agreement on sharing its waters. Egypt, which has been the prime beneficiary of the 1959 treaty, has declared that it would not stand idly by if upstream countries diverted water from Egyptian use.[18]

Despite the fact that there are already more than 2,000 treaties regulating waters shared by two or more countries, international water law is poorly developed and not adequate for heading off potentially violent conflicts.[19] Legal principles governing the use of water in shared river basins have been agreed on: Countries should inform and consult with neighbors who will be affected by their actions, exchange hydrologic data, avoid harming downstream states, and agree on reasonable and equitable water allocations. But all these principles are open to varying interpretations, and concrete rules are particularly needed to apply the general principle of reasonable and equitable water allocation. Although Agenda 21 includes a number of norms for protecting the supply and quality of freshwater resources, it did not deal with the more sensitive issue of sharing those resources. An effort at the 1994 Hague Ministerial Conference on Drinking Water and Environmental Sanitation to develop norms for international sharing of water was weakened by Brazil, India, and Mexico. So further development of international law on sharing water probably will depend on reaching agreement on individual river basins and aquifers— perhaps beginning with those facing the threat of violent conflict.[20]

Agreement on equitable sharing has to be a central element in the settlement of the Arab-Israeli conflict.[21] Israel, Jordan, and Syria have long competed for the water of the Jordan and Litani Rivers, and Israel went to war in 1967 in part to ensure control over those waters. In October 1994, as part of the Israeli-Jordanian peace agreement, the two nations agreed on sharing the waters of the Jordan and Yarmuk Rivers. Israel will support Jordan and Syria's long-standing hopes of building a dam on the Yarmuk and will give up part of its share of Jordan River water to Jordan. A comprehensive agreement on shared water resources could include provisions for developing standards for collection and dissemination of water supply and demand data and establishment of a Jordan River–basin authority including all the affected states and interested outsiders.

But since there is not enough water to meet projected demand under current patterns of usage, a successful agreement on water sharing will have to encompass cooperation in conserving those same freshwater resources. That will require the adoption of plans that bring consumption into line with projected supplies in both countries. Although Israel is considered the most water-efficient country in the world, even greater efficiency is needed in agricultural use. Similarly, Jordan can make much more efficient agricultural use of water through policy and management reforms.[22]

The multilateral Middle East peace process involving the six regional parties and the United States, Russia, Japan, the EU, and Canada includes working groups on environmental issues and on water. Japan and the United States have key roles to play on this issue as chairs of the environmental and water working groups, respectively. The first stage of negotiations on water as an environmental issue will probably be on a set of general environmental principles for the region. The next stage could be to focus on the modalities of agreement on sustainable water use in the region, such as national plans that include effective demand-reduction policies. The environmental committee is already discussing some issues that are relevant to such plans, including recycling of wastewater for agriculture.[23] But the discussions will need to include such issues as agricultural water subsidies, choice of crops and irrigation methods, water-distribution systems, and even shifts away from reliance on agriculture. The latter may be particularly difficult for Israel, where food self-sufficiency has long been an ideological principle.

Another element in a peace settlement in the region will be an Israeli-Palestinian agreement on sharing the aquifer that lies for the most part beneath the occupied territories of the West Bank. Israel has long been dependent for nearly 40 percent of its groundwater on that aquifer and has strictly limited water use by Palestinians on the West Bank in order to ensure Israeli use of those water supplies. Hard bargaining will take place over reallocation of that water within a committee on water created by the 1994 bilateral Israeli-Palestinian agreement.

Agreement between Arabs and Israelis on sharing and sustainable use of their common freshwater resources is likely because of the diplomatic involvement of the United States and other outside parties, which are also prepared to provide significant financial assistance and technical support. Thus far, the same has not been true in conflicts over other international rivers around the world—the Tigris-Euphrates, Nile, Senegal, Zambezi, Ganges-Brahmaputra, Aral, and Mekong. In the Indo-Pakistani conflict over the Sind River forty years ago, the World Bank played an important role in mediating shared use of the river's waters and then helped finance the proposed solution. In none of the current troubled river basins except in the Arab-Israeli negotiations has there been major international attention and financing that would prompt nation-states to negotiate regional sharing and conservation agreements. Regional regimes will require also that the development banks and agencies be sensitive to environmental and social consequences lest they repeat the tragedy of the Senegal basin, where the construction of a modern dam (with World Bank, UNDP, French, and U.S. financing) contributed to bloody class and ethnic conflict between traditional herdsmen and modern agriculturalists using irrigation.[24]

Reducing Marine Pollution from Land-based Sources

An estimated 75 to 80 percent of marine pollution originates from land-based sources, among which the most important are synthetic organic compounds—also known as persistent organic pollutants (POPs)—such as pesticides; excess sedimentation from mining, deforestation, or agriculture; sewage that can cause biological contamination; and excess nutrients from fertilizers and sewage. However, international agreements to reduce marine pollution have thus far focused on direct ocean dumping and ship-based pollution (as, for example, in the MARPOL and the London Dumping Convention) rather than on land-based sources.

Marine pollution from land-based sources, like overfishing, can only be regulated in each region by regional actors. Regional agreements have been reached to control land-based sources of pollution in the Northeast Atlantic, the Baltic, the Mediterranean, the Persian Gulf, and the Southeast Pacific, but the effectiveness of these agreements has varied significantly. For the remaining regional seas of the world, the only agreement on the problem is a set of nonbinding guidelines called the Montreal Guidelines for the Protection of the Marine Environment from Land-based Sources, adopted in 1985 under the auspices of UNEP.

These guidelines have been regarded as ineffective in protecting regional seas from land-based pollution. Agenda 21 called for updating and strengthening the Montreal Guidelines, for identifying new actions to reduce the impact of land-based pollution, and for initiating regional agreements on the problem where appropriate. Also in Agenda 21 was the request that UNEP convene a conference on the problem. In 1994, preparatory work began on the UNEP-sponsored Global Conference on the Protection of the Marine Environment from Land-based Sources of Pollution, to take place in November 1995 in Washington, D.C.

During these preparations differences emerged on whether the primary focus should be on rewriting the Montreal Guidelines or on developing a nonbinding program of action. Proponents of redrafting the Montreal Guidelines, led by Finland and Canada, hoped that process would be a step toward a binding convention on the problem of land-based sources. The Nordic countries and Iceland were primarily concerned with binding obligations to ban the discharge of POPs that are now being carried from all coastal areas toward the poles, thus damaging marine ecosystems in the Arctic. But most industrialized countries do not support a global convention, and developing countries are skeptical of an agreement that they fear would impose new obligations on them but provide few new resources to carry them out.

Proponents of a global program of action, led by the United States, felt that the Montreal Guidelines have not been helpful and that redrafting principles would leave little time for the task of reaching agreement on a program of action. At a 1994 preparatory meeting, proponents persuaded the entire conference to agree to draft such an action plan beginning in 1995. The idea of rewriting the guidelines was dropped.

The draft of a global action plan, tabled at a March 1995 meeting, encompassed actions at the global, regional, and national levels. The draft plan called for a set of measures by states, on a nonbinding basis, to deal with each of the major land-based sources of pollution. Although the negotiation of timetables was proposed, the agreement would leave room for states to set their own target dates in line with their own capabilities.

The draft included provisions on POPs, as requested by the Nordics, calling, among other activities, for the development of national inventories of all possible sources of POPs and of comprehensive national action plans and regulatory measures for reduction and/or elimination of discharges of POPs by dates that were yet to be negotiated. Despite the nonbinding nature of the document, major agricultural countries in the developing world, such as India, China, and Brazil, have expressed concern that the expected actions could constrain their agricultural productivity because insecticides are among the major categories of POPs. India was expected to insist that any action on reducing or eliminating POPs be accompanied by increased access to financial flows or technology transfer. Similarly, developing countries were expected to condition agreement on actions regarding other land-based sources of marine pollution on such compensatory programs.

A significant innovation in soft law concerning the global environment was introduced in the action program's annex, which suggested a detailed methodology for developing action programs to manage land-based sources of marine degradation. Management objectives were to be stated in quantitative terms, and strategies for meeting them, including economic and regulatory incentive structures, were to be specified. The methodological annex could help achieve through a soft-law agreement an objective that the biodiversity and desertification conventions lack—a detailed common framework for the national action plans that are the heart of a number of global environmental regimes.

Global Pesticide Trade

Regulating the global trade in dangerous pesticides in developing countries has been placed on the global environmental agenda as a result of pressures from some developing countries and NGOs. Until the early 1990s, the agrochemical industry managed to avoid any international regulation of the pesticide trade, but at least some binding regulations are likely to be imposed in the next few years.

Worldwide pesticide use tripled between 1970 and 1987, rising to almost $6 billion annually. While some pesticides are justified in cases of extreme threats to crops, their promotion by manufacturers and donor agencies has resulted in massive overuse during the past two decades. Highly toxic pesticides, many of which were banned in the exporting countries, have caused an estimated 4 million cases of pesticide poisoning and tens of thousands of deaths annually in the developing world and pose serious threats to human health through entry into the food chain and water. And improper use of pesticides has frequently increased pest resistance to the chemicals while killing benign insects, reducing productivity rather than raising it.[25]

The influence of agrochemical companies on major pesticide-exporting states and of the FAO effectively limited international action to address problems with the global pesticide trade in the 1980s. Instead of supporting a binding agreement regulating the pesticide trade, the FAO sponsored the drafting of a "code of conduct" between 1982 and 1985. Those guidelines called for provision of data on the health dangers of pesticides to government authorities and to farmworkers in the importing countries and for reforms in labeling and advertising pesticides. But after seven drafts, pesticide-exporting countries got the FAO to remove from the code the provision for "prior informed consent" (PIC), which would have required that a pesticide banned, withdrawn, or severely restricted by one country could not be exported to another unless the importing country's government has been fully informed of the reason for the regulation and has explicitly agreed to import that pesticide. The exporting countries supported instead a concept of "notification" that could take place *after* the sale, which had already been inserted into a draft of guidelines for controlling the trade in hazardous chemicals being negotiated by a UNEP working group. Those guidelines were later adopted as the

London Guidelines. Developing countries were pressured to adopt the FAO code without the PIC, with the promise that the issue would be revisited in two years.

Prodded by the Pesticide Action Network, an international NGO, the G-77 majorities in the UNEP Governing Council and in the FAO General Conference insisted in 1987 on the inclusion of PIC provisions in the London Guidelines and the FAO Code of Conduct. As a result, both documents were amended to include PIC procedures in 1989.[26]

But because the London Guidelines and the Code of Conduct were voluntary guidelines, there was little implementation of either.[27] In 1991, under pressure from the G-77 majority in the UNEP Governing Council, and despite opposition from major pesticide-exporting states (the United States, the United Kingdom, Germany, and Japan), the council called on its working group on the London Guidelines to discuss turning that voluntary agreement into a binding one.[28] Agenda 21 similarly called for making the PIC procedures legally binding.

The working group could not agree, however, on the fundamental issue of the scope of such a legal instrument. Delegations from developing countries wanted to include pesticides that cause health "and/or environmental problems" in countries lacking adequate infrastructure. That phrase was intended to include pesticides that ultimately bring about resistance in pests and thus create worse problems. Delegations from pesticide-exporting countries opposed the inclusion of pesticides creating environmental problems, since that would bring a much larger range of pesticides within the scope of the mandatory PIC procedure.[29]

The main means of reducing actual pesticide use in developing countries, however, will be greater international cooperation to promote integrated pest management (IPM), in which chemical pesticides are used sparingly along with natural methods of pest control. Until the 1990s there was little international support for IPM, and few developing countries were adopting it. Even at the end of the 1980s, support for IPM programs from all bilateral development agencies was estimated at only about $100 million annually, and there was little interest among these agencies in collaborative efforts. There was no international institution responsible for promoting IPM research and project development and implementation, so the necessary resources were not mobilized.

But the situation began to change in 1990, when a few bilateral and multilateral development agencies established a small task force to evaluate the reasons for IPM's lack of success and to make recommendations for international cooperation. The task force outlined several options, including a donor consortium to promote IPM, a consultative body that would include both client countries and donor agencies, and a new institution to implement IPM programs in the field.[30]

In 1993, the World Bank, FAO, UNEP, and UNDP began meeting with IPM specialists on establishing a new institutional mechanism most closely resembling the first of those three options. The four agencies agreed in May 1994 to form an IPM facility that would mobilize increased resources to support IPM programs in the developing countries and to stimulate more proposals for IPM projects. This consensus signals a new emphasis by multilateral agencies on supporting alternatives to overuse of pesticides in developing countries.

A Regime to Conserve the World's Forests

Despite the debacle on forest principles at the Earth Summit, the issue of a global forest convention is not dead: Thirty-five European countries reaffirmed at the 1993 Ministerial Conference for the Protection of Forests in Europe their support for a world forest convention. Several countries, most notably Canada and Germany, are still committed to working toward such a convention as a long-term goal. And the threat of ecolabeling schemes for timber products in world trade makes Malaysia, one of the primary foes of such an agreement during the UNCED negotiations, interested in negotiating a world forest convention that would not restrict its freedom to log its remaining forests.[31]

In the next few years, however, it is unlikely that a global convention to protect forests will be negotiated, since most of the G-77 countries are publicly opposed to such negotiations. Until the global political situation becomes more favorable, modest progress is possible in putting some of the building blocks in place for an eventual global forest regime. But major political obstacles remain in the path of world consensus on forests.

One potential avenue of progress is to negotiate nonbinding "criteria and indicators" of sustainable forest management. In 1994 and 1995, discussions of criteria and indicators were taking place in two separate processes that involved only temperate and boreal forests:[32] the European Ministerial Conference (the Helsinki process) and a series of meetings for temperate and boreal forest countries involving Australia, Canada, Chile, China, Japan, Korea, Mexico, New Zealand, Russia, and the United States (the Montreal process). Both groups have agreed on their own criteria and indicators, but the states participating in them have thus far avoided any formal commitment to accountability for applying them in their own forest management. Tropical forest countries have so far shown no interest in going beyond the general guidelines that they adopted in 1990. Nor is there yet any momentum toward harmonizing the criteria and indicators, even for temperate and boreal forests, either through the U.N. Commission on Sustainable Development or by other means.

Another possible track is progress in building a global system of certification of sustainable forest management that would be enforced by consumer preferences. Several ecolabeling schemes for timber products in world trade, which are a response to consumer demands in Europe and North America, are a major source of pressure on timber-exporting countries to agree to some system for certifying the sustainable management of their forests. And the nongovernmental Forest Stewardship Council (FSC), composed of representatives of business, NGOs, indigenous peoples, and the scientific community, is proposing to assume authority for accrediting national and local systems of certification of sustainable-forest-management schemes. Most tropical forest countries appear to accept the inevitability of consumer-driven certification of tropical timber, but they insist on a role in determining the criteria and standards.

The question that will be debated over the next few years is who will determine such criteria and standards. Some countries, including Malaysia, wanted to do so in the ITTO, given its pro-timber-trading bias. But that proposal was rejected by Brazil, Colombia, and others on the grounds that the ITTO does not deal with temperate and boreal forests.[33] Now some countries appear to prefer to adopt their own national criteria and indicators for sustainable forest management, and others (the nations of the Amazon basin) are doing so on a regional basis. One can expect continuing confusion among competing criteria for some years to come until states are able to agree on standards.

Another route toward global agreement may be the negotiation of regional or subregional agreements on forest management that could be the models for agreements to stem deforestation at the global level. The first such agreement is the Central American Forest Treaty, signed in 1993, which could eventually be a model for a hemispheric treaty on all forests.[34] That treaty formalizes some cooperation already taking place in the form of border ("peace") parks and agroforestry projects, provides for the consolidation of protected areas, and commits the Central American nations to concentrate commercial logging in secondary forests rather than primary forests and to respect the rights of indigenous peoples and other forest dwellers.

Moreover, the process by which the agreement was negotiated and is being implemented is as important as the substance. Unlike most treaties, the negotiations included campesinos, forest industry representatives, women's organizations, and indigenous peoples as well as the government forest services, giving these social groups a stake in its implementation. Parties to the treaty also created a regional mechanism, the Central American Forest Council, with representation for the governments and full membership and voting rights for designated regional peasants' and women's groups, and the regional Forest Industries Chamber.[35]

In the longer run, a globally binding forest convention covering all types of forests is still possible. Such a convention would have to include the previously agreed "criteria and indicators" of sustainable management for all types of forests and could draw on elements from the Central American Forest Treaty. Brazil, Indonesia, and other major rainforest countries would have veto power over the agreement but may be driven to accept some meaningful limits on exploitation by the threat of ecolabeling schemes for timber products.

IMPROVING COMPLIANCE WITH
ENVIRONMENTAL CONVENTIONS

Countries that sign and ratify international conventions usually do so with the intention of complying fully with their provisions, and most do comply to the best of their ability.[36] But compliance may turn out to be more politically or technically difficult or more costly than anticipated. And some countries may sign and comply with an environmental convention primarily in order to avoid international opprobrium rather than because they are convinced that it is in their interest.

The states of the former Soviet Union are a special case in this regard. The Soviet Union signed a number of global environmental conventions but failed to implement them. Since the collapse of the Soviet state, a number of cases of treaty violations and false reporting, including ocean dumping of nuclear wastes and whaling, have been disclosed.[37] With regard to atmospheric treaties, such as those on climate, ozone, and acid rain, the former Soviet Union and its successor states, preoccupied with dire political and economic crises, have not been prepared to make the investments needed to comply with treaties they have signed and ratified.

To ensure maximum compliance with environmental regimes, therefore, a range of mechanisms are available, including regular reporting by the parties, independent evaluation and public availability of such reports, review of implementation at regular meetings of the parties, the readiness of some parties to call noncomplying parties to account publicly, monitoring of compliance by NGOs, and international assistance for building administrative and financial capacity to implement environmental agreements.[38] In some cases one or more determined governments and a technically and politically sophisticated NGO can pressure states effectively by publicizing evidence of their noncompliance.

Most global environmental conventions rely on the parties to monitor and verify their own compliance. The Montreal Protocol, for example, created the Implementation Committee, but it has no power to investigate or to recommend actions in the event of noncompliance.[39] Environmental conventions generally require the parties to submit data on their compliance to their respective secretariats, which is then made available to the public. But these bodies usually lack the authority to evaluate and verify information submitted by the parties, eliminating one of the sources of pressure on governments to comply fully with the agreement. CITES is an exception: The CITES secretariat—based in part on monitoring by NGOs, which also distribute the results widely to the public—publishes regular reports on noncompliance with its provisions. The 1989–1991 report contained more than seventy pages of detailed violations of the agreement.

Another difficulty that limits enforcement of environmental conventions is the lack of developing-country capacity to implement them. CITES has provisions for trade measures to enforce its controls on wildlife trade, but many countries lack the implementing legislation, budgets, or trained personnel needed to comply.[40] And the 1989 Basel Convention contains no provision for monitoring the accuracy of hazardous waste labels or spot-checking shipments in receiving-country ports. The developing countries, whose inability to monitor the trade had led them to call for a ban on international waste shipments, were left to enforce the agreement themselves.[41]

The secretariats of environmental conventions often lack the staff and funding needed to fulfill the functions they are assigned. The total combined staff of seven agreements (Montreal Protocol, Sofia Protocol, Basel Convention, London Dumping Convention, MARPOL, CITES, and the International Whaling Convention) as of 1990 was only 71.5 people, and their combined budget was estimated at only $12.4 million. The secretariats of the London Dumping Convention, MARPOL, and CITES in particular have experienced funding shortfalls caused by the failure of parties to approve adequate budgets or to pay their contributions.[42]

Several options are available to strengthen compliance with environmental agreements:

☐ Donor countries can negotiate a new joint commitment to increase funding for secretariats of global environmental conventions and to end the practices of late payment and nonpayment of pledges to them.

☐ Donor countries and multilateral agencies could increase funding for programs that strengthen developing countries' capacity to implement conventions such as CITES and the Basel Convention.

☐ A convention's provisions for compliance can be amended to give new monitoring and assessment power to the secretariat. The United States has resisted such proposals in the past on the ground that monitoring authority should not be given to international civil servants.[43] But that attitude simply gives parties to environmental treaties greater opportunities to be global environmental "free riders."

☐ In some cases, such as a future convention regulating fishing, trade sanctions against those parties found in violation could be used as a central mechanism for enforcement. Although there is generally little support for trade sanctions as a remedy for treaty violations, they would make sense in situations such as overfishing, where trade sanctions (in this case curbs on fishing rights or sales) can be directly related to the failure to comply with the treaty.

☐ Because fear of public shaming has proven to be a strong deterrent to treaty violations, an appropriate mechanism could be created by which the secretariats or COPs of treaties would address complaints about states' compliance brought by interest groups, including NGOs in each country.[44] This could be particularly important for conventions whose implementation involves complex social and economic policies, such as the biodiversity and desertification conventions.

FINANCING GLOBAL ENVIRONMENTAL REGIMES AND AGENDA 21

Industrialized and developing countries alike will need new sources of financing to support their own implementation of global environmental regimes and different kinds of investments to make the transitions to sustainable development called for in Agenda 21. Most developing countries finance their economic development out of their own resources, and development assistance is less important than trade as a source of financing for all but the poorest countries. But the environment must compete with other urgent problems for budgetary resources throughout the developing world.

Official development assistance (ODA) worldwide, which increased modestly in real terms during the 1981–1991 decade, began to fall off substantially after 1992. Aggregate ODA from OECD countries in 1993 fell by nearly 8 percent in real terms from 1992 levels and represented just 0.29 percent of their combined GNPs—the lowest ratio reported since 1973.[45] The largest aid donor, Japan, which already contributes about one-fifth of all ODA worldwide, has pledged to increase its ODA during the 1993–1997 period by 40–50 percent over the $50 billion provided in the 1988–1992 period.[46] But most other donor states are either reducing or freezing their ODA. And the $2 billion over three years pledged by donor countries to the GEF is, in the absence of other bilateral and multilateral efforts, too little to make a decisive difference in the climate and biodiversity agreements. The agreements on desertification and land-based sources of marine pollution, as well as policies called for in Agenda 21, will also require additional funding.

For the foreseeable future, any significant increase in financial resources for global environmental regimes and sustainable development worldwide will have to come, therefore, from reorienting existing bilateral and multilateral ODA programs and from adopting innovative international approaches to financing. The main options for generating additional financial support for global environmental conventions and sustainable development are the following:

□ Refocus multilateral bank programs as well as bilateral assistance on projects that will be supportive of environmental regimes and Agenda 21 goals.

The multilateral banks lend billions of dollars annually for projects that promote unsustainable development. In the energy field, 95 percent of the World Bank's lending portfolio is still spent on large-scale, capital-intensive central power-generating stations. If the World Bank and other regional development banks were to shift their loan portfolios progressively away from such centralized projects toward a combination of smaller, decentralized installations, energy-efficiency projects, and renewable energy development, developing countries would get just as much or more energy at lower cost while reducing pollution and helping reduce the threat of global warming. In 1993, for example, the Bank approved a large hydroelectric project for Nepal, the Arun III dam, which would cost $750 million (an amount equal to Nepal's annual budget), displace communities, and damage an ecologically very fragile area. A counterproposal by Nepalese NGOs for a mix of small installations and renewable energy alternatives, which would avoid the environmental and social problems of the Arun dam project and employ largely local workers in construction, could supply the same amount of electricity at the same cost.[47] Similar shifts in lending in transportation and agriculture toward more sustainable alternatives to conventional projects would support international environmental regimes and sustainable development objectives without any overall increase in budgetary commitments.

ODA programs also could devote more resources to promoting the social bases of sustainable development, including basic health and nutrition, family planning and education—especially for women. Better health and education contribute to smaller families, more productive agriculture, higher incomes, and less stress on the environment and natural resources. According to one study, between 1988 and 1990 only about 6.5 percent of total bilateral ODA and 11 percent of multilateral ODA was allocated to such human development concerns, although funding for health and basic education was beginning to rise by the early 1990s.[48]

Since the early 1990s, UNDP and the United Nations Children's Fund (UNICEF) have advocated a plan under which bilateral and multilateral ODA agencies and the developing countries themselves would make commitments to parallel budgetary shifts to give greater priority to human resource development (health, nutrition, and basic education). In what UNDP calls the 20/20 Global Compact, developing countries would agree to increase the percentage of their national budgets going to human resource development programs from the current 13 percent on average to a minimum of 20 percent in return for a commitment by donor agencies to increase their investments in the same social sectors from the current 10 percent on average to 20 percent of total ODA. UNDP calculates that such a compact would generate $30 to $40 billion in additional investment in human development programs annually.[49] Most developing countries are sympathetic to the idea that more ODA should be focused on human resources development; a few, notably China, have opposed it. Although most states are sympathetic to establishment of a 20-percent basic floor of support for social development, the 1995 Copenhagen Social Summit endorsed the 20–20 concept only as a nonbinding goal.[50]

□ Tax international currency transactions, air travel, or the trade in arms or in fossil fuels to generate funds for support of sustainable development.

Taxes on international transactions vary enormously in potential for raising resources: A 1-percent charge on all air travel in 1989 would have generated about $1 billion; by the end of the century, it would probably generate twice that amount.[51] A global energy tax of $1 per barrel of oil or its coal equivalent would raise $66 billion annually. It could also be adjusted to the carbon content of the fuel, as proposed by the EC environment commissioner in 1989.[52] And a tax of just 0.005 percent on international movements of speculative capital, the ease and speed of which present a threat to the stability of currencies, would generate $15 billion a year.[53] That would be far more than would be needed to pay for all the U.N. peacekeeping efforts and thus could also be a major source of funding for global environmental protection efforts.[54] Each of these taxes has the additional advantage of raising the costs of activities that either add to environmental degradation or are otherwise destabilizing.

□ Forgive the debt obligations of the poorest developing countries and of lower-middle-income countries in return for sustainable development policy reforms and investments.

As noted in Chapter 4, heavy indebtedness often forces countries to mine their natural resources for export. It also diverts budgetary resources from sustainable development programs. The Paris Club of creditor nations, recognizing that the least developed countries do not have the capability to pay back the bilateral debts they owe, has begun to forgive some of these debts. In December 1991, the creditor nations—except for the United States and Australia—agreed to a 50-percent reduction in the debt-service payments due during a "consolidation period" of three or four years. But for half of the seriously indebted countries, that limited debt reduction was insufficient to bring debt-service payments into line with their ability to pay. Many of these countries will need up to 90-percent cancellation of the stock of debt to be financially viable. Meanwhile, the pressures of debt repayment force them to give little or no attention to the long-term environmental consequences of economic policies aimed at maximizing exports.

The Paris Club could adopt a debt-management policy aimed at promoting sustainable development by reducing the debt of the poorest countries to a level that would bring debt-service payments below 20 percent of export revenues—the level generally regarded as the maximum consistent with financial health.[55] Eligibility for Paris Club debt rescheduling or forgiveness in the past has been based on having an IMF program for macroeconomic reform in place, but additional debt-reduction benefits could be linked to sustainable policy reforms, such as eliminating environmentally harmful subsidies and increasing fees for logging concessions. Such conditionality would help governments make politically difficult policy shifts.

☐ Eliminate subsidies in industrialized countries for use of natural resources (water and energy) and for environmentally harmful activities (such as using pesticides and fertilizers) in order to set an example for developing countries.

According to the United Nations, approximately $1 trillion—5 percent of the world's GNP—is spent annually on environmentally damaging subsidies.[56] Ending such subsidies can save substantial financial resources while making economies more sustainable. For example, eliminating subsidies for irrigation of surplus crops grown in the United States could save $830 million annually.[57] In the late 1980s the Indonesian government saved $120 million annually by ending pesticide subsidies, and Brazil saved about $300 million annually by ending the fiscal and credit incentives for ranching, which had been the major factor in deforestation of the Amazon rainforest.

Despite the financial and environmental advantages of ending such subsidies, however, governments are usually reluctant to end policies that benefit powerful economic elites. The largest category of environmentally harmful subsidies in the industrialized world is subsidies for agricultural exports, which cost consumers and taxpayers in OECD countries over $300 billion annually.[58] Because of the resistance of powerful agricultural lobbies, European governments were unwilling to agree to phase them out during the Uruguay Round negotiations, even in the face of heavy pressure from the United States. As budgets continue to get tighter in the OECD countries, however, pressures to cut such subsidies are growing, increasing the chances for international agreement on the issue.

□ Negotiate international agreements between commodity producers and consumers on the sustainable management of and trade in specific commodities.

In recent years, researchers have advanced some innovative proposals for raising the prices of commodities in world trade and internalizing the environmental costs of their production through what some have called "international commodity-related environmental agreements" (ICREAs).[59] This proposal is fundamentally different from traditional commodity agreements proposed by producer countries, which were aimed at stabilizing commodity prices through buffer stock mechanisms for buying or selling supplies when prices went too high or low. An ICREA would levy a higher import tax on a commodity whose production costs have not internalized environmental costs and would then transfer the revenues back to the exporting country either for specific projects to assist in introducing new production techniques or in return for implementing policy reforms regarding sustainable management of the resource. It would thus permit increased resource flows to developing countries for sustainable development purposes without additional budgetary costs.

The biggest potential political obstacle to the negotiation of ICREAs is the reluctance of producer countries to agree to any increase in price that could reduce market demand for the commodity. In the case of timber, for example, any increase in prices of tropical forest products might permit temperate forest products to gain markets at the expense of tropical producers. Thus any agreement affecting the price of tropical timber would certainly have to apply to temperate and boreal timbers as well. And criteria and indicators of sustainable production of commodities would have to be agreed on by the international community.

CONCLUSION: THE PROSPECTS FOR GLOBAL ENVIRONMENTAL POLITICS

The stakes in global environmental politics will continue to increase in the coming decade as the costs of environmental degradation and of measures to reverse it grow and as global environmental regimes require greater changes in development strategies and production techniques to be effective. How far the international community will progress in implementing and strengthening environmental regimes and making progress on the objectives for sustainable development adopted at the Earth Summit will depend largely on four political factors:

☐ the willingness of some key state actors to assume lead roles and set an example;
☐ the incentives for potential veto states to support strong regimes;
☐ the size and sophistication of the worldwide network of citizens' movements, especially environmental and development NGOs;
☐ the effectiveness of multilateral institutions in facilitating agreements and supporting sustainable development.

The most important determinant of progress in regime formation, strengthening, and implementation will continue to be the active leadership of a major state or groups of states in each case. An agreement is likely to be strong and effective only if a strong coalition of lead states is actively engaged. Lead states must provide some combination of diplomatic influence, technical expertise, financial commitments, and pace-setting unilateral initiatives to induce swing states and potential veto states to commit to the regime or its strengthening.

The prospects for adequate leadership are somewhat different for each issue on the global environmental agenda, but the roles of major financial and trading states and blocs—the United States, Japan, the EU, and other members of the Group of Seven—will be crucial in almost every issue. On climate change, Germany, Denmark, and the Netherlands can be counted on to form the core of a lead-state coalition, but that will not be sufficient for significant progress without the United States, Japan, and the rest of the EU—or some combination of them—at least actively supporting a strong regime. Unless those states show that they will change their own energy-use patterns and speed the development and use of appropriate technologies in the rapidly industrializing countries, progress toward a strong climate regime will be slow. Serious domestic political obstacles to lead roles on climate remain in most OECD countries, but especially in the United States, the United Kingdom, and Japan.

The United States is the one state actor without whose leadership most environmental regimes are certain to be much weaker. When it is actively

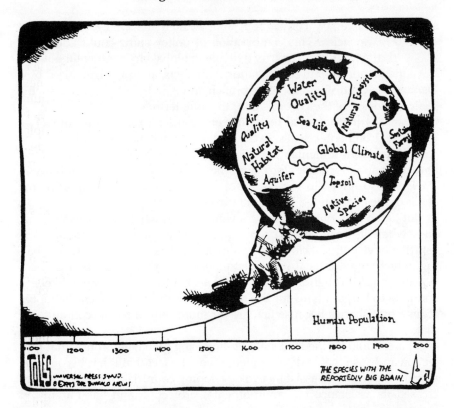

Tom Toles/*The Buffalo News* © 1993.

engaged in trying to forge consensus on stronger institutions or actions, it can often overcome reluctance on the part of other industrialized countries, as was the case in the negotiations on ozone depletion, African elephants, desertification, and restructuring the GEF. But when the United States has been a veto or swing state, as it has been on climate change, the negotiation of the Basel Convention, and parts of Agenda 21, the regime is inevitably weaker.

The future U.S. role in global environmental politics was clouded by the political upheaval of the 1994 congressional elections. Control of both House and Senate as well as the policy initiative shifted to a Republican Party whose leadership has been hostile to major elements of the sustainable development paradigm. The new majority could severely restrict U.S. financial support for global environmental regimes and sustainable development plans; reduce its commitment to implementing even the stabilization goal of the climate change regime; keep the United States outside the biodiversity convention; and weaken the UNEP, UNDP, and other U.N. agencies. This combination of policy shifts could add up to U.S. withdrawal from a constructive role in global environmental politics, but considerations of urgency, national interests, and prestige, raised by a Democratic-controlled executive branch and NGOs, could reverse such a radical revision of the U.S. role over the long term.

Japan has the potential for both veto and lead roles on a number of global environmental issues. In the past, Japan has shown a willingness to reconsider environmental policies that have generated strong protest abroad. It not only went along with the ban on African elephant ivory in 1989 but also agreed to stop its use of drift nets and to stop importing the shells of the endangered hawksbill turtle.

But Japan has continued to be a veto state on whaling and fisheries issues, where its position has been dominated by domestic economic interests that have political clout. The political tide has begun to shift on whaling, which is not crucial to the Japanese economy or diet, suggesting a possible breakthrough in the relatively near future. But Japan is likely to continue to bargain hard for the foreseeable future to weaken the global regime on fisheries because fish are far more central to its economy and diet.

Japan should be the lead state on financing global environmental protection and sustainable development given the fact that it has become the world's top donor of assistance to developing countries. It has already increased its assistance for environmental protection and has minimized the tied aid that used to make up the bulk of its development assistance. But so far Japan has not exercised political leadership on this issue within the GEF or in negotiations on environmental conventions, partly because of a reluctance to be out in front of the United States on international issues. Given the fact that acid rain originating in China represents a growing problem for Japan, Japan could emerge as a leader on cooperation with China on industrial pollution and energy use, with important implications for the future of the climate convention.

Despite shifts in public opinion favoring stronger environmental policies, Japan is not likely to have a powerful environmental NGO sector in the foreseeable future. And the likelihood that Japan will be governed by a series of coalition governments in the next few years makes it less likely that it will take any major policy initiatives on the global environment that would propel it into international leadership.

The prospects for a climate protocol limiting greenhouse-gas emissions depend in part on whether China and India will give sufficient priority to investments in energy-efficiency gains to minimize carbon emissions. The absence of pluralism and of a tradition of free speech and press in China reduces that likelihood.

Other important developing countries such as Brazil, Mexico, and Indonesia, all of which will be key to progress on biodiversity and forest regimes, are at different stages of political development. Brazil has a rapidly evolving democratic system in which **civil society** has a growing role. The agroindustrial elite continue to be a strong political force, and some sectors still resist limitations on their right to exploit the Amazon's resources. But there are now counterbalancing forces that can possibly influence Brazilian policy toward biodiversity and forest regimes. Since 1988, popular groups with support from NGOs and governments abroad have begun to play a role in formulating plans for sustainable development in the Amazon region.[60] And in Mexico, where a one-party authoritarian state has had limited meaningful political participation in the past, NGOs emerged for the first time as a major democratic force in the context of the 1994 presidential election. That could also be a signal that policies toward exploitation of natural resources will come under increased public scrutiny in coming years.[61]

Indonesia remains much closer to a traditional patrimonial political system. Close links exist between the bureaucratic elite and a business elite with economic interests in logging the country's forest resources, and civil society has limited scope to assert itself. But even there, local farmers who were trained to analyze pest-management problems have shown that it is possible to put pressure on government when the objective (in this case, pesticide policy) is ostensibly nonpolitical.[62] Environmental NGOs are also becoming more skilled and self-confident in lobbying the government, especially on forest policy.

The worldwide NGO movement is continuing to increase its influence on global environmental politics by adding to its numbers, becoming more sophisticated politically, and cooperating more effectively across national boundaries and regions. Worldwide NGO networks on biodiversity and desertification involving regional and national focal points are mapping strategies for monitoring the process of treaty implementation in every country and for ensuring popular participation in national action programs and strategies. The global climate network is continuing to develop its technical expertise in analyzing climate action plans. International NGOs such as Greenpeace and the World Wildlife Fund are playing key roles in developing substantial ideas for negotiations on fisheries and land-based sources of marine pollution.

More important to environmental regimes in the future will be the continued growth of campaigns and systems by which consumers can express their preference for products that are sustainably produced over those that are not. Organizations in the United States and the Netherlands, for example, plan campaigns to reduce wood consumption in their countries over a ten-year period.[63] Consumer consciousness about sustainability could powerfully shape the politics of world forest management in the coming years.

Citizens' movements for environmental protection are most effective when translated into electoral power, whether through green parties or clear voter preferences for a party or candidate supporting an active role in international cooperation on the environment. In recent years there have been significant fluctuations in the political salience of environmental issues in European elections, apparently on the rise again at this writing, but the global environment has not yet emerged as a major issue in U.S. or Japanese national elections.

International organizations and institutions have helped create and strengthen global environmental regimes by bringing states together to negotiate, by organizing international cooperation at a regional or global level, by monitoring the state of the global environment, and by providing financial support. Some observers have complained, however, that existing institutions, including UNEP and the Commission on Sustainable Development (CSD), do not provide sufficiently coherent policymaking on the global environment and that they lack either the authority under international law or the actual political power to impose sanctions on countries that reject international regulations or norms embraced by most nations. Moreover, UNEP has far too small a budget and staff and too narrow a mandate to coordinate the activities of all U.N. agencies and has lost the initiative in agenda setting to the General Assembly. Multilateral financial institutions still subordinate sustainable development to other functions. The CSD, if it is not able to effectively monitor progress on Agenda 21 or fails to develop strategies for holding state actors accountable, is in danger of becoming irrelevant.

In recent years, some governments and observers have called for a new global environmental organization that could overcome some of these limitations. A proposal by New Zealand and adopted by twenty-four heads of state at an international conference at The Hague in March 1989 called for a "global legislative organization" for the environment that could take effective action "even if . . . unanimous agreement has not been achieved."[64] More recently, others have called for a new "global environmental organization" that would have a stronger policymaking mandate and more resources than any existing IO, and perhaps the ability to impose sanctions as well.

Such proposals seek to avoid the problem of least-common-denominator politics, which is inherent in an international system based on national sovereignty and consensus. Critics of the idea, including the authors, have doubts about the appropriateness of a single world organization for creating rules on such a wide group of issues. But it is unlikely that a new enviromental authority will be created any time in the foreseeable future because the United States, China, Japan, and other major states remain strongly opposed to any system that would take away their sovereign right to choose the international regimes to which they will agree. Most developing countries are sensitive as well to sovereignty on global environmental issues, fearing that they might be pushed unwillingly into agreements that would limit their freedom to determine their own development strategies. For the time being, strengthening international enviromental regimes will continue to depend on a wide variety of international organizations and national governments and on the vigilance of interested parties, including NGOs.

The relatively brief history of global environmental politics offers abundant evidence that a fundamental paradigm shift and a profound social and political transformation are already under way, although progress is proceeding at different rates in different countries, in different national and international institutions, and on different issues. Underneath the fluctuations of electoral politics and economic cycles, there is an inexorable evolution in international relations toward more effective cooperation on global environmental threats. The only question is whether that cooperation will develop rapidly enough to stave off and reverse those threats.

□ □ □

Discussion Questions

CHAPTER ONE

1. Discuss the ways in which population and environmental factors interact. What is the effect on forests? On energy? Why is per capita consumption an issue?

2. Why are global environmental trends an issue now? Why weren't they an issue earlier in this century? What has changed physically and in terms of consciousness?

3. What is a veto state? Why is it so important in global environmental politics?

4. How are global environmental politics different from security and global economic politics? How are they similar to human rights politics?

5. According to the different theoretical approaches described in this chapter, what factors make it easier or more difficult to achieve strong international agreement on a global environmental issue?

6. What is sustainable development? What are the differences in understanding of the concept? If pursued in the United States, how do you think it would change our economy and lifestyles? What are its implications for developing countries? For North-South relations?

7. Do you believe that global environmental issues should be viewed as "national security" issues? What characteristics of these issues suggest that the term is appropriate, or inappropriate?

CHAPTER TWO

1. How have industries affected international environmental issues in the past? In what ways, and why, is that role changing?

2. In what ways do the domestic politics of various states influence their policies toward global environmental issues?

3. Why may some states feel that there are "winners" and "losers" in a particular proposal for international cooperation on the environment, even though it may be in the interests of all states?

4. Why are multilateral banks, commercial banks, and bilateral development-assistance programs important to global environmental politics?

5. Why have environmental NGOs grown in importance in global environmental politics in the past decade?

6. What NGOs would you expect in a coalition on ozone depletion? The climate convention? The biodiversity convention? Why? What governments would they befriend or attack?

7. How does the role of particular U.S. industries affect the position of the U.S. government on international issues?

8. Make up a profile of any of the states frequently mentioned in this chapter—the OECD countries, China, India, Indonesia, Mexico, Brazil, Malaysia—and describe how active they are in lead or blocking roles. Could you do the same for the former Soviet Union? What other countries are conspicuously absent?

9. When might "soft law" take on the characteristics of an international agreement?

10. How has technology contributed to the growing influence and effectiveness of the environmental NGOs in the past decade?

CHAPTER THREE

1. On which global environmental issues has new scientific evidence altered the positions of government negotiators? On what other issues might it be relevant? In which has it been irrelevant? Why?

2. Consider the veto coalitions opposing strong action on the issues in this chapter. What are the primary motives of each individual member? What are the reasons for those coalitions weakening?

3. Trace the role of specific U.S. environmental NGOs such as Friends of the Earth, Greenpeace, Environmental Defense Fund, or World Wildlife Fund through the regimes discussed in this chapter. Which appear to be most active on which issues?

4. Trace the role of a particular state on a variety of issues and try to assess the extent of its involvement in leadership or blocking roles.

5. What might be the effect of growing economic prosperity or recession in the United States or other countries on the specific global environmental issues discussed?

6. Discuss two framework conventions and the political, economic, and environmental factors that influenced their evolutions.

CHAPTER FOUR

1. Compare the trade/environment issue with other global environmental issues of the regimes discussed in Chapter 3. Are NAFTA or GATT environmental regimes in any sense? Why or why not?

2. Why do developing-country spokespersons often get angry when population and environmental issues are linked? Do you think they are justified?

3. In what ways are the interests of developing countries and industrialized countries at odds over global environmental issues? In what sense are they compatible?

4. Explain why environmental "conditionality" and the concept of "new and additional funding" have become key issues in North-South relations regarding global environmental issues.

5. Explain how trade and environmental patterns affect each other. What are the main impacts of each on the other?

6. How might previous trade experience with the United States sharpen European or developing-country concern about possible U.S. environmental trade measures?

7. Do you think that Agenda 21 can be considered an international environmental regime?

8. Explain how developing countries' concerns about economic growth and jobs might affect their position on ozone depletion or the climate treaty. Why would their position on the Basel Convention (to control international trade in toxic wastes) be different?

9. Imagine yourself in a debate on the pros and cons of imposing environmental conditionality on international loans and assistance. Prepare the arguments on both sides.

CHAPTER FIVE

1. Why is monitoring so important a factor in regime implementation?

2. Discuss the importance and limits of popular consciousness in forging strong environmental regimes over the long term. What factors could nullify its impact?

3. What unexpected scientific or technical breakthrough, environmental disaster, or economic or political crisis might stimulate the United States or other lead states to push boldly ahead or to pull back from some issue on the global environmental agenda? Analyze the domestic political and international factors that might be pertinent.

4. Pick your favorite global environmental issue and develop a strategy for strengthening or weakening its purpose or implementation.

5. Do you think the voters' identification of Senator Gore as an environmentalist and internationalist hurt or helped him at the polls in 1992?

6. What are the differences between global environmental issues on which international regimes have been established and those on which negotiations are continuing? Is there any pattern of differences?

□ □ □

Notes

CHAPTER ONE

1. Nafis Sadik, *The State of World Population 1993* (New York: United Nations Population Fund, 1993), pp. 1–2.

2. Douglas Southgate, "Tropical Deforestation and Agricultural Development in Latin America," World Bank, Environment Department, Divisional Working Paper no. 1991-20, March 1990.

3. Alex de Sherbinnin, *Population and Consumption Issues for Environmentalists*, (Washington, D.C.: Population Reference Bureau for the Pew Charitable Trusts' Global Stewardship Initiative, October 1993), pp. 18–20.

4. World Resources Institute (WRI), *World Resources 1992–1993* (New York: Oxford University Press, 1992), pp. 176–180.

5. Nafis Sadik, *The State of World Population 1989* (New York: United Nations Population Fund, 1989), p. 2.

6. Sandra Postel and Lori Heise, "The Fragile Forest," *Courier*, January 1989, p. 11.

7. "Science Capsule," *Earth Quest*, Summer 1992 (Boulder, Colorado). For past projections, see World Commission on Environment and Development, *Our Common Future* (New York: Oxford University Press, 1987), p. 170; Diane Fisher, ed., *Options for Reducing Greenhouse Gas Emissions* (Stockholm: Stockholm Environment Institute, 1990), p. v; and James Gustave Speth, "Environmental Pollution: A Long-Term Perspective," in *Earth '88, Changing Geographic Perspectives*, proceedings of the Centennial Symposium (Washington, D.C.: National Geographic Society, 1988), p. 280.

8. Fisher, *Options for Reducing Greenhouse Gas Emissions*, p. xi. The IPCC estimates that CO_2 emissions from energy, cement production, and deforestation could reach 15 gigatons by 2020. See Intergovernmental Panel on Climate Change, *1992 IPCC Supplement, Scientific Assessment of Climate Change* (Cambridge: Cambridge University Press, 1992), especially pp. 10–13.

9. WRI, *World Resources 1990–1991* (New York: Oxford University Press, 1990), p. 12.

10. Daniel A. Lashoff, "The Dynamic Greenhouse: Feedback Processes That May Influence Future Concentrations of Atmospheric Trace Gases and Climatic Change," *Climatic Change* 14 (1989), p. 213.

11. U.S. EPA, Office of Policy Planning and Evaluation and Office of Research and Development, "Policy Options for Stabilizing Global Climate Change," draft report to Congress, Executive Summary, February 1989, pp. 17–18.

12. Jill Jaeger, "Development Policies for Responding to Climatic Change," World Meteorological Organization and United Nations Environment Programme, WMO/TD no. 225, April 1988, pp. iii–iv.

13. Speth, "Environmental Pollution," p. 263.

14. Caroline Thomas, *The Environment in International Relations* (London: Royal Institute of International Affairs, 1992), pp. 199–210, 213–214.

15. World Meteorological Organization, "Scientific Assessment of Ozone Depletion," WMO Global Ozone Research and Monitoring Project Report no. 25, 1991; Richard Stolarski et al., "Measured Trends in Stratospheric Ozone," *Science* (April 17, 1992), pp. 340–342.

16. Boyce Rensberger, "Decline of Ozone-Harming Chemicals Suggests Atmosphere May Heal Itself," *Washington Post,* August 26, 1993, p. A11; and *CFC Phase-Out: An Environmental Balancing Act* (Washington, D.C.: Environmental and Energy Study Institute, 1994), p. 1.

17. See Manfred Teveni and Alan H. Teramura, "UV-B Effects on Terrestrial Plants," *Photochemistry and Photobiology* 50 (1989), pp. 479–487; A. H. Terramura, M. Tevini, J. F. Bornman, M. M. Caldwell, G. Kulandaivelu, and L. O. Bjorn, *UNEP Environmental Effects Panel Report* (Nairobi: UNEP, 1991), pp. 25–32; R. C. Smith et al., "Ozone Depletion: Ultraviolent Radiation and Phytoplankton Biology in Antarctic Waters," *Science* 235 (February 21, 1992), pp. 255–258; Warwick L. Morrison, "The Effects of Ultraviolent Radiation on the Immune System in Humans," *Photochemistry and Photobiology* 50 (1989), pp. 515–524.

18. Food and Agriculture Organization, "Review of the State of World Marine Fishery Resources" FAO Fisheries Paper no. 335 (Rome: FAO, 1993), Table 1, p. 3.

19. Jumanah Farah, *Pesticide Policies in Developing Countries: Do They Encourage Excessive Pesticide Use?* (Washington, D.C.: World Bank, 1993), p. 4; Lester H. Brown, Hal Kane, and David Malin Roodman, *Vital Signs, 1994* (Washington, D.C.: Worldwatch Institute, 1994), p. 93.

20. Satu Nurmi, "Issues and Problems in the Protection of the Marine Environment," in John E. Carroll, ed., *International Environmental Diplomacy* (Cambridge: Cambridge University Press, 1988), pp. 214–215; "Marine Pollution from Land-Based Sources: Facts and Figures," *UNEP Industry and Environment,* January-June 1992; Organization for Economic Cooperation and Development, *The State of the Environment, 1985* (Washington, D.C.: OECD, 1985), p. 79; and William J. Broad, "Russians Describe Extensive Dumping of Nuclear Waste," *New York Times,* April 17, 1993.

21. Michael M'Gonigle and Mark W. Zacher, *Pollution, Politics and International Law: Tankers at Sea* (Berkeley: University of California Press, 1979), p. 34; *The Global 2000 Report to the President* (Washington, D.C.: Council on Environmental Quality and Department of State, 1980), p. 133; Nurmi, "Issues and Problems," pp. 214–215; and Robert A. Shinn, *The International Politics of Marine Pollution* (New York: Praeger, 1974), pp. 31–32.

22. Sandra Postel, "Facing Water Scarcity," in Lester Brown et al., *State of the World 1993* (New York: W. W. Norton, 1993), p. 22.

23. WRI, *World Resources 1992–1993*, pp. 111–114; and Maya K. Ajmere, *Our Diminishing World: The Land/Population Crisis* (Washington, D.C.: Population Institute, 1991), p. 7.

24. Jean-Paul Malingreau and Compton J. Tucker, "Large-Scale Deforestation in the Southeastern Amazon Basin of Brazil," *Ambio* 17 (1988), p. 49; WRI, *World Resources, 1992–1993*, pp. 118–119.

25. National Science Board Task Force on Global Biodiversity, *Loss of Biological Diversity: A Global Crisis Requiring International Solutions* (Washington, D.C.: National Science Foundation, 1989), pp. 1, 3; interview with E.O. Wilson, "All Creatures, Great and Small," *Defenders,* September-October 1992, p. 10.

26. Food and Agriculture Organization, *Harvesting Nature's Diversity* (Rome: FAO, 1993); Cary Fowler and Pat Mooney, *Shattering: Food, Policy, and the Loss of Biodiversity* (Tuscon: University of Arizona Press, 1990).

27. For an early effort to categorize the different types of international environmental problems, see Clifford S. Russell and Hans H. Landsberg, "International Environmental Problems—A Taxonomy," *Science* 172 (June 25, 1972), pp. 1307–1314.

28. See Susan Strange, "Cave! Hic Dragones: A Critique of Regime Analysis," *International Organization* 36 (Spring 1982), pp. 479–496.

29. M'Gonigle and Zacher, *Pollution, Politics and International Law,* pp. 58–59, 84–85, 93–96; Jan Schneider, *World Public Order of the Environment: Toward an International Ecological Law and Organization* (Toronto: University of Toronto Press, 1979), pp. 33, 92–93.

30. For an analytical overview of theoretical approaches, see Stephan Haggard and Beth A. Simmons, "Theories of International Regimes," *International Organization* 41 (Summer 1987), pp. 491–517.

31. Robert O. Keohane and Joseph S. Nye, *Power and Interdependence* (Boston: Little, Brown, 1977), pp. 50–51.

32. For the former approach, see Robert Gilpin, *The Political Economy of International Relations* (Princeton, N.J.: Princeton University Press, 1987); Joseph M. Grieco, "Anarchy and the Limits of Cooperation: A Realist Critique of the Newest Liberal Institutionalism," *International Organization* 42 (Summer 1988), pp. 485–508; and Strange, "Cave! Hic Dragones," pp. 337–343. Susan Strange, "The Persistent Myth of Lost Hegemony," *International Organization* 41 (Summer 1987), p. 570, argues that the erosion of international regimes has been caused by inconsistency in U.S. policy rather than the loss of U.S. global hegemony per se.

33. Oran R. Young, "The Politics of International Regime Formation: Managing Natural Resources and the Environment," *International Organization* 43 (Summer 1989), p. 355.

34. Fen Osler Hampson, "Climate Change: Building International Coalitions of the Like-minded," *International Journal* 45 (Winter 1989–1990), pp. 36–74.

35. Young, "The Politics of International Regime Formation," p. 367. Young cites six determinants of success in bargaining for regime formation, but the other five are either stating the obvious (effective leadership) or are said only to increase the probability of success (the availability of effective compliance mechanisms).

36. See Peter M. Haas, "Do Regimes Matter? Epistemic Communities and Mediterranean Pollution Control," *International Organization* 43 (Summer 1989), pp. 378–403.

37. The issue of ocean dumping of radioactive wastes, in which scientific evidence was explicitly rejected as the primary basis for decisionmaking by antidumping states, is analyzed in Judith Spiller and Cynthia Hayden, "Radwaste at Sea: A New Era of Polarization or a New Basis for Consensus?" *Ocean Development and International Law* 19 (1988), pp. 345–366.

38. The concept of dominant social paradigm is developed in Willis Harman, *An Incomplete Guide to the Future* (New York: W. W. Norton, 1979), Chapter 2; and in Dennis Pirages and Paul Ehrlich, *Ark II: Social Response to Environmental Imperatives* (New York: Viking, 1974), Chapter 2.

39. Harold and Margaret Sprout, *The Ecological Perspective in Human Affairs* (Princeton, N.J.: Princeton University Press, 1965); Kenneth Boulding, "The Economics of the Coming Spaceship Earth," in H. E. Jarrett, ed., *Environmental Quality in a Growing Economy* (Baltimore: Johns Hopkins University Press, 1966).

40. For an analysis of neoclassical economic assumptions as they bear on environmental management, see Daniel A. Underwood and Paul G. King, "On the Ideological Foundations of Environmental Policy," *Ecological Economics* 1 (1989), pp. 317–322.

41. See Michael E. Colby, *Environmental Management in Development: The Evolution of Paradigms* (Washington, D.C.: World Bank, 1990).

42. John McCormick, *Reclaiming Paradise: The Global Environmental Movement* (Bloomington: Indiana University Press, 1989), p. 67.

43. See Clem Tisdell, "Sustainable Development: Differing Perspectives of Ecologists and Economists, and Relevance to LDCs," *World Development* 16 (1988), pp. 377–378.

44. Donella H. Meadows et al., *The Limits to Growth* (New York: Universe Books, 1972); *Global 2000 Report*.

45. Julian Simon and Herman Kahn, eds., *The Resourceful Earth* (Oxford: Basil Blackwell, 1984).

46. For an account of the background of the sustainable development concept, see U.N. Center for Transnational Corporations, *Environmental Aspects of the Activities of Transnational Corporations: A Survey* (New York: U.N., 1985).

47. See World Commission on Environment and Development, *Our Common Future*.

48. See Jim MacNeill, "Sustainable Development, Economics and the Growth Imperative," paper presented at the conference "The Economics of Sustainable Development," Smithsonian Institution, Washington, D.C., January 23–26, 1990.

49. See Edith Brown Weiss, "In Fairness to Future Generations," *Environment* 32 (April 1990), pp. 7ff. See similar arguments made in *Our Own Agenda*, report of the Latin American and Caribbean Commission on Development and Environment (Washington, D.C., and New York: Inter-American Development Bank and United Nations Development Programme, 1990).

50. See Alan Durning, "How Much Is Enough?" *Worldwatch* 3 (November-December 1990), pp. 12–19.

51. See Yusuf J. Ahmad, Salah El Serafy, and Ernst Lutz, eds., *Environmental Accounting for Sustainable Development* (Washington, D.C.: World Bank, 1989). For a concrete example of how natural resources accounting would work, see Robert

Repetto et al., *Accounts Overdue: Natural Resources Depreciation in Costa Rica* (Washington, D.C.: World Resources Institute, 1991).

52. See Partha Dasgupta and Karl Goran Maler, "The Environment and Emerging Development Issues," paper presented at the World Bank Conference on Development Economics, April 26–27, 1990, pp. 14–20; Herman E. Daly, "Toward a Measure of Sustainable Social Net National Product," in Ahmad, Serafy, and Lutz, eds., *Environmental Accounting for Sustainable Development*, pp. 8–9; and Herman E. Daly and John B. Cobb Jr., *For the Common Good: Redirecting the Economy Toward Community, the Environment and a Sustainable Future* (Boston: Beacon Press, 1989), pp. 368–373, 401–455. A similar effort to rate the distributive effects of national policies is embodied in the United Nations Development Programme's human development indicators in its annual *Human Development Report* (New York: Oxford University Press, 1994), Chapter 5.

53. See, for example, Dasgupta and Maler, "The Environment and Emerging Issues," p. 22.

54. See Robert Repetto, *Promoting Environmentally Sound Economic Progress: What the North Can Do* (Washington, D.C.: World Resources Institute, 1990); and Daly, "Toward a Measure of Sustainable Social Net National Product."

55. *Economic Policies for Sustainable Development*, ministerial brief, Conference on Environment and Development in Asia and the Pacific, October 10–16, 1990, Bangkok, Thailand (Manila: Asian Development Bank, October 1990); Latin American and Caribbean Commission on Development and Environment, *Our Own Agenda;* and Organization of American States, Permanent Council, *Status Report Submitted by the Chairman of the Special Working Group on the Environment* (Washington, D.C.: General Secretariat of the OAS, February 6, 1991).

56. Palme Commission on Disarmament and Security Issues, *A World at Peace: Common Security in the Twenty-first Century* (Stockholm: PCDSI, 1989).

57. *Environmental Security: A Report Contributing to the Concept of Comprehensive Security* (New York: International Peace Research Institute, U.N. Environment Programme, Programme on Military Activities and the Human Environment, 1989); George F. Kennan, "Morality and Foreign Policy," *Foreign Affairs* 64 (Winter 1985–1986), pp. 215–217; Jessica Tuchman Mathews, "Redefining Security," *Foreign Affairs* 68, no. 2 (Spring 1989); and Peter H. Gleick, "Environment, Resources and International Security and Politics," in E. Arnet, ed., *Science and International Security: Responding to a Changing World* (Washington, D.C.: American Association for the Advancement of Science, 1990).

58. Bruce Parrott, "Soviet National Security Under Gorbachev," *Problems of Communism,* November-December 1988, p. 19.

59. In 1990, the United States, the United Kingdom, and France were the only three states to vote against a General Assembly resolution that called for an expert study of the "potential uses of resources such as know-how, infrastructure and production currently allocated to military activities to protect the environment." Most of the rest of NATO abstained. *Disarmament Times* (New York), November 1990, p. 1.

60. Lawrence Freedman, "Order and Disorder in the New World," *Foreign Affairs: America and the World 1991–1992* 71, no. 1 (1992), p. 29.

CHAPTER TWO

1. Paul Kennedy, *Preparing for the Twenty-first Century* (New York: Random House, 1993), especially Chapters 3, 4, 5, 7; John Maxwell Hamilton, "Everybody's a Diplomat," *Boston Globe Sunday Magazine,* April 1, 1990; and Michael Clough, "Grassroots Policymaking," *Foreign Affairs* 73, no. 1 (January-February 1994), pp. 2–7.

2. David Day, *The Whale War* (Vancouver and Toronto: Douglas and MacIntyre, 1987), pp. 103–107.

3. *Times* (London), May 14, 1990.

4. Michael M'Gonigle and Mark W. Zacher, *Pollution, Politics and International Law: Tankers at Sea* (Berkeley: University of California Press, 1979).

5. The largest cattle ranches in the deforested regions of the Amazon—some more than a quarter of a million acres—are owned by the great industrial and banking consortia and corporations of Brazil. See Susanna B. Hecht, "Environment, Development and Politics: Capital Accumulation and the Livestock Sector in Eastern Amazonia," *World Development* 13, no. 6 (June 1985), pp. 667–671, 678; Susanna B. Hecht and Andrew Cockburn, *The Fate of the Forest* (New York: Verso, 1989), p. 45.

6. For the Energy and Interior Departments' positions on environmental protection in the context of a minerals regime in Antarctica, see Barbara Mitchell, "Undermining Antarctica," *Technology Review,* February-March 1988, p. 56.

7. John McCormick, *Acid Earth: The Global Threat of Acid Pollution* (London: Earthscan, 1985), pp. 88–90.

8. The German Green Party lost all of its parliamentary members in the first all-German elections since 1932 because it opposed reunification, but it had begun to rebound by mid-1991, when polls showed it had the support of 6 percent of the voters—above the 5 percent needed to achieve representation in the parliament. See Wolfgang Rudig, "Green Party Politics Around the World," *Environment* 33, no. 8 (October 1991), pp. 7–9.

9. Denmark has the highest ratio of environmental organization membership in the entire world: The combined memberships of its environmental organizations are greater than the total population of the country. Brian Wynne, "Implementation of Greenhouse Gas Reductions in the European Community: Institutional and Cultural Factors," *Global Environmental Change Report* (March 1993), pp. 113, 122.

10. *UNEP News,* September-October 1987, p. 12.

11. *Earth Summit Update,* no. 7 (March 1992), p. 3.

12. For official statements emphasizing these points, see *Statement of Australia,* Response Strategies Working Group of the IPCC, January 30–February 1, 1989; "Foreign Policy and the Environment," address by the minister of foreign affairs and trade, Senator Gareth Evans, Brisbane, March 14, 1990, in *Australian Issues* (Washington, D.C.: Embassy of Australia).

13. *Worldwatch* (September-October 1990), p. 6.

14. Carolyn Thomas, *The Environment in International Relations* (London: Royal Institute of International Affairs, 1992), p. 228.

15. "Report of the Energy Demand Screening Group of the Indian Planning Commission," cited in *Indian Post* (Bombay), December 4, 1989.

16. On EU ambitions for global leadership on the environment, see Wynne, "Implementation of Greenhouse Gas Reductions," p. 102; Paleokrassas is quoted in *Energy, Economics and Climate Change,* July 1994, p. 14.

17. *Washington Post,* June 9, 1992.

18. Press release, City of Portland, Oregon, November 10, 1993; *Worldwatch* (March-April 1994), p. 7.

19. *Environmental News from the Netherlands,* no. 2 (1992), pp. 7–8.

20. Personal communication from Jaime Lerner, mayor, Curitiba, Brazil, May 8, 1993. As a follow-up to UNCED, the mayor of Manchester, England, hosted a world conference, "Cities and Sustainable Development," in October 1993.

21. For a discussion of California's international interests, see James O. Goldsborough, "California's Foreign Policy," *Foreign Affairs* (Spring 1993), pp. 88–96.

22. Eric Rodenburg, *Eyeless in Gaia: The State of Global Environmental Monitoring* (Washington, D.C.: World Resources Institute, 1991); "Tropical Deforestation: Not Just a Problem in Amazonia," *Science* 259 (March 5, 1993), p. 1390.

23. Remarks by UNEP executive director Elizabeth Dowdeswell, Washington, D.C., October 14, 1994.

24. Richard Elliott Benedick, "The Ozone Protocol: A New Global Diplomacy," *Conservation Foundation Letter,* no. 4 (1989), pp. 6–7, and *Ozone Diplomacy* (Cambridge: Harvard University Press, 1991), pp. 109–110.

25. "Discussion of Major UNEP Priority Activities with Executive Director," undated document in files of UNEP, Washington, D.C., office.

26. U.N. official Peter H. Sands has described these soft-law alternatives to treaties in *Lessons Learned in Global Environmental Governance* (Washington, D.C.: World Resources Institute, 1990), pp. 16–17.

27. See Khalil Sesmou, "The Food and Agriculture Organization of the United Nations: An Insider's View," *Ecologist* 21 (March-April 1991), pp. 47–56, and other critical analyses in this special issue on the FAO.

28. For FAO's vision of the TFAP, see Committee on Forest Development in the Tropics, Seventh Session, "Draft Proposals for Action Programmes in Tropical Forestry," FAO: FDT/85/3, April 1985. For other assessments of TFAP and FAO's role, see Robert Winterbottom, *Taking Stock: The Tropical Forestry Action Plan After Five Years* (Washington, D.C.: World Resources Institute, 1990); Charles J. Lankester, principal technical adviser, UNDP, "The Earth's Green Mantle," address to World Forestry Charter Gathering, London, December 1989.

29. *International Environment Reporter,* October 10, 1990, p. 427.

30. See "Researchers Score Victory over Pesticides—and Pests—in Asia," *Science* 256 (May 29, 1992), pp. 1272–1273.

31. Michael Hansen, *Sustainable Agriculture and Rural Development: FAO at the Crossroads* (Yonkers, N.Y.: Consumers Union of the United States, 1993), pp. 16–18.

32. This formulation is used in the context of a different conceptualization of the role of IOs in global environmental policymaking in Marc A. Levy, Robert O. Keohane, and Peter M. Haas, "Improving the Effectiveness of International Environmental Institutions," in Peter M. Haas, Robert O. Keohane, and Marc A. Levy, eds., *Institutions for the Earth: Sources of Effective International Environmental Protection* (Cambridge, Mass., and London: MIT Press, 1993), p. 400.

33. India, whose high level of defense spending was criticized in the 1994 *Human Development Report*, complained publicly that UNDP's pressure on countries to conform to its norm for allocation of resources was in contradiction to national sovereignty. See Jack Freeman, "Development Report: Southern Nations Attack an Emerging Premise of UN Policy," and "What India Told the G-77 About the Report," *Earth Times*, October 15, 1994, pp. 6–7.

34. See *The World Bank Annual Report 1994* (Washington, D.C.: World Bank, 1994), pp. 80, 90, 96, 102, 108, 118.

35. For a critical analysis of the environmental impacts of various multilateral development bank loans, see Bruce Rich, *Mortgaging the Earth: The World Bank, Environmental Impoverishment, and the Crisis of Development* (Boston: Beacon Press, 1994).

36. David A. Wirth, *Environmental Reform of the Multilateral Development Banks* (Midland, Mich.: C. S. Mott Foundation, 1992), p. 12.

37. World Bank, *Monthly Operational Summary of the Bank and IDA Proposed Projects* (Washington, D.C.: World Bank, February 15, 1992.

38. See World Bank, *World Development Report 1992, Development and the Environment* (New York: Oxford University Press, 1992), Chapter 6, for a summary of Bank energy policies; and Environmental Defense Fund and Natural Resources Defense Council, *Power Failure, A Review of the World Bank's Implementation of Its New Energy Policies* (Washington, D.C.: Author, March 1994), especially pp. 13–14.

39. For analyses documenting negative consequences of adjustment lending conditions on sustainable development, see Wilfrido Cruz and Robert Repetto, *The Environmental Effects of Stabilization and Structural Adjustment Programs: The Philippines Case* (Washington, D.C.: World Resources Institute, 1992); Robert Repetto, "Designing Sustainable Macroeconomic Adjustment Policies," unpublished paper, n.d.; Marijke Torfs, *Effects of the IMF Structural Adjustment Programs on Social Sectors of Third World Countries* (Washington, D.C.: Friends of the Earth U.S., May 1992).

40. David Reed, ed., *Structural Adjustment and the Environment* (Boulder, Colo.: Westview Press, 1992), esp. pp. 161–178.

41. For a defense of the IMF's macroeconomic policy prescriptions in environmental terms, see Ved P. Gandhi, "Macroeconomic Adjustment and the Environment: A Personal View," paper presented at the International Round Table Meeting "Structural Adjustment and the Environment," Berlin, November 10–13, 1992. In some cases, such as Brazil and Costa Rica, adjustment-lending pressures did contribute to the elimination of credit and other subsidies that had accelerated tropical deforestation.

42. *OED Precis*, June 1992.

43. "IMF Reviews Its Approach to Environmental Issues," *IMF Survey*, April 15, 1991, p. 124.

44. "Seminar Explores Links Between Macro Policy and the Environment," *IMF Survey*, June 14, 1993, p. 192.

45. European Commission, *Environmental Policy in the European Community*, 4th ed. (Luxembourg: European Commission, 1990).

46. Personal communications from Heraldo Muñoz, Chilean ambassador to the OAS, 1990–1994, and founding chair of the OAS Permanent Commission on the Environment.

47. "United Nations Officials See Basel Treaty as 'Limping' into Effect with Limited Support," *International Environment Reporter*, May 6, 1992, pp. 275–277; and "SADCC Policies on Food, Agriculture, Natural Resources and the Environment," South African Centre for Cooperation in Agricultural Research, Occasional Publication no. 4, 1989, revised 1990, Gaborne, Botswana, 1990.

48. Personal communication with Jorge Cabrera, coordinator of CCAD's small secretariat, March 24, 1994. The treaty, the Regional Convention for the Management and Conservation of Forest Natural Ecosystems and the Development of Forestry Plantations, was signed in Guatemala City by Panama, Costa Rica, Honduras, Guatemala, Nicaragua, and El Salvador in October 1993.

49. *Environment, Australia's International Agenda* (Canberra: Department of Foreign Affairs and Trade, January 1994); "A Summary Report on the Conference on the Sustainable Development of Small Island Developing States," *Earth Negotiations Bulletin* 8, no. 17 (March 14), 1993.

50. For the official U.N. definition, see Jens Martens, "NGOs in the UN System: The Participation of Non-Governmental Organizations in Environment and Development Institutions of the United Nations," Projectstelle UNCED, DNR/BUND, Bonn, September 1992, p. 4.

51. "NGO Influence Grows Worldwide," *EnviroNet* 3, no. 1 (Spring 1994), p. 6.

52. See Julie Fisher, *The Road from Rio: Sustainable Development and the Nongovernmental Movement in the Third World* (Westport, Conn.: Praeger, 1993), pp. 123–128; Nonita Yap, "NGOs and Sustainable Development," *International Journal* 45 (Winter 1989–1990), pp. 75–105.

53. Interview with Barbara Bramble, National Wildlife Federation, March 1990; Stephen Schwartzman, "Deforestation and Popular Resistance in Acre: From Local Movement to Global Network," paper presented to Eighty-eighth Annual Meeting of the American Anthropological Association, Washington, D.C., November 15–19, 1989.

54. Working with Merck and Genentech, the World Resources Institute, the World Wildlife Fund, and the Environmental and Energy Study Institute drafted an interpretative statement and persuaded President Clinton to sign the treaty with such a statement attached.

55. Statement by Craig Van Note before the Subcommittee on Human Rights and International Organizations, Committee on Foreign Affairs, U.S. House of Representatives, September 28, 1989.

56. Conversation with Jim Barnes, director, International Program, Friends of the Earth U.S., February 14, 1994.

57. Robert Boardman, *International Organization and the Conservation of Nature* (Bloomington: Indiana University Press, 1981), pp. 88–94.

58. Richard Elliot Benedick, "Creating a Spirit of Partnership: Policy Dialogues and Environmental Diplomacy," *Capacity Building* (Geneva), April 1993, p. 4.

59. Elizabeth Cook, "Global Environmental Advocacy: Citizen Activism in Protecting the Ozone Layer," *Ambio* 14 (October 1990), pp. 334–338; Cook, "Report on the First Meeting of the Parties to the Vienna Convention and the Montreal Protocol, Helsinki, Finland, April 26–May 5, 1989," unpublished paper, pp. 15–16.

60. Patricia Birnie, "The Role of International Law in Solving Certain Environmental Conflicts," in John E. Carroll, ed. *International Environmental Diplomacy:*

The Management and Resolution of Transfrontier Environmental Problems (Cambridge: Cambridge University Press, 1988), pp. 107–108.

61. Personal communication from a member of the U.S. delegation to the biodiversity negotiations, February 1994.

62. Laura H. Kosloff and Mark C. Trexler, "The Convention on International Trade in Endangered Species: No Carrot, But Where's the Stick?" *Environmental Law Reporter* 17 (July 1987), pp. 10225–10226.

63. Paul Lewis, "Rich Nations Plan $2 Billion for Environment," *New York Times*, March 17, 1994. For a full discussion of the GEF, see Chapter 4.

64. This discussion is based on Barbara J. Bramble and Gareth Porter, "Non-Governmental Organizations and the Making of U.S. International Environmental Policy," in Andrew Hurrell and Benedict Kingsbury, eds., *The International Politics of the Environment* (Oxford, U.K.: Clarendon Press, 1992), pp. 325–346.

65. *Financial Times,* April 25, 1994.

66. Center for Applied Studies in International Negotiations, Issues and Non-Governmental Organizations Program, *Report on the Participation of Non-Governmental Organizations in the Preparatory Process of the United Nations Conference on Environment and Development* (Vienna, August 1992), p. 5; U.N. Non-Governmental Liaison Service, *E and D File 1992: Briefings for NGOs on UNCED* no. 25 (April 1992), p. 1, and no. 30 (July 1992), p. 1.

67. Langston James Goree VI, who edited the daily report on the negotiations from PrepComs II to IV and in Rio, quoted in Nancy Gabriel, "The Net Result: Computer Networks, NGOs and UNCED," *Concordare* (Cambridge, Mass.), Spring 1993, pp. 8–9.

68. Gabriel, "The Net Result," p. 8.

69. Bella Abzug and Charlotte Price, "Women's Caucus Succeeds at PrepCom 4," *Earth Island Journal,* June 1992, p. 7.

70. Jonannah Bernstein, Pamela Chasek, and Langston James Goree VI, "A Summary of the Proceedings of the Fourth Session of the UNCED Preparatory Committee," *Earth Summit Bulletin* (April 1992), p. 2.

71. Remarks by Barbara Brown, delegation of Canada at NGO Forum, New York City, March 16, 1994.

72. Telephone interview with Jim Valette, Greenpeace, June 22, 1994.

73. See Gareth Porter, *The United States and the Biodiversity Convention: The Case for Participation* (Washington, D.C.: Environmental and Energy Study Institute, 1992).

74. *International Environment Reporter,* June 2, 1993, p. 416.

75. M'Gonigle and Zacher, *Pollution, Politics and International Law,* pp. 58–62.

76. *International Environment Reporter,* April 1989, p. 169.

77. *International Environment Reporter,* January 27, 1993, p. 40.

78. *Global Environmental Change Report* 4, no. 15 (August 14, 1992), p. 3.

79. Interview with Jim Barnes, March 22, 1994.

80. David Day, *The Whale War* (Vancouver and Toronto: Douglas and MacIntyre, 1987), pp. 103–107.

81. Interview with William Nitze, Alliance to Save Energy, June 20, 1994.

82. Alan S. Miller and Durwood Zaelke, "The NGO Perspective," *Climate Alert* 7, no. 3 (May-June 1994), p. 3.

83. *Daily Environment Reporter*, August 27, 1992, p. B-2.

84. *Global Environmental Change Report* (November 20, 1992).

85. Monica Moore, "The First Word," *Global Pesticide Campaign* 3, no. 3 (August 1993), p., 2; Jumanah Farah, *Pesticide Policies in Developing Countries: Do They Encourage Excessive Pesticide Use?* (Washington, D.C.: World Bank, 1993).

86. Robert L. Paarlberg, "Managing Pesticide Use in Developing Countries," in Peter M. Haas, Robert O. Keohane, and Marc A. Levy, eds., *Institutions for the Earth: Sources of Effective International Environmental Protection* (Cambridge and London: MIT Press, 1993), p. 319.

87. François Nectoux and Yoichi Kuroda, *Timber from the South Seas: An Analysis of Japan's Tropical Timber Trade and Its Environmental Impact* (Gland, Switzerland: World Wildlife Fund, 1989), p. 94; David Swinbanks, "Sarawak's Tropical Rainforests Exploited by Japan," *Nature* 238 (July 30, 1987), p. 373.

88. See Stephen Schmidheiny with the Business Council for Sustainable Development, *Changing Course: A Global Business Perspective on Development and the Environment* (Cambridge: MIT Press, 1992). Another publication reflecting a new corporate environmental consciousness is Paul Hawken, *The Ecology of Commerce: Doing Good Business* (New York: Harper Business Publications, 1993).

89. Business Council for Sustainable Development, "The BCSD's Position Statement on Joint Implementation," paper presented at the Tenth Session of the INC, August 24, 1994.

CHAPTER THREE

1. Lars Bjorkbom, "Resolution of Environmental Problems: The Use of Diplomacy," in John E. Carroll, ed., *International Environmental Diplomacy: The Management and Resolution of Transfrontier Environmental Problems* (Cambridge: Cambridge University Press, 1988), p. 128; Harold Dovland, "Monitoring European Transboundary Air Pollution," *Environment* 29 (December 1987), p. 12.

2. Lothar Gundling, "Multilateral Cooperation of States Under the ECE Convention on Long-Range Transboundary Air Pollution," in C. Flinterman et al., eds., *Transboundary Air Pollution* (Dordrecht, Netherlands: Martinus Nijhoff, 1987), pp. 19–30.

3. Sten Nelson and Peter Druinker, "The Extent of Forest Decline in Europe," *Environment* 29, no. 9 (1987), pp. 7–8.

4. Seven states pledged to reduce their emissions by 40 or 50 percent by various dates. See John McCormick, *Acid Earth: The Global Threat of Acid Pollution* (Washington, D.C.: Earthscan and International Institute for Environment and Development, 1985), especially Figure 1, p. 11.

5. Peter H. Sand, "Air Pollution in Europe: International Policy Responses," *Environment* (December 1987), p. 18.

6. See Iwona Rummel-Bulska, "The Protection of the Ozone Layer Under the Global Framework Convention," in Flinterman et al., *Transboundary Air Pollution*, pp. 281–296.

7. Richard Elliot Benedick, *Ozone Diplomacy* (Cambridge: Harvard University Press, 1991), p. 33.

8. Yasuko Kawashima, "Policy Making Processes for Global Environmental Problems," p. 4, English translation of a paper submitted to *Jukaku Gyosei* in 1994.

9. "An Analysis of the Montreal Protocol on Substances That Deplete the Ozone Layer," staff paper prepared by the Oceans and Environment Program, Office of Technology Assessment, U.S. Congress, December 10, 1987, Table 1, p. 9. Chinese plans to provide a refrigerator for every household over the next fifteen years would offset progress made by a CFC ban by OECD countries if the Chinese used CFCs in their production.

10. Benedick, *Ozone Diplomacy*, p. 43.

11. Alan S. Miller, "Incentives for CFC Substitutes: Lessons for Other Greenhouse Gases," in *Proceedings of the First North American Conference on Preparing for Global Climate Change: A Cooperative Approach, October 27–29, 1987* (Washington, D.C.: Government Institutes, n.d.).

12. Benedick, *Ozone Diplomacy*, pp. 4–7; David D. Doniger, "Politics of the Ozone Layer," *Issues in Science and Technology* 4 (Spring 1988), p. 87; David A. Wirth and Daniel A. Lashof, "Beyond Vienna and Montreal: Multilateral Agreements on Greenhouse Gases," *Ambio* 19 (October 1990), pp. 305–310.

13. Rudy Abramson, "Ninety Nations Agree on Three Steps to Protect Ozone Layer," *Los Angeles Times*, November 26, 1992.

14. *Into the Sunlight: Exposing Methyl Bromide's Threat to the Ozone Layer*, a report by eight U.S. NGOs (Washington, D.C.: Friends of the Earth, November 1992).

15. "Declaration on Methyl Bromide," UNEP/OzL.Pro. 5/12, Annex VII, Bangkok, November 17–19, 1993, p. 62. The parties declared their "firm determination" to reduce the use of methyl bromide 25 percent by 2000 and to phase it out completely "as soon as technically possible."

16. s.a.f.e. (Sustainable Agriculture, Food and Environment) Alliance press release, London, December 3, 1993.

17. Executive Committee of the Multilateral Fund for the Implementation of the Montreal Protocol, "Contributions in Arrears and Promissory Notes," UNEP/OzL.Pro/ExCom/14/14, September 6, 1994.

18. Greenpeace letter to Elizabeth Dowdeswell, UNEP, October 18, 1993. The letter points out that there exist non-HCFC/HFC alternatives for most current use, which is in coolants for refrigeration systems and insulation in domestic refrigerators.

19. *Financial Times*, September 9, 1994; *International Environmental Reporter*, November 2, 1994, p. 884.

20. This analysis is based primarily on David Day, *Whale War* (Vancouver and Toronto: Douglas and MacIntyre, 1987); Patricia Birnie, "The Role of Developing Countries in Nudging the International Whaling Commission from Regulating Whaling to Encouraging Non-Consumptive Uses of Whales," *Ecology Law Quarterly* 12, no. 4 (1985), pp. 938–968; interview with Patricia Forkan, Humane Society of the United States, Washington, D.C., June 15, 1990.

21. A revised version of the Endangered Species Conservation Act passed in 1973 banned whaling in U.S. waters or by U.S. citizens, outlawed the import of whale products, and required that the United States initiate bilateral and multilateral negotiations on an agreement to protect and conserve whales.

22. The effort to build an IWC majority to ban whaling was stymied in the latter half of the 1970s because otherwise antiwhaling states such as Canada, Mexico, and other Latin American states were primarily concerned about protecting rights to regulate economic activities within their own 200-mile (320-kilometer) economic zones and opposed the jurisdiction of an international body over whaling.

23. Statement by Craig Van Note, Monitor Consortium, before the Subcommittee on Human Rights and International Organizations, Committee on Foreign Affairs, U.S. House of Representatives, September 28, 1989.

24. "Whaling: Soviet Kills Could Affect Sanctuary Decision," *Greenwire*, February 22, 1994.

25. Teresa Watanabe, "Japan Is Set for a Whale of a Fight," *Los Angeles Times*, April 20, 1993.

26. Paul Brown, "Playing Football with the Whales," *London Guardian*, May 1, 1993. The Caribbean states cooperating with Japan are Grenada, St. Lucia, St. Kitts–Nevis, Antigua and Barbuda, Dominica, and St. Vincent.

27. *Financial Times*, April 6, 1995.

28. *Japan Times*, May 13, 1993, and *El Epoca/El Mercurio*, May 12, 1993, reported in *Greenwire*, May 13, 1993; and Paul Brown, *London Guardian*, reported in *Greenwire*, May 28, 1993; Nicholas T. Bennett, "Whales, Driftnets and Hawksbill Turtles: Lessons for a U.S.-Japan Environmental Partnership," unpublished paper, 1993, p. 19.

29. See Sarah Fitzgerald, *Whose Business Is It?* (Washington, D.C.: World Wildlife Fund, 1989), pp. 3–8, 13–14.

30. World Resources Institute, *World Resources 1990–1991* (New York: Oxford University Press, 1990), p. 135.

31. Fitzgerald, *Whose Business Is It?* p. 67.

32. *TRAFFIC (USA)* 9 (June 1989), p. 2.

33. Chris Huxley, "Lies, Damned Lies and Population Figures," *Independent* (London), June 30, 1990, p. 13.

34. David Harland, "Jumping on the 'Ban' Wagon: Efforts to Save the African Elephant," *Fletcher Forum on World Affairs* 14 (Summer 1990), pp. 284–300.

35. "CITES 1989: The African Elephant and More," *TRAFFIC (USA)* 9 (December 1989), pp. 1–3.

36. *New York Times*, June 5, 1990, p. C2; Raymond Bonner, *At the Hand of Man: Peril and Hope for Africa's Wildlife* (New York: Vintage Books, 1994), p. 157.

37. "Ivory Smugglers Busted in Japan," *TRAFFIC (USA)* 11, no. 2 (January 1992).

38. "Comments of the Humane Society of the United States Regarding Proposals by Zimbabwe, Botswana, South Africa, Namibia, Malawi, and Zambia to Transfer Population of the African Elephant from CITES" (Washington, D.C.: Humane Society of the United States, January 30, 1992), Appendixes 1, 2; and Ginette Henley, "CITES 1992: Endangered Treaty? Kyoto Decisions Political Not Practical," and "CITES Eighth Meeting of the Conference of the Parties to CITES," *TRAFFIC (USA)* 11, no. 3 (August 1992), pp. 1–2, 13.

39. "Report of the Ad Hoc Working Group on the Work of Its Fourth Session," UNEP/WG.190/4, February 13, 1989, p. 3.

40. Carol Annette Petsonk, "The Role of the United Nations Environment Programme (UNEP) in the Development of International Environmental Law," *American University Journal of International Law and Policy* 5 (Winter 1990), pp. 374–377; *International Environment Reporter,* April 1989, pp. 159–161.

41. See David P. Hackett, "An Assessment of the Basel Convention on the Control of Transboundary Movements of Hazardous Wastes and Their Disposal," *American University Journal of International Law and Policy* 5 (Winter 1990), pp. 313–322; Mark A. Montgomery, "Travelling Toxic Trash: An Analysis of the 1989 Basel Convention," *Fletcher Forum of World Affairs* 14 (Summer 1990), pp. 313–326.

42. *International Environment Reporter,* April 1989, pp. 159–160.

43. *Greenpeace Waste Trade Update* 2 (July 15, 1989, and December 1989).

44. *International Environment Reporter,* May 6, 1992, p. 275.

45. Only the republics of the former Soviet Union, desperate for foreign exchange and willing to disregard the health and environmental consequences, appeared willing to accept significant shipments of hazardous wastes. See Steven Coll, "Free Market Intensifies Waste Problem," *Washington Post,* March 23, 1994; Tamara Robinson, "Dirty Deals: Hazardous Waste Imports into Russia and Ukraine," *CIS Environmental Watch* (Monterey Institute of International Studies), no. 5 (Fall 1993).

46. Greenpeace, *The International Trade in Wastes: A Greenpeace Inventory,* 5th ed. (Washington, D.C.: Greenpeace, 1990); *Toxic Trade Update,* no. 6.2 (1993), pp. 6, 7, 12–26; "Chemicals: Shipment to South Africa Draws Enviro Protests," *Greenwire,* February 18, 1994; and "Deadly Trade in Toxics," *U.S. News and World Report,* March 7, 1994, pp. 64–67.

47. John H. Cushman Jr., "Clinton Seeks Ban on Export of Most Hazardous Waste," *New York Times,* March 1, 1994; "Basel Convention Partners Consider Ban on Exports of Hazardous Wastes," *International Environment Reporter,* March 22, 1994, p. A9.

48. Charles P. Wallace, *Los Angeles Times,* March 23, 1994, cited in *Greenwire,* March 23, 1994. For a detailed account of the Geneva meeting, see Jim Puckett and Cathy Fogel, "A Victory for Environment and Justice: The Basel Ban and How It Happened," Greenpeace International Toxic Trade Campaign, Washington, D.C., September 1994.

49. "Basel Treaty Partners Agree to Ban Waste Exports to Nations Outside OECD," *International Environment Reporter,* March 28, 1994, p. AA1.

50. Given the economic and technological barriers to onshore mining, it is generally believed that only oil and gas exploration would be practical. See Barbara Mitchell, *Frozen Stakes: The Future of Antarctic Minerals* (London and Washington, D.C.: International Institute for Environment and Development, 1983), pp. 7–21.

51. Barbara Mitchell, "Undermining Antarctica," *Technology Review,* February-March 1988, p. 56.

52. Mitchell, "Undermining Antarctica," pp. 50–51, 68–69.

53. These meetings were closed to the public and press as well as to nontreaty nations, and the documents being considered were not released to the public. *The Future of the Antarctic: Background for a Third UN Debate* (East Sussex, U.K.: Greenpeace International, 1985), p. 15.

54. *Christian Science Monitor,* June 7, 1988.

55. For description and analysis of CRAMRA and its environmental provisions, see R. Tucker Scully and Lee A. Kimball, "Antarctica: Is There Life After Minerals?" *Marine Policy,* April 1989, pp. 87–98; Lee A. Kimball, *Southern Exposure: Deciding Antarctica's Future* (Washington, D.C.: World Resources Institute, 1990), pp. 16–18; Antarctic and Southern Oceans Coalition, "Analysis of the Convention on the Regulation of Antarctic Mineral Resource Activities," ASOC Information Paper 1988-4, October 29, 1988.

56. *Christian Science Monitor,* June 7, 1988.

57. *International Environment Reporter,* June 19, 1991, p. 331; Embassy of Australia, *Australian Report* (Washington, D.C.: Embassy of Australia, July 15, 1991).

58. See Wirth and Lashof, "Beyond Vienna and Montreal," pp. 305–310.

59. See Peter Rogers and Myron Fiering, "Climate Change: Do We Know Enough to Act?" *Forum for Applied Research and Public Policy,* Winter 1989, pp. 5–12. There is widespread agreement on the history and existence of greenhouse gases, the probability of climate change, and the need to act, but there are still serious uncertainties on future atmospheric abundances of CO_2, cloud-radiation feedbacks, regional-scale predictions of climate change, and changes in the frequency and intensity of tropical storms. For a summary of the science, see J. D. Mahlman, D. Albritton, and R. T. Watson, *State of Scientific Understanding of Climate Change,* a useful analysis based on IPCC scientific assessments (Washington, D.C.: Office of Science and Technology Policy, December 1993).

60. World Resources Institute, *World Resources 1990–1991,* Chapter 2.

61. Richard A. Houghton and George M. Woodwell, "Global Climatic Change," *Scientific American* 260 (April 1989), pp. 42–43.

62. Lamont C. Hempel and Matthias Kaelberer, "The Changing Climate in Greenhouse Policy: Obstacles to International Cooperation in Agenda Setting and Policy Formulation," unpublished paper, April 1990, p. 6; and Daniel Bodansky, "The United Nations Framework Convention on Climate Change: A Commentary," *Yale Journal of International Law* 18, no. 2 (Summer 1993), p. 461.

63. Genn Frankel, "U.S. Moves to Block Pact on Emissions," *Washington Post,* November 7, 1989, pp. A1, 21; *Washington Post,* July 10, 1990; *New York Times,* July 10, 1990.

64. Japan subsequently backtracked by proposing a process of "pledge and review" in place of binding commitments. Individual countries, it suggested, would set for themselves appropriate targets that would be publicly reviewed. Most EC member states and NGOs were cool to the idea. Bodansky, "The United Nations Framework Convention on Climate Change," p. 486.

65. Intergovernmental Panel on Climate Change, *The Formulation of Response Strategies: Report by Working Group III, Policymakers' Summary,* June 1990, p. 11, Table 2. For country contributions and rankings, see World Resources Institute, *World Resources, 1992–1993* (New York: Oxford University Press, 1992), pp. 205–213, 345–355. For a good discussion of different methods of greenhouse-gas accounting, see Peter M. Morrisette and Andrew J. Plantinga, "The Global Warming Issue: Viewpoints of Different Countries," *Resources* (Washington, D.C.: Resources for the Future), no. 103 (Spring 1991), pp. 2–6.

66. Developing-country concerns over the various ways of calculating responsibility for greenhouse-gas emissions and the burdens that might be placed on their own development were overwhelmed in the final bargaining with the United States, but for information, see Bodansky, "The United Nations Framework Convention on Climate Change," pp. 480–481. For a discussion of estimated economic costs to developing countries of atmospheric protection, see World Bank, *World Development Report 1992, Development and Environment* (New York: Oxford University Press, 1992), pp. 61–63, 1124–1126; and Arnulf Grüber and Nebojsa Nekicenovic, "International Burden Sharing in Greenhouse Gas Reduction," World Bank Environment Working Paper no. 55, November 1992.

67. *Earth Summit Update,* no. 9 (May 1992), p. 1.

68. In May 1995, all the OECD states except Belgium had ratified, as had most of the small island states. China, India, Mexico, Indonesia, Brazil, Egypt, Argentina, and Chile had ratified. A total of 137 states had ratified. U.N. General Assembly, Intergovernmental Negotiating Committee for a Framework Convention on Climate Change, "Status of Ratification on the United Nations Framework Convention on Climate Change," New York, May 9, 1995.

69. Kenton R. Miller et al., "Issues on the Preservation of Biological Diversity," in Robert Repetto, ed., *The Global Possible: Resources, Development and the New Century* (New Haven and London: Yale University Press, 1985), pp. 341–342; IUCN, "Explanatory Notes to Draft Articles Prepared by IUCN for Inclusion in a Proposed Convention on the Conservation of Biological Diversity and the Establishment of a Fund for That Purpose," Part 1: General Comments, p. 1.

70. The main interest of the Reagan administration in making that proposal was to save money by bringing the multiplicity of species-specific or region-specific conservation conventions already in existence under one convention, so that there could be a single secretariat instead of several secretariats. Personal communication from E. U. Curtis Bohlen, former assistant secretary of state for oceans, environment, and science, Washington, D.C., February 2, 1994.

71. "Report of the Ad Hoc Working Group on the Work of its Second Session in Preparation for a Legal Instrument on Biological Diversity of the Planet," UNEP/Bio.Div2/3, February 23, 1990, p. 7.

72. Personal communication from a member of the U.S. delegation to the biodiversity convention negotiations, April 12, 1994.

73. For contrasting analyses of the text of the convention regarding intellectual property rights, see Melinda Chandler, "The Biodiversity Convention: Selected Issues of Interest to the International Lawyer," *Colorado Journal of International Environmental Law and Policy* 4, no. 1 (Winter 1993), pp. 161–165; and Gareth Porter, *The United States and the Biodiversity Convention: The Case for Participation* (Washington, D.C.: Environmental and Energy Study Institute, 1992), pp. 13–21.

74. Personal communication from a member of the U.S. delegation to the biodiversity convention negotiations, October 21, 1994.

75. The Clinton administration dealt with the objections to the text that had been raised by the Bush administration by announcing that it would issue a statement asserting that it interpreted the treaty's provisions on intellectual property rights and the financial mechanism to be compatible with U.S. interests. See U.S. Congress, Senate, *Convention on Biological Diversity: Message from the President of*

the United States, November 20, 1993, Treaty Document 103-20 (Washington, D.C.: U.S. Government Printing Office, 1993).

76. United Nations Environment Programme, *Desertification: The Problem That Won't Go Away* (Nairobi: UNEP, 1992); Ridley Nelson, "Dryland Management: The "Desertification" Problem," World Bank Policy Planning and Research Staff, Environment Department Working Paper no. 8, September 1988, p. 2.

77. *Crosscurrents,* no. 1 (March 2, 1992), p. 5. For a more detailed later report on these findings, see William K. Stevens, "Threat of Encroaching Deserts May Be More Myth Than Fact," *New York Times,* January 18, 1994, pp. C1, 10.

78. U.N. Governmental Liaison Service, "Second Session of Desertification Negotiations, Geneva, 13–24 September, 1993," *E and D File* 2, no. 13 (October 1993).

79. "A Convention for Africans," *Impact* (Nairobi), no. 6 (September 1992), p. 3.

80. United Nations Environment Programme, *Desertification Control Bulletin* (Nairobi), no. 20 (1991); Dr. Mostafa K. Tolba, "Desertification and the Economics of Survival," statement to the International Conference on the Economics of Dryland Degradation and Rehabilitation, Canberra, Australia, March 10–11, 1986.

81. *World Bank News,* May 27, 1993, p. 4; *Crosscurrents,* no. 5 (March 16, 1992), p. 13.

82. E. U. Curtis Bohlen, deputy chief of the U.S. delegation, recalls that he made the decision personally without consulting with any higher U.S. officials. Private communication from Bohlen, August 15, 1994. On the earlier suggestion by African countries of a possible bargain linking African support for a forest convention with U.S. support for a desertification convention, see *Crosscurrents,* no. 5 (March 16, 1992), p. 13.

83. *Earth Summit Bulletin* 2, no. 13 (June 16, 1992), p. 3.

84. "Summary of the First Session of the INC for the Elaboration of an International Convention to Combat Desertification, 24 May–3 June 1993," *Earth Negotiations Bulletin* 4, no. 11 (June 11, 1993), pp. 2–6.

85. "Summary of the Fifth Session," pp. 7–8.

86. "Summary of the Second Session of the INC for the Elaboration of an International Convention to Combat Desertification, 13–24 September 1993," *Earth Negotiations Bulletin* 4, no. 22 (September 30, 1993), p. 11.

87. "Summary of the Fifth Session of the INC for the Elaboration of an International Convention to Combat Desertification, 6–17 June 1994," *Earth Negotiations Bulletin* 4, no. 55 (June 20, 1994), pp. 9–10.

CHAPTER FOUR

1. See Karl P. Sauvant and Hajo Hasenpflug, eds., *The New International Economic Order: Confrontation or Cooperation Between North and South?* (Boulder, Colo.: Westview Press, 1977).

2. This was part of a longer-term decline in the real prices of primary products in the world market, caused by slow growth in demand, the development of cheaper substitutes, and overproduction. See United Nations Development Programme, *Human Development Report 1992* (New York: UNDP, 1992), p. 59.

3. World Bank, *World Debt Tables 1992–93* (Washington, D.C.: World Bank, 1992), vol. 1, Table 1.4, p. 15, and UNDP, *Human Development Report 1992,* p. 46.

4. World Bank, *Global Economic Prospects and the Developing Countries* (Washington, D.C.: World Bank, 1992), p. 13.

5. J. Michael Finger and Patrick A. Messerlin, "The Effects of Industrial Countries' Policies on Developing Countries," World Bank Policy and Research Series no. 3, 1988.

6. World Bank, *Global Economic Prospects,* p. 2.

7. UNDP, *Human Development Report 1992,* p. 34.

8. For the example of the Philippines, see Gareth Porter with Delfin Ganapin Jr., *Population, Resources and the Philippines' Future* (Washington, D.C.: World Resources Institute, 1988); Robin Broad with John Cavanagh, *Plundering Paradise: The Struggle for Environment in the Philippines* (Berkeley and Los Angeles: University of California Press, 1993).

9. "The Price of the Environment," *Environmental News from the Netherlands,* no. 1 (1992).

10. Mark Fritz, "Imports Hurting African Farmers," *Sacramento Bee,* December 20, 1993, p. A18.

11. For the best succinct analysis of the environmental implications of agricultural subsidies, see G. Edward Schuh, "International Economic Policies and Sustainable Development," unpublished paper presented at the UNECE/USEPA Workshop on the Economics of Sustainable Development, Washington, D.C., January 23–25, 1990. For a different view of the issue see Ernst Lutz, "Agricultural Trade Liberalization, Price Changes and Environmental Effects," World Bank, Environment Department, December 1990.

12. Statement by H. E. Datuk Amar Stephen K. T. Yong, leader of the Malaysian delegation, at the second meeting of the parties to the Montreal Protocol, London, June 27–29, 1990.

13. Talk by Mohammed El-Ashry, then vice-president of World Resources Institute, at the Egyptian Embassy, Washington, D.C., March 9, 1990.

14. Ninth Conference of Heads of State or Government of Nonaligned Countries, "Environment," NAC 9/EC/Doc.8/Rev. 4, September 7, 1989. Also see *The Challenge to the South: Report of the South Commission* (London: Oxford University Press, 1990).

15. Matthew L. Wald, "Environment Dominates Ninety-one-Nation Energy Talks," *New York Times,* September 21, 1989.

16. Marlise Simons, "North-South Divide Is Marring Environmental Talks," *New York Times,* March 17, 1992 (Mahathir speech).

17. See South Centre, *Environment and Development: Towards a Common Strategy of the South in the UNCED Negotiations and Beyond* (Geneva and Dar es Salaam: South Centre, 1991). This publication presents recommendations to an influential group of developing-country heads of government and ministers, headed by President Julius Nyerere of Tanzania, from a group of NGO activists and academics from the South. See also, New World Dialogue for Environment and Development in the Western Hemisphere, *Compact for a New World* (Washington, D.C.: World Resources Institute, 1991).

18. Interview with UNCED secretariat official, Geneva, March 21, 1991.

19. Mukund G. Rajan, "The Environment and North-South Relations: A View from the South," *Development Alternatives* (New Delhi) 3, no. 6 (June 1993), p. 8.

20. See "Kuala Lumpur Declaration on Environment and Development," Second Ministerial Conference of Developing Countries on Environment and Development, April 28–29, 1992. That conference was attended by fifty-five developing countries.

21. See the memorandum circulated to all Environmental Protection Agency employees after UNCED. EPA administrator William K. Reilly criticized the Bush administration for playing a "defensive game" in preparing for the Earth Summit. *New York Times,* August 1, 1992, p. A1. This generalization is also based on the guidelines for the U.S. delegation to PrepCom II, to which one of the authors had access as an NGO member of the delegation.

22. See statement of Hans Alders, minister of housing, physical planning, and the environment of the Netherlands, to PrepCom IV, March 2, 1992.

23. In Rio, a Japanese delegate was instructed to take the text of Prime Minister Miyazawa's speech containing a pledge to increase Japanese environmental assistance to the U.S. delegation, apparently hoping to receive assurances that the United States had no objection to the pledge. Interview with member of U.S. delegation to the Rio conference, July 8, 1992.

24. Such criticisms were made in meetings of the U.S. delegation to PrepCom III, attended by one of the authors.

25. Interview with E. U. Curtis Bohlen, head of the U.S. delegation to PrepCom IV, New York, April 3, 1992.

26. "A Summary of the Proceedings of the United Nations Conference on Environment and Development 3–14 June 1992," *Earth Summit Bulletin* (Winnipeg, Canada: International Institute for Sustainable Development), no. 13 (June 17, 1992).

27. *Agenda 21, Rio Declaration, and Forest Principles* (New York: U.N., 1992), Chapters 23–32: the final text of agreements negotiated by governments at the UNCED, June 3–14, 1992, Rio de Janeiro, Brazil. "Major groups" include women, youth, indigenous peoples, NGOs, local authorities, unions, business, the science and technology community, and farmers.

28. Ibid. See especially Chapter 8 of Agenda 21.

29. See the text of "International Policies to Accelerate Sustainable Development in Developing Countries and Related Domestic Policies," based on negotiations on A/CONF.151/PC/100 Add.3 (no date), pp. 10–11. The final version of that section of Agenda 21 calls only for further negotiations between debtor countries and creditor banks but no action by governments. And it fails to use the usual "should" in regard to reducing bilateral debt. "Report of the United Nations Conference on Environment and Development," A/CONF.151/26 (vol. 1), August 12, 1992, Section 1, Chapter 2, pp. 26–27.

30. Cf. "International Policies," pp. 2–4; and "Report of the United Nations Conference," p. 20.

31. "Adoption of Agreements on Environment and Development," UNCED, A/CONF.151/4 (Part II), May 1, 1992, Agenda 21, para. 20.7, p. 238. The developing countries succeeded, however, at the 1994 COP. See Chapter 5.

32. The United States initially bracketed the entire chapter on radioactive waste, opposing its inclusion in Agenda 21 in any form. *Earth Summit Update,* special supplement (October 1991), p. 3.

33. "Report of the United Nations Conference on Environment and Development," A/CONF.151/216 (vol. 2), August 13, 1992, para. 22.5(b), p. 263.

34. *Earth Summit Update,* no. 8 (April 1992), p. 8.

35. United Nations Development Programme, "UNDP Commits to Follow-up Activities to Assist Small Island Developing States," *Update* 7, no. 10 (May 23, 1994), p. 2; "Summary of the UN Global Conference on the Sustainable Development of Small Island Developing States, 25 April–6 May 1994," *Earth Negotiations Bulletin* 8, no. 28 (May 9, 1994); and *Environment Australia's International Agenda* (Washington, D.C.: Embassy of Australia, January 1994).

36. Cf. "Combatting Poverty, Changing Consumption Patterns and Demographic Dynamics and Sustainability," A/CONF.151/PC/L68, March 30, 1992, paras. 17 and 19, p. 8, and "Report of the United Nations Conference," paras. 4.3 and 4.5, p. 37.

37. Briefing by Ambassador Robert Ryan of the U.S. delegation to PrepCom IV, April 13, 1992.

38. Environmental Defense Fund memorandum, "Agenda 21 Chapter on Atmospheric Protection: What's Gone and What Remains," no date.

39. Within the G-77 caucus a small number of delegations, such as Mexico, Argentina, Colombia, and Ecuador, refused to accept the term "family planning." *Earth Summit Times,* March 23, 1992; *Crosscurrents* (March 23, 1992), p. 4.

40. "Demographic Dynamics and Sustainability (Chapter 5 of Agenda 21)" InterNet/EcoNet, April 29, 1992, paras. 5.50 and 5.51.

41. The draft by the EC, the Nordics, and Japan offered only a commitment by industrial countries "in a position to do so" (a formula allowing the United States to refuse) to reach the target of 0.7 percent of GNP going to ODA and gave no time frame for achieving it.

42. "Financial Negotiations End in Deadlock," *Earth Summit Update,* no. 8 (April 1992), p. 6.

43. The Netherlands, Denmark, and France supported the target of 0.7 percent of GNP by the year 2000; the United Kingdom and Germany did not. *Earth Summit Bulletin* (June 17, 1992), p. 17.

44. The head of the U.S. delegation, E. U. Curtis Bohlen, indicated that he was concerned about that possibility at a U.S. delegation meeting at PrepCom III.

45. Author's interview with a member of U.S. delegation, Rio, June 9, 1992.

46. Malaysia demanded that industrialized countries (most of whom had long since reduced their forest cover to a small fraction of the preindustrial level) draw up national forestry action plans aimed at substantially increasing that forest cover. Intervention by Malaysian delegate to Working Group 1, PrepCom II, March 20, 1991.

47. The EC and the Nordics supported negotiation of a forest convention only *after* UNCED was finished, despite intensive diplomatic efforts by the United States with its G-7 partners and more than twenty-five tropical forest countries in between PrepComs. Briefing by State Department official for NGOs, June 21, 1991; briefing by Christine Dawson, State Department Policy Planning Staff, for NGOs, May 22, 1991.

48. See U.S. delegation reporting cable, "UNCED PREPCOM III: Report of Second Week," August 26, 1991.

49. David Humphreys, "The UNCED Process and International Responses to Deforestation," paper presented to the Inaugural Pan-European Conference on International Studies, Heidelberg, Germany, September 16–20, 1992, pp. 34–35.

50. Malaysia openly charged that industrialized countries were using the issue of conserving tropical forests to prevent rapidly industrializing countries from achieving developed-country status. Claude Smadja, "Malaysia: Objective 2020," *World Link* (Geneva), no. 3 (1991), pp. 26–29.

51. See "Land Resources: Deforestation," A/CONF.151/PC/WG.I/L.46, April 1, 1992.

52. *Earth Summit Update,* no. 8 (April 1992), p. 7.

53. "Finger-pointing in the Charter Debate," *Crosscurrents,* no. 4 (March 12, 1992), p. 5; "Text of Secretariat Compilation of Proposed Amendments to the Earth Charter," *Crosscurrents,* no. 7 (March 23, 1992), pp. 8–11.

54. U.S. delegation reporting cable no. 3 on PrepCom IV, pp. 10–11.

55. Koh retained another principle, in which developed countries acknowledge the pressures their societies place on the global environment, on the grounds that it was actually lifted from an OECD ministers' communiqué. Angela Harkavy, *The Earth Summit: A Progress Report on Preparatory Negotiations for the United Nations Conference on Environment and Development* (n.p: National Wildlife Federation and Campaign for Action to Protect the Environment '92, 1992), p. 23.

56. The legal adviser to the U.S. delegation explained, "We believe generally that states have the same responsibilities." Jeffrey Kovar, U.S. UNCED delegation roundtable, Washington, D.C., May 13, 1992.

57. The lone exception was Israel, which objected to a principle that referred to people "under occupation."

58. Jeff Kovar, U.S. delegation roundtable, Washington, D.C., May 13, 1992.

59. "News Analysis: U.S. Isolation Reflects Reduced Clout on Global Environment," *Earth Summit Update* (July 1992), p. 8.

60. For a range of assessments of the outcomes of the Rio conference, see Michael Grubb et al., *The Earth Summit Agreements: A Guide and Assessment* (London: Royal Institute of International Affairs and Earthscan, 1993); Pratap Chatterjee and Matthias Finger, *The Earth Brokers* (London and New York: Routledge, 1994), pp. 39–60; Peter M. Haas, Marc A. Levy, and Edward A. Parson, "Appraising the Earth Summit," *Environment,* October 1922, pp. 7–11, 26–33; Marc Pallemaerts, "International Law from Stockholm to Rio: Back to the Future?" and Ileana Porras, "The Rio Declaration: A New Basis for International Cooperation," in Philippe Sands, ed., *Greening International Law* (London: Earthscan, 1993), pp. 1–34.

61. The literature on trade and environment is growing rapidly. Introductions to the subject representing a range of viewpoints include C. Ford Runge with Francois Ortalo-Magne and Philip Vande Kamp, *Freer Trade, Protected Environment* (New York: Council on Foreign Relations Press, 1994); Robert Repetto, *Trade and Sustainable Development* (Geneva: UNEP, 1994); Daniel Esty, *Greening the GATT* (Washington, D.C.: Institute for International Economics, 1994); Heraldo Muñoz

and Robin Rosenberg, eds., *Difficult Liaison: Trade and the Environment in the Americas* (New Brunswick: Transaction Books, 1993).

62. See Esty, *Greening the GATT,* p. 42.

63. The term "environmental trade measures" is used in Steve Charnowitz, "The Environment vs. Trade Rules: Defogging the Debate," *Environmental Law* (Northwestern School of Law of Lewis and Clark College) 23 (1993), p. 490. Charnowitz lists all of these forms of ETMs except mandatory ecolabeling.

64. Sang Don Lee, "The Effect of Environmental Regulations on Trade: Cases of Korea's New Environmental Laws," *Georgetown International Environmental Law Review* (Summer 1993), p. 659.

65. Brice Lalonde and Penny Allen (Eco-development, Paris), "Trade and Environment: Influencing the Work of the Committee on Trade and Environment (WTO)," unpublished paper presented at National Wildlife Federation, October 1994.

66. "Principles on General Rights and Obligations," Principle 14 of the Rio Declaration, p. 5; unclassified Department of State telegram, June 14, 1992. The U.S. interpretive statement is nowhere mentioned in the official U.N. version of the Rio Declaration.

67. Multilateral trade negotiations, the Uruguay Round, "Communication from the Chairman: Decision on Trade and Environment," restricted, MTN.-TNC/W/141, March 29, 1994; briefing for NGOs by Chris Marcich, Office of the U.S. Trade Representative, December 23, 1993.

68. GATT, "Trade and the Environment," in *International Trade 90–91* (Geneva: GATT, 1992), vol. 1, pp. 19–44.

69. It was widely believed among NGOs that more such disputes over unilateral actions in the future would ultimately force the negotiation of new GATT rules on the issue. See Bruce Stokes, "The Road from Rio," *National Journal,* May 30, 1992, p. 1288.

70. Esty, *Greening the GATT,* p. 188. In an ironic twist, tuna fishermen have asserted that U.S. rules on dolphin-safe tuna fishing force them to catch young tuna, which don't school beneath groups of dolphins as mature tuna do, and thus threaten the long-term health of the tuna fisheries. *U.S. News and World Report,* June 13, 1994, pp. 26–28, 138, 188.

71. For environmental critiques of the decision, see Steve Charnovitz, "GATT and the Environment: Examining the Issues," *International Environmental Affairs* 4, no. 3 (Summer 1992), pp. 203–233; Robert Repetto, "Trade and Environment Policies: Achieving Complementarities and Avoiding Conflict," *WRI Issues and Ideas,* July 1993, pp. 6–10. For an alternative view of the decision, see John H. Jackson, "World Trade Rules and Environmental Policies: Congruence or Conflict?" *Washington and Lee Law Review* 49 (Fall 1992), pp. 1242–1243.

72. For an excellent summary, see Donald M. Goldberg, "GATT Tuna-Dolphin II: Environmental Protection Continues to Clash with Free Trade," *CIEL Brief,* no. 2 (June 1994).

73. At the same time, dolphin-safe fishing techniques are believed by biologists to be more threatening to other beleaguered species, such as sharks and sea turtles. *U.S. News and World Report,* June 13, 1994, pp. 71–74.

74. The panel's conclusions were released in GATT, "United States Taxes on Automobiles: Report of the Panel," restricted, DS31/R, September 29, 1994.

75. Ibid.

76. Mark Dillenbeck, "Mission Report: International Tropical Timber Council— Thirteenth Session," December 11, 1992, pp. 1–2; Ronnie Taylor, "Positive Incentives for Sustainable Development Production and the OECD: A Constructive Approach to the Integration of Trade, Environment and Development Policies," discussion paper prepared for the Organization for Economic Cooperation and Development's Trade and Environment Seminar, June 30, 1993, pp. 6–7; Lilly Sucharipa-Behrmann, "ECO-Labeling Approaches for Tropical Timber: The Austrian Experience," in *Life-Cycle Management and Trade* (Paris: Organization for Economic Cooperation and Development, 1994), pp. 55–58; *International Environment Reporter*, March 24, 1993, p. 220; GATT Group on Environmental Measures and International Trade, "GATT and International Environmental Agreements (IEAs)," TRE/W/19, October 1, 1993, submission by Austria, p. 3.

77. A commission named by the government–NGO–private-sector group that was to supervise the policy concluded that such a ban would not be feasible by the end of 1995, in part because it would not apply to hardwoods produced in nontropical regions. *International Environment Reporter*, June 1, 1994, p. 478.

78. See Charles Arden-Clarke, *The General Agreement on Tariffs and Trade, Environmental Protection and Sustainable Development* (Gland, Switzerland: World Wildlife Fund International, 1991), p. 5.

79. Address by Indian ambassador B. K. Zutshi at the international conference "Striking a Green Deal," Brussels, November 7, 1993.

80. For analyses of environmental standards and competitiveness, see *Environmental Policies and Competitiveness* (Paris: Organization for Economic Cooperation and Development, 1993).

81. U.S. trade representative Mickey Kantor was quoted as saying that, since U.S. companies must comply with tough environmental laws, "for them to remain competitive, others must meet these standards too." *Wall Street Journal*, January 10, 1994, p. A9.

82. "The GATT Trade and Environment Work Programme: A Joint NGO Statement," February 9, 1994; Frances Williams, "First Steps to 'Green the GATT,' " *Financial Times*, February 22, 1994.

83. John Zaracostas, "US Under Fire for Attempts to Link Trade, Labor Rules," *Journal of Commerce*, March 28, 1994; *Environment Watch Western Europe* 22, no. 21 (November 5, 1993), pp. 1–3; Steve Charnowitz, "The Green Trade Debate," *Policy Focus* (Washington, D.C.), no. 1 (1994), p. 5; *Daily Environment Reporter*, July 1, 1993, pp. B5–B6.

84. *International Trade Reporter*, March 30, 1994, p. 497; Zaracostas, "US Under Fire"; John Zaracostas, "G-15 Leaders Blast Non-Economic Trade Curbs in West" and "US Firm on Linking Trade, Labor Standards," both in *Journal of Commerce*, March 29, 1994.

85. "ITTO Guidelines for the Sustainable Management of Natural Tropical Forests," ITTO Technical Series no. 5, Yokohama, 1990.

86. Mark Dillenbeck, "ITTO Renegotiation Session 6/21–25," memorandum of July 22, 1993; Debbie Davenport, "October 1993 ITTA Renegotiations Report:

Summary of Key Points," memorandum of March 14, 1994. Dillenbeck and Davenport were the NGO representatives on the U.S. delegation to the ITTO during the 1992–1993 and 1993–1994 periods, respectively.

87. Wale Adeleke, "Report on the Third Negotiation Session of the International Tropical Timber Agreement," *IUCN Forest Conservation Programme Newsletter*, no. 17 (December 1993), p. 5.

88. See *International Tropical Timber Agreement 1994*, U.N. Conference on Trade and Development, U.N. Conference for the Negotiation of a Successor Agreement to the International Tropical Timber Agreement 1983, TD/TIMBER.2/Misc.7, March 2, 1994.

89. The EU entered a reservation on the text, fearing that it could be interpreted as bringing temperate timber under the scrutiny of the agreement, but the United States and others denied it was subject to such an interpretation.

90. *Journal of Commerce*, September 19, 1994; Lalonde and Allen, "Trade and Environment."

91. For an overview of the ecolabeling systems, see *Status Report on the Use of Environmental Labels Worldwide* (Washington, D.C.: Environmental Protection Agency, 1993). This analysis draws primarily on Veena Jha and Simonetta Zarrilli, "Ecolabelling Initiatives as Potential Barriers to Trade: A Viewpoint from Developing Countries," paper presented at the SELA/UNCTAD/ECLAC Regional Seminar on Environmental Policies and Market Access, Santa Fe de Bogota, October 19–20, 1993.

92. Personal communication from Laura Campbell, senior legal officer, UNEP, September 5, 1994, p. 1.

93. See Gareth Porter, *Multilateral Negotiations on Minimum Standards for Manufacturing and Processing Industries* (Washington, D.C.: Environmental and Energy Study Institute, July 1994); Esty, *Greening the GATT*, pp. 89–98; Runge, *Freer Trade, Protected Environment*, pp. 100–106; Charnowitz, "The Green Trade Debate," p. 7.

94. Only at PrepCom IV in April 1992 did the United States announce for the first time that it was pledging $50 million for a restructured GEF once the pilot phase was completed.

95. Richard N. Mott, "Financial Transfers Under the Conventions on Climate Change and Biodiversity," *International Environmental Affairs* 7, no. 1 (Winter 1995), p. 71; "Third World Suspicious of 'Green Fund' in World Bank," UNCED PrepCom III Daily Press Bulletin (Inter Press Service) 15/1, August 30, 1991.

96. According to Byron Swift of IUCN, one Latin American country's representative to the GEF participants' meeting in April 1992 admitted privately that he could lose his job if his country didn't get a $5 million project. Remarks at NGO consultation on the GEF, Washington, D.C., April 25, 1992.

97. For the final text of the agreement, see Global Environment Facility, "Instrument for the Establishment of the Restructured Global Environment Facility," report of the GEF participants meeting, Geneva, Switzerland, March 14–16, 1994, March 31, 1994.

98. UNDP, UNEP, and World Bank, *Global Environment Facility: Independent Evaluation of the Pilot Phase* (Washington, D.C.: World Bank, 1994).

CHAPTER FIVE

1. Edith Brown Weiss, "International Environmental Law: Contemporary Issues and the Emergence of a New World Order," *Georgetown Law Journal* 81 (1993), p. 697.

2. *Daily Environment Reporter,* April 7, 1994, p. B2; *International Environment Reporter,* July 27, 1994, p. 623.

3. *Energy, Economics and Climate Change,* July 1994, p. 13; *Daily Environment Reporter,* August 11, 1994, p. B2.

4. Daniel Lashof, *The Gap: Climate Plan Faces Major Shortfall* (Washington, D.C.: Natural Resources Defense Council, April 19, 1994); Howard Geller, John Decicco, Neal Elliott, Daniel Lashoff, and Marika Tatsutani, *Bridging the Gap: Initiatives to Achieve President Clinton's Climate Commitment* (Washington, D.C.: American Council for an Energy-Efficient Economy and Natural Resources Defense Council, April 19, 1994); Timothy Noah, "Environmentalists Fault Clinton Plan on Emissions Tied to Global Warming," *Wall Street Journal,* April 19, 1994.

5. *Daily Environment Reporter,* July 12, 1994, p. A2.

6. See Geller et al., *Bridging the Gap.*

7. *Energy Use and Carbon Emissions: Some International Comparisons* (Washington, D.C.: Energy Information Administration, U.S. Department of Energy, 1994), p. 14.

8. Nancy C. Wilson, "China Faces Hard Energy Choices: Booming Economy, Soaring Emissions," *Climate Alert* (Washington, D.C.) 6, no. 3 (May-June 1993), p. 1.

9. "Will the Greenhouse Put Coal in the Doghouse?" *Global Environmental Change Report* 4, no. 6 (March 27, 1992), p. 2.

10. A series of country studies by teams in Brazil, Egypt, Thailand, and Venezuela projected potential emissions reductions ranging from 27 percent to 56 percent based on such policy shifts without increased external financing. See "UNEP Completes Phase Two of International Costing Study," *Energy, Economics and Climate Change* 4, no. 7 (July 1994), Table 1, p. 3.

11. Russell A. Mittermeier and Ian A. Bowles, "The GEF and Biodiversity Conservation: Lessons to Date, Suggestions for Future Action," *Biodiversity and Conservation* 2 (1993), pp. 637–655.

12. FAO, *Recent Developments in World Fisheries* (Rome: FAO, 1991); World Resources Institute, *World Resources 1994–1995* (New York and Oxford: Oxford University Press, 1994), pp. 184–194; Sandra Postel, "Carrying Capacity—The Earth's Bottom Line," in Lester Brown et al., *State of the World 1994* (New York: W. W. Norton, 1994), pp. 10–11.

13. Deborah MacKenzie, "Fishing Quotas Shipwrecked," *Tomorrow* 4, no. 3 (July-September 1994), p. 75.

14. However, some coastal states, urgently needing foreign currency, have allowed long-range fishing fleets to take far more fish than is sustainable. "Bank and Donors Group Seek to Stem the Tide of Global Overfishing," *World Bank News,* May 5, 1994.

15. U.N. news release, March 31, 1994, cited in *Greenwire,* April 5, 1994; David E. Pitt, "Pact Eluding Fishing Nations in Talks on Imperiled Species," *New York Times,* April 6, 1994. In March 1995, Canada carried out its threat to seize offending vessels. See Anne Swardson, "Canadians Drive Off Spanish Fish Trawler," *Washington Post,* March 27, 1995.

16. For an outline of the draft agreement and analysis of the negotiating process, see "Summary of the Third Session of the Straddling Fish Stocks and Highly Migratory Fish Stocks, 15–26 August 1994," *Earth Negotiations Bulletin* 7, no. 39 (August 29, 1994).

17. Deborah Moore, "Think Small to Solve the World Water Crisis," *Christian Science Monitor,* May 18, 1994.

18. On these shared-river-basin conflicts, see WRI, *World Resources 1994–1995,* pp. 182–190; J. K. Cooley, "The War over Water," *Foreign Policy* 54 (1984), pp. 3–26; C. O. Okidi, "Environmental Stress and Conflicts in Africa: Case Studies of African International Drainage Basins," paper for Workshop on Environmental Stress and Acute Conflicts, AAAS and University of Toronto, May 1992; George D. Moffett III, "Tigris-Euphrates Basin: Downstream Fears Feed Tensions," *Christian Science Monitor,* March 13, 1990.

19. WRI, *World Resources 1994–1995,* pp. 182–183.

20. See Moore, "Think Small"; personal communication from Deborah Moore, November 7, 1994.

21. The literature on water and international conflict in the Middle East is large. Two good sources are Thomas Naff and Ruth Matson, *Water in the Middle East: Conflict or Cooperation?* (Boulder, Colo.: Westview Press, 1984); and Peter H. Gleick, "Water and Conflict: Fresh Water Resources and International Security," *International Security* 18, no. 1 (Summer 1983), pp. 79–112.

22. Peter H. Gleick, "Water and War in the Middle East," presentation to EESI briefing, Washington, D.C., November 5, 1993, p. 11; Project in Development and the Environment (PRIDE), "A Water Management Study for Jordan," AID Project no. 398-0365, August 1992.

23. Information on the Middle East peace process is based on a telephone interview with Dr. Charles Lawson, special assistant for science and technology, Bureau of Near Eastern Affairs, U.S. Department of State, July 7, 1994.

24. Michael M. Horowitz, "Victims of Development," *Development Anthropology Network* 7, no. 2 (Fall 1989), pp. 1–8.

25. "Exporting Banned and Hazardous Pesticides, 1991 Statistics," special supplement, *FASE Reports* 11, no. 1 (Spring 1993), p. S1; Jumanah Farah, *Pesticide Policies in Developing Countries: Do They Encourage Excessive Pesticide Use?* (Washington, D.C.: World Bank, 1993), pp. 4–5; ILO report cited in "World Outlook for Jobs 'Gloomy,' " *Financial Times,* April 27, 1994.

26. Farah, *Pesticide Policies,* pp. 6–7; Robert Paarlberg, "Managing Pesticide Use in Developing Countries," in Peter M. Haas, Robert O. Keohane, and Marc A. Levy, eds., *Institutions of the Earth: Sources of Effective International Environmental Protection* (Cambridge: MIT Press, 1993), pp. 321–323; *International Code of Conduct on the Distribution and Use of Pesticides* (Rome: FAO, 1990).

27. Paarlberg, "Managing Pesticide Use," pp. 332–337.

28. Ibid., pp. 324–325, 344–345.

29. "Report of the Ad Hoc Working Group of Experts of Its Fourth Session," UNEP/PIC/WG.1/4/5, April 15, 1994, p. 17.

30. *Integrated Pest Management in Developing Countries: Experience and Prospects,* consultants' report commissioned by the Integrated Pest Management Task Force (Chatham, U.K.: Natural Resources Institute, 1992), pp. 49, 58–61.

31. This analysis is based on private communications from Bill Mankin, Global Forest Policy Project, July 22, 1994.

32. The following discussion is based on Bill Mankin, "CSD Memo #1," July 17, 1994.

33. Memorandum from Richard Z. Donovan, Rainforest Alliance, to U.S. conservation NGOs on ITTO meetings in Cartagena, Colombia, May 26, 1994.

34. Bill Mankin, "Initial Thoughts on Using the Central American Forest Treaty as the Foundation for a Western Hemisphere Agreement Beginning at the 1994 Summit of the Americas," unpublished paper for the Global Forest Policy Project, Sierra Club, and National Audubon Society, March 1994.

35. Personal communications from Bruce Cabarle, World Resources Institute, April 20, 1994, and Jorge Rodríguez, coordinator, Tropical Forest Action Plan of Central America, January 6, 1995.

36. Abram Chayes and Antonia H. Chayes, "Compliance Without Enforcement: State Behavior Under Regulatory Treaties," *Negotiation Journal* 7 (1991), pp. 311–330.

37. William J. Broad, "Russians Describe Extensive Dumping of Nuclear Waste," *New York Times*, April 27, 1993; and Peter James Spielman, AP/*Philadelphia Inquirer*, February 21, 1994, cited on *Greenwire*, February 22, 1994.

38. Weiss, "International Environment Law," p. 696; Peter H. Sand, ed., *The Effectiveness of International Environmental Law* (Cambridge: Grotius Publications, 1992).

39. Elizabeth P. Barratt-Brown, "Building a Monitoring and Compliance Regime Under the Montreal Protocol," *Yale Journal of International Law* 16 (1991), pp. 542–544.

40. Statement by Dr. Mostafa K. Tolba, executive director, U.N. Environment Programme, to the Eighth Meeting of the Parties to CITES, Kyoto, Japan, March 1992, p. 5.

41. David Mulenex, "Improving Compliance Provisions in International Environmental Agreements," in Lawrence E. Susskind, Eric Jay Dolin, and J. William Breslin, *International Environmental Treaty-Making* (Cambridge: Program on Negotiation at Harvard Law School, 1992), p. 174.

42. U.S. Government Accounting Office, "International Agreements Are Not Well Monitored," GAO/RCED-92-43, January 1992, pp. 28–33.

43. Comment from the U.S. Department of State in "International Agreements Are Not Well Monitored," p. 54.

44. See, for example, Lawrence E. Susskind, *Environmental Diplomacy: Negotiating More Effective Global Agreements* (New York: Oxford University Press, 1994), pp. 113–117.

45. *Development Brief* (World Bank), no. 16 (April 1993), p. 1; "Sharp Changes in the Structure of Financial Flows to Developing Countries and Countries in Transition," OECD press release, June 24, 1994.

46. *Yen Aid Watch* (Tokyo), August 1994, p. 5.

47. Friends of the Earth, U.S., *Profiles of World Bank Disasters: Arun III Hydroelectric Power Project in Nepal* (Washington, D.C.: FOE, May 1994).

48. Inge Kaul and Robert Savio with Phil Harris, "Global Human Security: A New Political Framework for North-South Relations," paper prepared for SID/IPS European Parliamentarians Conference "Building Global Human Security," Bonn, Germany, September 17–18, 1993, p. 8.

49. David Parker and Eva Jespersen, "20/20: Mobilizing Resources for Children in the 1990s," UNICEF Staff Working Paper, no. 12, January 1994.

50. Eva Jespersen, "Why 20/20?" paper prepared for meeting, "Estimating Resource Needs for Population Activities," Harvard Center for Population and Development Studies, June 28, 1994; "Report of the World Summit for Social Development: 6–12 March, 1995," Earth Negotiations Bulletin 10, no. 4 (March 15, 1995). China was one of the few to oppose the concept.

51. United Nations Economic and Social Council, Commission on Sustainable Development, Intersessional Ad Hoc Open-Ended Working Group on Finance, February 28 to March 2, 1994, "Financial Resources and Mechanisms for Sustainable Development: Overview of Current Issues and Developments," report of the secretary-general, p. 24.

52. Marnie Stetson, "People Who Live in Green Houses . . . ," Worldwatch (September–October 1991), p. 29.

53. The original proposal, by Nobel Prize–winning economist James Tobin, was for a 0.5-percent tax on speculative currency transactions that would raise $1.5 trillion annually and was aimed at deterring such transactions. The UNDP proposed reducing the tax to 10 percent of the original level. See UNDP, Human Development Report 1994 (New York: Oxford University Press, 1994), pp. 69–70.

54. Martin Walker, "Global Taxation: Paying for Peace," World Policy Journal 10, no. 2 (Summer 1993), pp. 7–12.

55. For the argument in favor of such a policy, see Francesco Abbate, UNCTAD Finance Development Programme, "The Paris Club: A Group of Debt Collectors or a Development Institution?" unpublished paper, February 11, 1993.

56. U.N. ECOSOC, CSD, Intercessional Ad Hoc . . . Group, "Financial Resources and Mechanisms," p. 17.

57. Ralph De Gennaro and Gawain Kripke, Earth Budget: Making Our Tax Dollars Work for the Environment (Washington, D.C.: Friends of the Earth, 1993), p. 25.

58. Jim MacNeill, "Trade-Environment Links: The Global Dimension," in John Kirton and Sarah Richardson, eds., Trade, Environment and Competitiveness (Ottawa: National Round Table on the Environment and the Economy, 1992), p. 14.

59. See Henk L.M. Kox, "Integration of Environmental Externalities in International Commodity Agreements," World Development 19, no. 8 (August 1991), pp. 933–944; Henk L.M. Kox, The International Commodity Related Environmental Agreement: Background and Design (Amsterdam, Netherlands: Free University Faculty of Economics and Econometrics, June 1994).

60. Sandra Hackman, "After Rio: Our Forests, Ourselves," Technology Review, October 1992, pp. 32–40.

61. David C. Scott, "NGOs Have the Credibility in Mexico," CROSSLINES Global Report (Geneva) 2, nos. 4–5 (July–October 1994), p. 57.

62. Briefing by Peter Kenmore, FAO, Washington, D.C., October 26, 1994.

63. "Wood Conservationists Target 75% Reduction," Rainforest Action Network, Action Alert no. 102, November 1994.

64. For accounts of the conference, see the Washington Post, March 11 and 12, 1989.

Suggested Readings

Arden-Clark. *The General Agreement on Tariffs and Trade: Environmental Protection and Sustainable Development*. Gland, Switzerland: World Wildlife Fund International, 1991.

Banks, James N., Ellen Grosman, and Walter V. Reid. *Bankrolling Successes: A Portfolio of Sustainable Development Projects*. Washington, D.C.: Friends of the Earth and the National Wildlife Federation, 1995.

Benedick, Richard Elliott. *Ozone Diplomacy*. Cambridge: Harvard University Press, 1991.

Binswanger, Hans P. *Brazilian Policies That Encourage Deforestation in the Amazon*. Washington, D.C.: Environment Department, World Bank, 1989.

Bodansky, Daniel. "The United Nations Framework Convention on Climate Change: A Commentary." *Yale Journal of International Law* 18, no. 2 (Summer 1993): 451–558.

Brown, Janet Welsh (ed.). *In the U.S. Interest: Resources, Growth, and Security in the Developing World*. Boulder, Colo.: Westview Press, 1990.

Brown, Lester R., et al. *State of the World 1994: A Worldwatch Institute Report on Progress Toward a Sustainable Society*. New York: W. W. Norton, 1994. (Published annually since 1984.)

Caldwell, Lynton Keith. *International Environmental Policy: Emergence and Dimensions*, 2nd rev. ed. Durham and London: Duke University Press, 1990.

Carroll, John E. (ed.). *International Environmental Diplomacy: The Management and Resolution of Transfrontier Environmental Problems*. Cambridge: Cambridge University Press, 1988.

Carson, Rachel. *Silent Spring*. Boston: Houghton Mifflin, 1987.

Chatterjee, Pratap, and Matthias Singer. *The Earth Brokers*. London and New York: Routledge, 1994.

Colby, Michael E. *The Evolution of Paradigms of Environmental Management in Development*. Washington, D.C.: Policy Planning and Research Staff, World Bank, 1989.

Cruz, Wilfrido, and Robert Repetto. *The Environmental Effects of Stabilization and Structural Adjustment Programs: The Philippines Case*. Washington, D.C.: World Resources Institute, 1992.

Daly, Herman E., and John B. Cobb. *For the Common Good: Redirecting the Economy Toward Community, the Environment and a Sustainable Future*. Boston: Beacon Press, 1989.

Day, David. *The Whale War*. Vancouver and Toronto: Douglas and McIntyre, 1987.

Doniger, David. "Politics of the Ozone Layer." *Issues in Science and Technology* 4, no. 3 (Spring 1988):86–92.

Ehrlich, Paul R., and Anne H. Ehrlich. *The Population Explosion*. New York: Simon and Schuster, 1990.

Esty, Daniel. *Greening the GATT*. Washington, D.C.: Institute for International Economics, 1994.

Fisher, Julie. *The Road from Rio: Sustainable Development and the Non-Governmental Movement in the Third World*. Westport, Conn., and London: Praeger, 1993.

Flavin, Christopher, and Nicholas Lanssen. *Power Surge: Guide to the Coming Energy Revolution*. New York: W. W. Norton, 1994.

French, Hillary F. "Making Environmental Treaties Work." *Scientific American*, December 1994, pp. 62–65.

Gleick, Peter H. (ed.). *Water in Crises: A Guide to the World's Freshwater Resources*. New York: Oxford University Press, 1993.

Gore, Al. *Earth in the Balance: Ecology and the Human Spirit*. Boston: Houghton Mifflin, 1992.

Grubb, Michael, et al. *The "Earth Summit" Agreements: A Guide and Assessment*. London: Earthscan, 1993.

Haas, Ernst. *When Knowledge Is Power*. Berkeley: University of California Press, 1990.

Haas, Peter M., Robert O. Keohane, and Marc A. Levy (eds.). *Institutions for the Earth*. Cambridge: MIT Press, 1993.

Hampson, Fen Osler. "Climate Change: Building International Coalitions of the Like-minded." *International Journal* 45, no. 1 (Winter 1989–1990):36–74.

Homer-Dixon, Thomas, J. Boutwell, and G. W. Rathgens. "Environmental Change and Violent Conflict." *Scientific American*, February 1993, pp. 38–45.

Houghton, Richard A., and George M. Woodwell. "Global Climatic Change." *Scientific American* 260, no. 4 (April 1989):36–44.

Hurrell, Andrew, and Benedict Kingsbury (eds.). *The International Politics of the Environment: Actors, Interests and Institutions*. New York: Oxford University Press, 1992.

Imber, Mark F. *Environmental Security and UN Reform*. New York: St. Martin's Press, 1994.

Kimball, Lee A. *Southern Exposure: Deciding Antarctica's Future*. Washington, D.C.: World Resources Institute, 1990.

———. *Forging International Agreements: Strengthening Intergovernmental Institutions for Environment and Development*. Washington, D.C.: World Resources Institute, 1992.

Klare, Michael T., and Daniel C. Thomas (eds.). *World Security: Trends and Challenges at Century's End*. New York: St. Martin's Press, 1991.

Krause, Florentin, Wilfred Bach, and Jon Koomey. *Energy Policy in the Greenhouse*. El Cerrito, Calif.: International Project for Sustainable Energy Paths, 1989.

Latin American and Caribbean Commission on Development and Environment. *Our Own Agenda*. Washington, D.C., and New York: Inter-American Development Bank and United Nations Development Programme, 1990.

Leonard, H. Jeffrey, et al. *Environment and the Poor: Development Strategies for a Common Agenda*. New Brunswick/Oxford: Transaction Books, 1989.

McCormick, John. *Acid Earth: The Global Threat of Acid Pollution*. Washington, D.C.: Earthscan and International Institute for Environment and Development, 1985.

———. *Reclaiming Paradise: The Global Environmental Movement*. Bloomington: Indiana University Press, 1989.

MacNeill, Jim. "The Greening of International Relations." *International Journal* 45, no. 1 (Winter 1989–1990):1–35.

MacNeill, Jim, Peter Winsemius, and Taizo Yakushiji. *Beyond Interdependence: Meshing of the World's Economy and the Earth's Ecology*. New York: Oxford University Press, 1991.

Mathews, Jessica Tuchman. "Redefining Security." *Foreign Affairs* 68 (Spring 1989):162–177.

Mathews, Jessica Tuchman (ed.). *Preserving the Global Environment: The Challenge of Shared Leadership*. New York: W. W. Norton, 1991.

Meadows, Donella H., et al. *The Limits to Growth*. New York: Universe Books, 1972.

Miller, Alan S., and Curtis Moore. *Japan and the Global Environment*. College Park, Md.: Center for Global Change, 1991.

Mitchell, Barbara. *Frozen Stakes: The Future of Antarctic Minerals*. London and Washington, D.C.: International Institute for Environment and Development, 1983.

Muñoz, Heraldo, and Robin Rosenberg (eds.). *Difficult Liaison: Trade and the Environment in the Americas*. New Brunswick, N.J.: Transaction Books, 1993.

Nectoux, François, and Yoichi Kuroda. *Timber from the South Seas: An Analysis of Japan's Tropical Timber Trade and Its Environmental Impact*. Gland, Switzerland: World Wildlife Fund International, 1989.

Nitze, William A. *The Greenhouse Effect: Formulating a Convention*. London: Royal Institute of International Affairs, 1990.

Orr, David W., and Marvin S. Soroos. *The Global Predicament: Ecological Perspectives on World Order*. Chapel Hill: University of North Carolina Press, 1979.

Ostrom, Elinor. *Governing the Commons: The Evolution of Institutions for Collective Action*. New York: Cambridge University Press, 1990.

Pirages, Dennis. *Global Technopolitics: The International Politics of Technology and Resources*. Pacific Grove, Calif.: Brooks and Cole, 1989.

"Planet of the Year: Endangered Earth." *Time*, January 2, 1989. (A special issue on the environment.)

Postel, Sandra. *Last Oasis: Facing Water Scarcity*. New York: W. W. Norton, 1992.

Repetto, Robert. *Promoting Environmentally Sound Economic Progress: What the North Can Do*. Washington, D.C.: World Resources Institute, 1990.

———. *Trade and Sustainable Development*. Geneva: United Nations Environment Programme, 1994.

Repetto, Robert, et al. *Accounts Overdue: Natural Resources Depreciation in Costa Rica*. Washington, D.C.: World Resources Institute, 1991.

———. *Mortgaging the Earth: The World Bank, Environmental Impoverishment, and the Crisis of Development*. Boston: Beacon Press, 1994.

Rich, Bruce. "The Multilateral Development Banks, Environmental Policy and the United States." *Ecology Law Quarterly* 12, no. 4 (1985):681–745.

Runge, C. Ford, with Francois Ortalo-Magne and Philip Vande Kamp. *Freer Trade, Protected Environment*. New York: Council on Foreign Relations Press, 1994.

Sadik, Nafis. *The State of World Population, 1994*. New York: United Nations Population Fund, 1994.

Sand, Peter H. *Lessons Learned in Global Environmental Governance*. Washington, D.C.: World Resources Institute, 1990.

Sands, Phillippe (ed.). *Greening International Laws*. London: Earthscan, 1993.

Schmidheiny, Stephan, with the Business Council for Sustainable Development. *Changing Course: A Global Business Perspective on Development and the Environment*. Cambridge: MIT Press, 1992.

Sjostedt, Gunnar (ed.). *International Environmental Negotiation*. Newbury Park, Calif.: Sage, 1993.

Sjostedt, Gunnar, et al. (eds.). *Negotiating International Regimes: Lessons Learned from the United Nations Conference on Environment and Development*. London: Graham and Trotman, 1994.

Speth, James Gustave. *Environmental Pollution: A Long-Term Perspective*. Washington, D.C.: World Resources Institute, 1988.

Starke, Linda. *Signs of Hope, Working Towards Our Common Future*. New York: Oxford University Press, 1990.

Susskind, Lawrence E., Eric Jay Dolin, and J. William Breslin. *International Environmental Treaty-Making*. Cambridge: Harvard Law School Program on Negotiation, 1992.

Thomas, Caroline. *The Environment in International Relations*. London: Royal Institute of International Affairs, 1992.

United Nations Development Programme. *Human Development Report 1994*. New York: Oxford University Press, 1994.

United Nations Environment Programme. *Register of International Treaties and Other Agreements in the Field of the Environment*. Nairobi: UNEP, 1989.

U.S. Congress, Office of Technology Assessment. *Polar Prospects: A Minerals Treaty for Antarctica*. Washington, D.C.: U.S. Government Printing Office, 1990.

Weiss, Edith Brown, Daniel B. Magraw, and Paul C. Szasz. *International Environmental Law: Basic Instruments and References*. Dobbs Ferry, N.Y.: Transnational, 1992.

Wilson, E. O. (ed.). *Biodiversity*. Washington, D.C.: National Academy of Sciences Press, 1988.

World Commission on Environment and Development. *Our Common Future*. New York: Oxford University Press, 1987.

World Resources Institute. *World Resources, 1990–91, 1992–93, 1994–95*. New York: Oxford University Press, 1990, 1992, 1994.

Young, Oran R. *International Cooperation: Building Regimes for Natural Resources and the Environment*. Ithaca, N.Y.: Cornell University Press, 1989.

Glossary

Acid rain is precipitation that deposits nitric or sulfuric acids on the earth, buildings, and vegetation.

Biodiversity (or **biological diversity**) is the variety of organisms, including species of plants and animals, genetic variation within individual species, and diversity of ecosystems.

Biosphere refers to the earth's land, water, atmosphere, and living things, or to a particular zone of the whole.

A **blocking** or **veto state** is one that by virtue of its importance on a particular environmental issue is able to block or weaken international agreement.

Bretton Woods institutions are the international financial institutions, such as the World Bank, the International Monetary Fund, and the International Finance Corporation, named after the New Hampshire resort at which they were negotiated.

CAFE standards are the Corporate Average Fuel Economy standards, a measure of fuel efficiency, imposed on U.S. auto manufacturers and importers of cars since 1975.

Civil society refers to an array of private-sector institutions such as trade unions, business associations, environmental and development organizations, women's and youth groups, cooperatives, and religious groups having an interest in public policy issues and decisions.

Climate change refers to the likelihood of increased change in the average weather over a period of time (usually thirty or more years) from natural causes (e.g., ice ages brought on by the changes in the earth's orbit around the sun) or as the result of human intervention (e.g., through the release of carbon dioxide and other greenhouse gases).

A **convention** is a multilateral legal agreement and the most common form of legal instrument used in agreements on international environmental issues.

Desertification is the deterioration of the biological potential of land from a combination of adverse climate and excessive human exploitation, leading ultimately to desertlike conditions.

Environmental accounting involves various methods of figuring national income accounts that assign value to resources such as soil, water, forests, and minerals and therefore reflect more accurately in the accounting system the depletion of natural resources and the degradation of natural systems.

Environmental services are the conserving or restorative functions of nature, e.g., the ability of plants to convert carbon dioxide to oxygen, the ability of marsh-

215

lands to cleanse polluted waters, or the capacity of a vegetation-covered flood plain to dissipate the destructive power of a river in flood.

The **exclusionist paradigm** (also known as "frontier economics") is the dominant social paradigm in contemporary societies and holds that humans are not subject to natural laws in their use of natural resources and systems for economic purposes.

Exclusive economic zones (EEZs) are the 200-mile-wide (320-kilometer-wide) territorial waters under the jurisdiction of individual nations.

A **framework convention** is a multilateral agreement that establishes common principles but does not include binding commitments to specific actions.

The **General Agreement on Tariffs and Trade** (GATT) is the multilateral agreement governing the world trading system.

Global commons are the natural resources and vital life-support services, such as the earth's climate system, ozone layer, and oceans and seas, that belong to all humankind rather than to any one country or private enterprise.

Global warming refers to the apparent trend of increasing temperatures on the world's surface and in the lower atmosphere, believed to be caused by the entrapment of heat due to the buildup of certain gases (see **greenhouse effect**).

The **greenhouse effect** occurs when certain gases—mainly carbon dioxide, ground-level ozone, chlorofluorocarbons (CFCs), and halons, methane, and nitrous oxide—build up in the atmosphere.

Green taxes include a variety of measures that would penalize practices that pollute or degrade the environment or encourage excessive use or waste of a valuable natural resource or service.

Gross world product is the value of the total goods and services produced in the world annually.

The **Group of Seven** (or **G-7**) includes the seven industrialized democracies: the United States, Canada, Japan, the United Kingdom, France, Germany, and Italy.

The **Group of 77** is a coalition of developing countries (numbering 128) that has pressed for reform of North-South economic structures since the mid-1970s.

A **hegemonic power** is a state that is able to set the primary rules of an international system, usually through a combination of military and economic power.

Intellectual property rights (IPR) are the rights of businesses, individuals, or states to legal protection of their discoveries and inventions.

Intergenerational equity is a norm of state behavior that calls for giving adequate consideration to the interests of future generations in the enjoyment of a healthy environment and natural resources.

International financial institutions are international organizations such as the World Bank, the regional development banks, the International Monetary Fund, and the International Finance Corporation, which are also known as the **Bretton Woods institutions.**

An **international regime** is a set of norms or rules of behavior, usually based on an international agreement, governing particular issues in world politics.

Joint implementation (JI) refers to a provision of the climate convention that allows parties to implement their commitments jointly with another state—the expectation being that an industrialized country would provide a developing country with financial or technical assistance.

A **lead state** is one that sponsors and asserts leadership on behalf of the most advanced proposal for international regulation on an environmental issue.

Neoclassical economics is a school of economic theory maintaining that free markets will always allocate resources so as to satisfy the greatest number of people.

The **New International Economic Order** is the list of demands made in the 1970s by the Group of 77 developing nations for changes in the structure of North-South economic relations. The list is still in effect.

Nontariff barriers are trade barriers, other than tariffs, erected by a government to discourage imports, e.g., quotas (both formal and "voluntary"), outright prohibition of specific imports (such as the Japanese refusal to import rice), discriminatory restrictions, or licensing requirements.

The **ozone layer** is the concentration of ozone in the stratosphere, between 15 and 50 kilometers (9.3 and 31 miles) above the earth's surface, depending on latitude, season, and other factors.

Paradigm refers to a set of assumptions about reality that define and often limit the scope of inquiry in any field of knowledge.

A **protocol** is a multilateral agreement providing detailed, specific commitments attached to a convention.

Soft law refers to nonbinding documents drawn up by international bodies that establish norms; these documents can take on the force of law through customary practice.

The **Stockholm conference** (the United Nations Conference on the Human Environment, 1972) was the first worldwide conference of nations devoted to environmental problems.

A **supporting state** is one that is willing to publicly support and work for the most far-reaching proposal for international regulation on an environmental issue.

Sustainable development is a perspective on environmental management that emphasizes the need to reconcile present and future economic needs through environmental conservation.

A **swing state** is one that attempts to bargain for major concessions in return for acceding to a global environmental agreement.

Technology transfer is the transfer, usually from highly industrialized to less industrialized developing countries, of the means of producing scientifically or technically advanced goods in the form of patents, machinery and equipment, or the necessary scientific-technical knowledge.

Transboundary air pollution is the emission of pollutants, especially nitric and sulfuric acids, across national boundaries.

A **unitary actor model** is an explanatory concept based on the assumption that state actors can be treated as though they are a single entity with a single, internally consistent set of values and attitudes.

The **Uruguay Round** is the negotiations under the auspices of the General Agreement on Tariffs and Trade on liberalization of world trade that began in 1985 in Uruguay and ended in 1994.

A **veto coalition** is a group of veto states that forms around a given issue.

A **veto** or **blocking state** is one that by virtue of its importance on a particular environmental issue is able to block or weaken international agreement.

□ □ □

Chronology

1940   The Convention on Nature Protection and Wildlife Preservation in the Western Hemisphere is signed.

1946   The International Convention for the Regulation of Whaling is signed.

1954   The International Convention for the Prevention of Pollution of the Sea by Oil is signed.

1959   Antarctic Treaty is signed.

1962   Publication of Rachel Carson's *Silent Spring*.

1969   National Environmental Policy Act of 1969 (NEPA) is passed by U.S. Congress.

1972   *The Limits to Growth* report for the Club of Rome is published.

1972   The United Nations Conference on the Human Environment is convened in Stockholm.

1972   Creation of the United Nations Environment Programme (UNEP).

1972   The Convention on the Prevention of Marine Pollution by Dumping of Wastes and Other Matter (or London Dumping Convention) is signed.

1972   Convention Concerning the Protection of the World Cultural and Natural Heritage is signed.

1972   Convention for the Conservation of Antarctic Seals is signed.

1973   The International Convention for the Prevention of Pollution from Ships (MARPOL) is signed.

1973   The Convention on International Trade in Endangered Species (CITES) is signed.

1973   U.S. Endangered Species Conservation Act banning whaling and whale imports becomes law.

1974   Declaration on the Establishment of a New International Economic Order (NIEO) is issued by the Sixth Special Session of the United Nations General Assembly.

1977   Ad Hoc Conference of Experts convened by UNEP approves the World Plan of Action on the Ozone Layer.

1979   The Convention on Long-Range Transboundary Air Pollution (LRTAP) is signed.

1979   First World Climate Conference in Geneva warns of danger of global warming.

1980   World Conservation Strategy launched by IUCN and UNEP.

1980   *Global 2000 Report to the President* is published.
1980   Convention on the Conservation of Antarctic Marine Living Resources (CCAMLR) is signed.
1982   Negotiations sponsored by UNEP begin on protection of the ozone layer.
1982   The United Nations Convention on the Law of the Sea (UNCLOS) is signed.
1982   Phaseout of commercial whaling over three-year period is passed by International Whaling Commission (IWC).
1984   International Tropical Timber Agreement (ITTA) is signed.
1985   The Helsinki Protocol to the LRTAP is signed, commiting the signatories to reduce sulfur dioxide emissions.
1985   The Vienna Convention for the Protection of the Ozone Layer is signed.
1985   London Dumping Convention meeting of the parties votes to ban all further dumping of low-level radioactive wastes in oceans until it is proven safe.
1985   Conference of climate experts in Villach, Austria, produces consensus on serious possibility of greenhouse warming.
1985   Tropical Forestry Action Plan (TFAP) approved by donor countries at conference in The Hague.
1985   Montreal Guidelines for the Protection of the Marine Environment from Land-Based Sources are signed.
1986   Major explosion at the Soviet nuclear plant in Chernobyl spreads radioactive cloud across Western Europe and Japan.
1987   International Tropical Timber Organization (ITTO) holds first meeting in Yokohama, Japan.
1987   The Montreal Protocol on Substances that Deplete the Ozone Layer is signed.
1987   The Report of the World Commission on Environment and Development (the Brundtland Report) is published as *Our Common Future.*
1988   British scientists issue report on dramatic decrease in ozone layer over Antarctica; Ozone Trends Panel report documents ozone-layer decreases in Northern Hemisphere.
1988   The Sofia Protocol to the LRTAP is signed, commiting the signatories to reduce nitrogen oxide emissions.
1988   Convention on the Regulation of Antarctic Mineral Resources Activities (CRAMRA) is signed in Wellington, New Zealand.
1988   Intergovernmental Panel on Climate Change (IPCC) is established by WMO and UNEP.
1989   Communiqué of the Group of Seven (G-7) heads of industrial democracies focuses on global environment.
1989   Twenty-four nations issue The Hague Declaration on the Environment.
1989   The Basel Convention on the Control of Transboundary Movements of Hazardous Wastes and Their Disposal is signed; the European Community reaches agreement with ACP (Africa, the Caribbean and the

Pacific) states to ban hazardous waste exports to countries without the capacity to dispose of them safety.

1989   Ministerial Conference on Atmospheric Pollution and Climate Change issues the Noordwijk Declaration, in the Netherlands, calling for stabilization of carbon dioxide emissions by 2000.

1989   Seventh CITES conference votes to ban trade in African elephant ivory products.

1990   Second meeting of the parties to the Montreal Protocol convenes in London to strengthen the Montreal Protocol.

1990   Communiqué of G-7 heads of state summit meeting in Houston calls for negotiation of an international agreement on the world's forests.

1990   Bergen Ministerial Declaration on Sustainable Development in the Economic Commission for Europe (ECE) calls stabilization of carbon dioxide emissions the first step.

1990   Meeting of Antarctic Treaty Consultative Parties (ATCPs) in Santiago, Chile, agrees to begin negotiations on a convention for environmental protection of Antarctica.

1990   Ban on whaling extended by the International Whaling Commission.

1991   Protocol on Environmental Protection to the Antarctic Treaty is signed.

1992   United Nations Conference on Environment and Development is convened in Rio de Janeiro.

1992   United Nations Convention on Climate Change is signed at Rio de Janeiro.

1992   United Nations Convention on Biological Diversity is signed at Rio de Janeiro.

1993   Central American Forest Treaty is signed.

1993   United Nations Conference on Straddling and Highly Migratory Fish Stocks is convened.

1994   International Convention to Combat Desertification is signed.

1994   United Nations Convention on the Law of the Sea comes into effect.

1995   Agreement on the Conservation and Management of Straddling Fish Stocks and Highly Migratory Fish Stocks is signed.

□ □ □

About the Book and Authors

When *Global Environmental Politics* was first published, the environment was just emerging as a pivotal issue in traditional international relations. Now the environment is a topic central to discussions of security politics and the relationship between foreign and domestic policy—and so much has changed that Gareth Porter and Janet Welsh Brown found themselves rewriting more than half of their original text. With new cases on biodiversity and desertification, this classic work is more complete and up-to-date than any survey of environmental politics on the market.

In addition to providing a concise yet comprehensive overview of global environmental issues, the authors have worked to contextualize key topics such as the Rio conference, water security, the biodiversity treaty, and trade in toxics. Environmental concerns from global warming to the ozone layer to whaling are seen as challenges to transnational relations, with governments, NGOs, IGOs, and MNCs all facing the prospect of multilateral interaction to solve a growing global problem.

Gareth Porter is the director of the International Program at the Environmental and Energy Study Institute in Washington, D.C. **Janet Welsh Brown** is a senior fellow at the World Resources Institute in Washington, D.C., former chair of the board of Friends of the Earth, and formerly the executive director of the Environmental Defense Fund. Both authors have taught a variety of courses in international relations and environmental politics at institutions that include the American University, Johns Hopkins University, the University of Washington in Seattle, the University of the District of Columbia, Howard University, and Sarah Lawrence College.

BOOKS IN THIS SERIES

Kenneth W. Grundy
**South Africa: Domestic Crisis
and Global Challenge**

□ □ □

David S. Mason
**Revolution in East-Central Europe
and World Politics**

□ □ □

Georg Sørensen
**Democracy and Democratization:
Processes and Prospects in a Changing World**

□ □ □

Steve Chan
**East Asian Dynamism: Growth, Order, and
Security in the Pacific Region, second edition**

□ □ □

Barry B. Hughes
**International Futures: Choices in
the Creation of a New World Order**

□ □ □

Jack Donnelly
International Human Rights

□ □ □

V. Spike Peterson and Anne Sisson Runyan
Global Gender Issues

□ □ □

Sarah J. Tisch and Michael B. Wallace
**Dilemmas of Development Assistance:
The What, Why, and Who of Foreign Aid**

□ □ □

Ted Robert Gurr and Barbara Harff
Ethnic Conflict in World Politics

□ □ □

225

Frederic S. Pearson
The Global Spread of Arms:
Political Economy of International Security

☐ ☐ ☐

Deborah J. Gerner
One Land, Two Peoples:
The Conflict over Palestine, second edition

☐ ☐ ☐

Karen Mingst and Margaret P. Karns
The United Nations in the Post–Cold War Era

Index